Globe Law
and Business

Law Firm Strategies for the 21st Century

Strategies for Success, Second Edition

Consulting Editor **Christoph H Vaagt**
on behalf of the International Bar Association

Consulting editor
Christoph H Vaagt on behalf of the International Bar Association

Managing director
Sian O'Neill

Law Firm Strategies for the 21st Century: Strategies for Success, Second Edition
is published by

Globe Law and Business Ltd
3 Mylor Close
Horsell
Woking
Surrey GU21 4DD
United Kingdom
Tel: +44 20 3745 4770
www.globelawandbusiness.com

Law Firm Strategies for the 21st Century: Strategies for Success, Second Edition

ISBN 9781787423022
EPUB ISBN 9781787423039
Adobe PDF ISBN 9781787423046
Mobi ISBN 9781787423053

Table of contents

Introduction 5
Christoph H Vaagt
Law Firm Change Consultants

Part I. General aspects of law firm strategies

Strategies of small, midsize and larger law firms: does one size fit all? 7
Christoph H Vaagt
Law Firm Change Consultants

Strategy in law firms: what it is and why we should care 31
Bente R Løwendahl
BI Norwegian Business School

Drivers of change – driving strategy in law firms 45
Mats Anderson
Supreme Administrative Court (Sweden)

How to drive change in a partnership setting 59
Wolf-Peter Gross
Law Firm Change Consultants

Part II. Resource-side strategies

Resource-based approach to strategy: what makes your law firm unique today and tomorrow? 75
Dina Gracheva
Independent strategy consultant

The role of professional ethics in shaping law firms' strategy 83
Tomasz Wardyński
Wardyński & Partners

Implementing a smart collaboration strategy 95
Heidi K Gardner
Harvard Law School
Ivan Matviak
Gardner & Co

Business model transformation as a tool for driving strategic innovation and growth 115
Robert Millard
Cambridge Strategy Group

Matter management in law firms – the emergence and impact of legal project management 149
Ignaz Fuesgen
smartvokat

Legal tech as a factor in strategic law firm development 179
Felix Dette
METIS Rechtsanwälte PartGmbB

Part III. Market-side strategies

Winning and keeping clients 189
E Leigh Dance
ELD International LLC
Global Counsel Leaders

Reputation management in professional service firms 199
William S Harvey
University of Exeter Business School
Timothy Morris
Michael Smets
Saïd Business School, University of Oxford

How to merge: lessons from 20 years of law firm mergers 217
Lisa R Smith
Fairfax Associates

How to screw up your international expansion: a 15-step guide 231
Robert C Bata
WarwickPlace Legal LLC

Professionalising the pricing and procurement processes 247
Richard Burcher
Validatum® and Virtual Pricing Director®
Silvia Hodges Silverstein
Buying Legal Council
Columbia Law School

About the authors 263

About Globe Law and Business 271

Introduction

Christoph H Vaagt
Law Firm Change Consultants

A book written under the auspices of the International Bar Association (IBA) on law firm management must take into account that the IBA has members from all over the world, and from law firms of different sizes. We can identify at least four different categories in each jurisdiction:

- sole practitioners, working on their own or as freelance lawyers;
- small, local law firms;
- midsize law firms with one or several offices within one jurisdiction; and
- large law firms with several offices in other jurisdictions.

Although the boundaries between these strategic groups are somewhat blurred, we intended to produce a book relevant to all of them. For this second edition, we have brought together authors who cover:

- the general aspect of law firm strategy;
- the resource side of law firm strategy; and
- the market side of law firm strategy.

We hope the reader will find it interesting to take a look at the different aspects of what law firm strategy is, discussed by active lawyers, academics and consultants, so that he or she may be able to understand better what a law firm needs in order to stay competitive.

The book starts by looking at what drives strategy in law firms, both through the observation of the market and by academia (Christoph H Vaagt and Bente R Løwendahl).

The historical perspective of how the market for legal services has changed is discussed by Mats Anderson, a lawyer previously at UK Magic Circle firm Linklaters in Stockholm and who is now a Justice of the Supreme Administrative Court in Sweden. Wolf-Peter Gross describes how law firms have successfully adapted in times of change.

The resource-based view on strategy is then introduced by Dina Gracheva, who worked in Russia as the business strategist in a leading firm in Moscow and asks: "What makes your law firm unique today and tomorrow?" Tomasz Wardyński of Wardyński & Partners in Warsaw delves into the important issue of professional ethics in shaping law firms' strategies. How much collaboration helps law firms to become competitive is explored by Harvard Law School professor Heidi K Gardner and Ivan Matviak, who write about implementing a smart collaboration strategy. The business of law must adapt to changes in technology and thus Robert Millard looks into business model transformation of larger firms as a tool for driving strategic innovation growth from a consultant's perspective. The practicalities of organisation based on process management is described by Ignaz Fuesgen, an old hand in law firm management. Finally, Felix Dette explores, from a midsize law firm partner's perspective, how legal tech as a factor in strategic law firm development could be understood.

The market-side view explores changes on the client side of the business. E Leigh Dance's chapter shines a light on how basic selling and servicing strategies of law firms must be designed nowadays, as all strategies are worthless if the clients are not at the centre of any law firm and, thus, of lawyers. The result is, one would think, a good reputation. However, as William Harvey, Timothy Morris and Michael Smets from the Universities of Exeter and Oxford show, reputation at the upper end of the market is not necessarily linked to superior knowledge; "the emperor has no clothes" one might exclaim after reading this thought-provoking piece, based on the latest research on reputation management in professional service firms.

Following on from this, Lisa R Smith looks at law firm mergers, based on her extensive experience in this field with more than 30 years of consulting with US law firms and beyond. Then, with his solid knowledge of the internationalisation of law firms, Robert C Bata describes how to screw up your international expansion with a 15-step guide, also applicable to midsize firms that want to set up offices outside of their main location. Finally, Silvia Hodges Silverstein of the Buying Legal Council and Richard Burcher of Validatum discuss the increasing importance of pricing in markets. This is a development which must be carefully observed by all market participants as the changes will produce a set of different legal 'products' to which law firms must somehow react.

We hope that the reader will be enlightened, and hopefully also enabled, to help his or her law firm stay competitive, whatever the markets, jurisdictions or circumstances in this fast-changing world.

Strategies of small, midsize and larger law firms: does one size fit all?

Christoph H Vaagt
Law Firm Change Consultants

The strategy of law firms is a subject often written about, but rarely will you find something to the point. David Maister[1] refused to define one; the only statement he was willing to pronounce is that "strategy is to say no". In a way, he realised that most law firms are generalists which do not have a clear client intake policy. He also found that law firms are difficult to run in terms of strategy due to the partnership model lending each partner autonomy about the clients and matters dealt with. But he could not explain "how" strategy is formulated in law firms. In this chapter, I endeavour to give an overview of the process of, the elements important for and different perspectives to strategy formulation in law firms, as can be found in literature, our own consulting experience and the other chapters of this book.

A law firm partnership is a beast of its own. The particularities of law firm partnerships, as first described by non-lawyers as 'professional partnerships', are now better known and have been studied more intensively since the turn of the century.

1. Important frame to the strategy development in law firms: P2 archetype and business model

The first thing one needs to realise is that law firms tend to be 'professional partnerships' or 'P2', as defined by Greenwood and Hinings in one of the first attempts to describe strategy formulation in professional service firms, as law firms, among others, are described in academia.[2] All partners are owners, manage the most important client matters and, very often, they are also the most skilled lawyers who still take care of a good chunk of the legal work.

1 Maister, David, *Managing the Professional Service Firm*, NY 1997.

2 Greenwood, Royston, Hinings, CR and Brown, John, "P2 Form of Strategic Management: Corporate Practices in Professional Partnerships", *Academy of Management Journal* 1990, Vol 33, No 4, pp725–755.

Several propositions for strategies of law firms have been formulated by Greenwood *et al*, and we find that most of them are (still) true today, but they need refinement, as they are increasingly true only for small to midsize law firms:

Proposition 1: *Decentralisation of operating control will characterise professional partnerships.* (Management is weak; the process of management is organised differently from corporations.)

Proposition 2a: *The primary focus in a professional partnership will be the development and maintenance of professional standards.* (While ignoring the potential of learning from assignments.)

Proposition 2b: *Professional partnerships will have centralised control of the development and maintenance of professional standards.*

Proposition 3: *Professional partnerships will use general market controls.* (There is no focus on key performance indicators.)

Proposition 4: *Professional partnerships will have tolerant performance accountability embracing both non-financial and financial targets.* (Profit is just as important as other criteria, like work–life balance, individual freedom etc.)

Proposition 5: *A consensus-building approach to strategic decision making will characterise the pattern of interaction in professional partnerships.* (Strategy is a difficult exercise as conflicting aims are in play.)

Proposition 6: *A low to modest use of strategic rational analysis characterises professional partnerships.*

All law firms sell time to clients. In essence, all law firms, all around the world, from small to large, share the same business model: lawyers are assigned to individual cases, working on them as if they were completely new to the firm and the lawyer, as well as billing the time spent on the matter (on any other billing scheme applicable due to local laws and regulations). Within this business model, strategy can unfold. But this business model also forms the limit within which strategies can be applied. That constraint makes it hard for new processes to take hold (as we shall see later, and in the chapter by Robert Millard).

1.2 The structure of the legal market: are the strategies of small, medium-size and large law firms different?

But first, let us clarify what strategy means in the context of a law firm. Very often, the strategies of the corporate world, essentially production companies, or very large business-to-consumer service industries, are applied to law firms. We strongly suggest that this is at least partially flawed.

Figure 1. Law firm entities (including individuals and employed lawyers) Germany, 2012

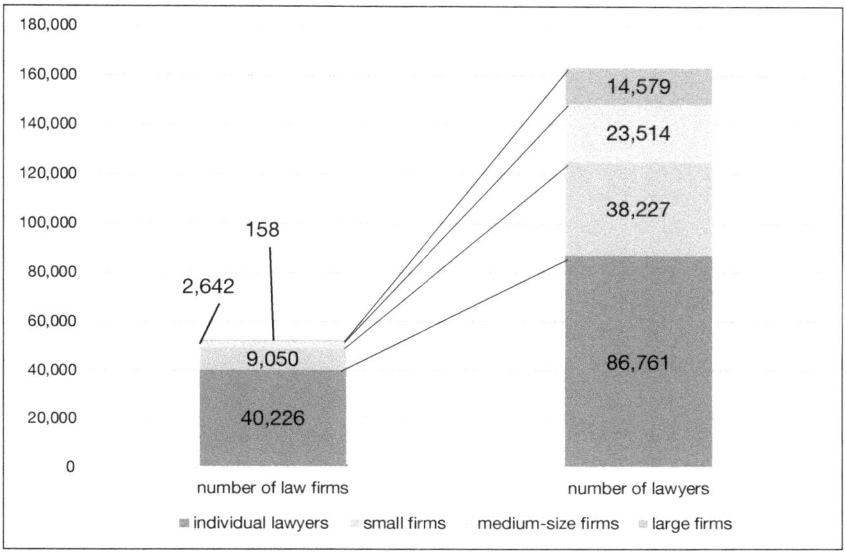

Source: Christoph H Vaagt, based on Benchmark study Der Kanzleimarkt in Deutschland, 2016; data from German tax authorities.

The structure of the legal market in each jurisdiction is divided into four major segments. In the case of Germany, this means:[3]

- 34,000 individual lawyers or small law firms with up to five lawyers caring for private clients and their needs (some 40,000 lawyers);
- 9,300 small law firms looking after private clients and small businesses (20,000 lawyers);
- 2,350 midsize law firms working mostly for family-owned or SME-type clients (with a turnover of €1 million to €10 million) with some 15,000 lawyers; and
- 140 large law firms with more than €20 million turnovers working primarily for listed companies, investors and the financial industry, with some 12,000 lawyers.

The US legal market is similar: with a market size of $326 billion and 440,000 businesses as clients, law firms tend to be rather small on average, with only 1.3 million employees overall. In the

3 All data from 1994 to 2017.

United States, there were approximately 1.33 million lawyers in 2017, working in 50,000 law firms, of which small law firms (<29 attorneys) generated approximately $108 billion, midsize firms (30–174 attorneys) approximately $73 billion, and large firms (>175 attorneys) around $95 billion. The structure of the market is the same as described above.[4]

The focus of most literature is on the strategy in large law firms, or even very large law firms with more than 100 lawyers, especially from the United Kingdom and the United States, as there is more data available.[5] The larger law firms, however, represent around or less than 1% of all law firms in general within a given jurisdiction; in the case of Germany, 90 law firms with more than €10 million turnover employ all in all some 12,000 lawyers, while about 110,000 lawyers are active in the legal market in more than 25,000 law firms or as individual lawyers.[6] Similar figures are available for the UK market:[7] 26 law firms with more than 26 partners represent only 1.81% of all firms of 87,786 solicitors, not counting the 10,000 or so barristers. In Germany, about 10% of all active lawyers work in these large law firms, over 40% in midsize firms (with €1 million to €10 million turnover).

1.3 Strategic challenges for law firms of different sizes

The law firms in each segment are facing different challenges when it comes to strategy. A book written under the auspices of the IBA must take account of this fact.

Strategies must be formulated, we assume, when competitive pressures force businesses to do so. Given the structure of the legal market, we can observe in very broad terms:

- The private client market is the most sensitive to lawyers' fees; thus, third-party service providers are the most likely source of competition. We note that in larger markets, such as the United States, the United Kingdom or Germany, these service providers are already gaining market access – first by serving client needs left unattended by law firms (eg, flightright.de, a company helping customers recover

4 http://businessoflawblog.com/2015/01/addressable-us-legal-market/.

5 See for instance: Smets, Michael, Morris, Tim, Nordenflycht, Andrew, Brock, David, "25 Years Since 'P2': Taking Stock and Charting the Future of Professional Firms", *Journal of Professions and Organization*, 2017.

6 See Vaagt, Christoph H and Zulauf, Thorsten, *Der Kanzleimarkt in Deutschland*, 2016.

7 Unpublished study by the Law Society of England and Wales, The Legal Service Industry, Part I, p9.

damages from flights cancelled or delayed within the European Union).

- The small or midsize law firms are only partially impacted by these changes, but they are "squeezed in the middle" between larger law firms, able to produce better legal advice in special areas of law, such as financing. Alternatively, cheaper or easier to use advice (eg, in personal injury cases) may be offered by highly specialised law firms such as Gordon & Slater, which can invest in software and marketing, overpowering smaller law firms in these areas of private client law.
- The large-firm market has become price-sensitive as the buyers of legal services are well experienced and increasingly make use of procurement processes and departments. Thus, large law firms, in particular in the UK or US law-dominated market segments, must try to reduce the costs for legal services, by making use of document automation, leaner processes with the help of legal process management or the like. The resource side of the equation accordingly receives a lot more attention.[8]

Now the question is, what drives strategies in law firms, and how can they be adapted to changing markets? Professional service firms are not immune to the changes happening in society, so they are adapting as professions.[9] How do law firms need to adapt, thus making use of 'strategies'? Again, we suggest differentiating the different markets that law firms operate in, from small to large firms.

This book has been structured along the lines of resource and market sides, as we see that the impact on business strategies comes from these two perspectives (see also the chapter by Dina Gracheva).

2. The resource side

Traditionally, the focus of law firm partnerships was to generate growth through the development of skills by training people inside the firm. Young lawyers were trained and promoted according to their ability to serve, retain or attract clients. They were usually asked to focus on areas within the larger strategic focus of the firm, based on the kind of clients it can attract and the kind of matters

---

8 For more on this group of law firms, see, for instance, Bruch, Nicholas, *Globalisation in the Strategy-Led Law Firm Business*, London, Ark Group, 2012.

9 See Greenwood, Royston and Lachman, Ran, "Change as an Underlying Theme in Professional Service Organizations: An introduction", *Organization Studies*, 1996, Vol 17, No 4, p563.

Figure 2. Market- and resource-based views of the business of law

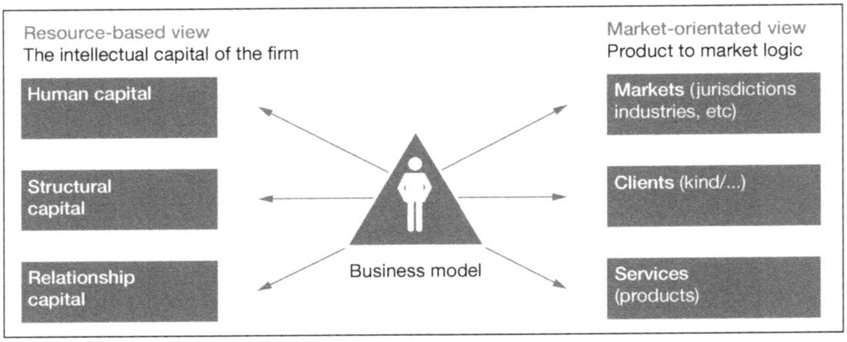

handed to it. This observation is key to understanding the business strategies of law firms in general, and thus the focus on partnerships to keep talent inside the firm.

2.1 Basic PSF strategy: developing the business strategy through learning feedback loops, thus increasing expertise

The law firm business strategy is the result of learning by the lawyers on assignments.[10] The learning enables the firm to offer even better services, creating a feedback loop based on continuous learning of the practitioners in a law firm. Of course, internal communication is helpful, even without every lawyer constantly learning something new, thereby altering the offering and services of the firm to new clients. Thus, we could speak of a kind of 'emerging strategy'.

Based on this very basic understanding of strategy in law firms of all sizes (which we can confirm based on more than 20 years of advising law firms of different sizes and scales in Germany and beyond), law firms address only those clients whom they believe to be able to serve with confidence; likewise, clients choose only those law firms where they believe they will find a sufficient degree of capabilities, experience and, sometimes, capacity to serve their needs.

This 'learning' is learning on the job, nothing formal or institutionalised. We are always surprised by the degree to which

10 See Løwendahl, Bente R, *Strategic Management of Professional Service Firms*, Copenhagen 2005; Reihlen, Markus and Nikolova, Natalia, *Knowledge Production in Consulting Teams: A Self-Organization Approach*, Lüneburg 2010.

Figure 3. Model of strategy development of PSF by feedback loops

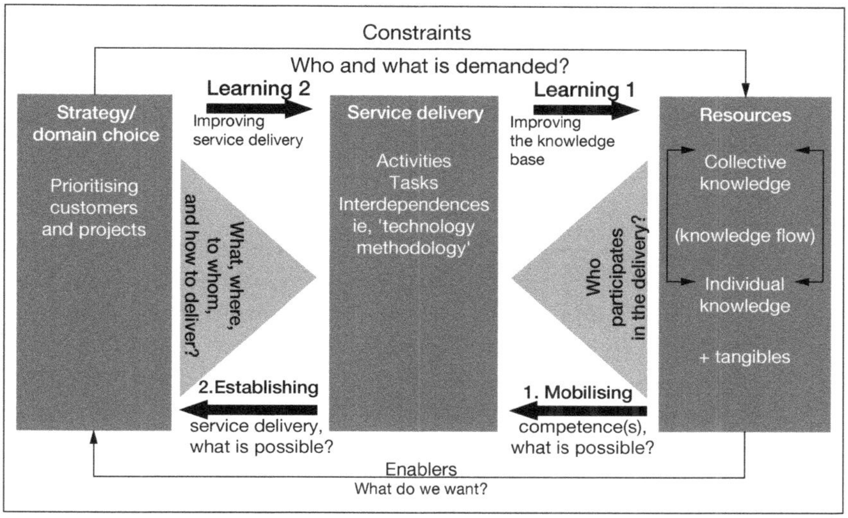

Source: Adapted from Bente R Løwendahl, Strategic Management of Professional Service Firms, 3rd edition, 2005, p107.

formal learning is neglected in law firms, while having in place an informal learning process which is driving the strategy of lawyers, and thus a firm. Bente R Løwendahl in her chapter empirically shows that learning in feedback loops is helpful for both people development and building institutional wisdom and insight. One example where this has been applied for centuries, for instance, are the conditions under which pupil barristers are learning in the barrister chambers in the Temple district in London, traditionally sitting in the same room as senior barristers, and learning by observation and under supervision.

2.2 Other elements of law firm strategy: service, reputation and relationship

Smets *et al*[11] argue that:

> *most professional service firms cannot build competitive advantage on their expertise alone but need a set of four interrelated resources: expertise, service, reputation and relationship. Individually,*

11 Smets, Michael, Morris, Tim, Carroll, Stuart, "Orchestrating for a Winning Performance: Rethinking Strategy in Professional Service Firms", *Said Business School Working Paper Series*, 2008.

these form the necessary basis of a strong competitive position in the marketplace, albeit one that remains assailable.

They further contend that "their expertise is not unique in any substantial way and is susceptible to imitation or replication". We would admit that this is true, but it is the result of a strategy, not a strategy in itself, nor a description of how one can successfully develop a strategy.

Most law firms enjoy some kind of reputation in a given marketplace, where each partner has his or her relationships.[12] The service level of the firm, or more often of each partner, plays a role too, as clients expect a certain level of service. All this, however, is based on the knowledge and experience of the lawyers which allow them to take on certain matters (and refuse others), building said reputation among a network of clients. The abstract 'management' of these four dimensions might be useful, and every law firm partnership of all sizes is looking at these four dimensions at some point. We find, however, that resources are generally reserved for the service element; the other dimensions are considered to a greater degree the larger a company is, if they are managed separately by individual processes. So, we would suggest that Løwendahl's observation remains the main 'driver' of the strategic process.

2.3 Formal education and training

As the formulation of a strategy does very much depend on the skillset of a law firm, the way in which these skills are formed, changed and enlarged should be a central focus of law firms. This is implemented through internal or external training, hiring of people with special skills, and even the lateral hiring of partners.

All of this does happen, but only very reluctantly and in small steps. Larger law firms have started introducing internal education programmes, yet most of these efforts are rather limited or not so much focused on building competitive advantage instead of being able to offer some fringe benefits beyond salaries. However, we can see some internal training as building internal institutionalised knowledge, based on "how we do things here". Smaller firms do often neglect the need for internal training and reflection.

---

12 The importance of reputation for PSF is argued in Harvey, Smets, Morris, *Reputation Management in Professional Service Firms*; see also: Greenwood, Royston, Li Stan X, Prakash, Rajshree and Deephouse, David L, "Reputation, Diversification, and Organizational Explanations of Performance in Professional Service Firms", *Organization Science*, Vol 16, No 6, November–December 2005, pp661–673.

2.4 Most importantly: who to make partner

As long as law firms are primarily constituted as partnerships, the core decision is who to make partner. Partners mostly stay in the same firm for their whole career, so it is a decision for the next 20 to 30 years and thus the most long-lasting choice.

We find what has been termed "the partner-manager-producer dilemma", as famously described in the Harvard Business School case "Bob Andersen at Cambridge Consulting Group".[13] Here we find the most important traits of law firms, where:

1. Partners are owners
2. Owners are managers
3. Managers are producers

Thus, making someone a partner has an effect on the resource side as well as the market side. Elevating the designated lawyer values his or her quality and capabilities, which become part of the firm's offering. Nothing is more important. This essential choice is also deeply entwined with strategic thinking. Making someone partner affirms their legal and entrepreneurial skills and thus affects the firm's strategy for further development. So if a commercial lawyer is invited, this means enlarging the commercial law capabilities of the firm; by the same token, inviting a family lawyer to join the partnership strengthens that aspect. Accordingly, the decisions on who to elevate are indeed discussed very much in detail, both in regard to 'personal fit' and 'strategic fit'.

Partnerships have been mostly formed among like-minded men. They share a similar attitude to work, clients and running a firm. This model is less attractive for female lawyers because most of the measured core qualities have been set by men for men. This might change in certain markets, in particular when clients require more diversity; it would also be an advantage for the partnership to include a more diverse workforce. Nonetheless, more observation in the future will be needed regarding whether this argument is included in the strategy debate.

2.5 Internal competition as a driver of business strategies: the inevitable development of the 'generalist' law firm

This model of learning produces, however, internal competition between partners if they were all to focus on the same clients and

13 DeLong, T and Nanda, A, *Professional Services: Texts & Cases*, McGraw Hill, 2003, p338.

matters. Thus, there is a natural tendency to broaden the offering, to attract new clients and to avoid internal competition among partners. To do so is, nevertheless, not easy.[14]

The resulting specialisation of lawyers – on either areas of law, or within one field, different aspects of it or different types of clients or matters – has been one of the observations in law firms. Basically, one does not find a law firm where all partners look after the same clients, offering the same specialisations and working in the same manner.[15] Thus law firms become generalist firms over time, offering services to different clients and in a variety of legal aspects. It is only in later stages that firms then start to refocus on particular clients and matters, based on their development over the years, thus eventually becoming law firms with a somewhat more refined reputation, and streamlining the services accordingly.

2.6 The profit-sharing system as an important driver in law firm business strategies

Most law firms are partnerships. Each partner has autonomy over which clients and matters to accept, within certain limits based on the fundamental skillset and experience within the firm. The way law firms operate can be compared to 'holding companies', where success is mainly determined by the financial contributions of each partner, representing a 'business within the business'. Each partner must contribute within a certain range to be acceptable to the rest of the partners.

The degree to which there is a common strategic answer of the whole firm, or only parts of it, also depends very much on the internal structure of the firm, mainly the profit-sharing system.[16] This formula is referred to frequently. We would speak here in broader terms of two kinds of system: those promoting the 'equal share' of partners in the profit or those rewarding 'individual merit'. There are also some systems which try to promote both aspects, but our research shows that, in general, one of these two 'cultural modes' will dominate.[17]

---

14 Anand, Narasimhan, Morris, Tim and Gardner, Heidi, *New Practice Development in Professional Service Firms*, 2005.

15 Garicano, Luis and Hubbard, Thomas N, *Specialization, Firms, and Markets: The Division of Labor Within and Between Law Firms*, June 2007.

16 Millard, Robert, "Aligning partner remuneration with strategy", in Roche, Michael and Pavlova, Polina, *Partner Remuneration in Law Firms*, Globe Law and Business, 2016; McChesney, Fred S, "Team Production, Monitoring, and Profit Sharing in Law Firms: An Alternative Hypothesis", *The Journal of Legal Studies*, Vol 11, No 2, June 1982.

17 Vaagt, Christoph H, "Do you share profits or do you receive remuneration? Patterns in law firm culture", in Roche, Michael and Pavlova, Polina, *Partner Remuneration in Law Firms*, Globe Law and Business, 2016.

In a law firm context, we understand this as describing each partner's commitment to the firm, or the lack of it. Weick[18] would speak of loosely coupled systems versus closely coupled systems. A loosely coupled system would be less able to follow a common strategy as the profit-sharing system rewards individual financial success. Thus, each partner would pursue individual market strategies rather than adapting to a joint approach. A closely coupled system – or law firms distributing profits not based on individual financial performance but rather common success, sharing according to a formula of equal shares, or by seniority like lockstep, or any other criteria not primarily linked to individual success – is a different case regarding formulating and following through strategies.

These examples illustrate how much strategic answers are dependent on the internal organisation of a law firm, whether small or larger. The resource side features several elements to consider, of which the profit-sharing system is certainly one of the most important.

2.7 The role of 'management' in midsize law firms vs group dynamics

When we discuss 'management', we should draw a difference between the following:

- Management as a structure: whether there is an entity within a law firm charged with the administration and, possibly, leadership of a law firm;
- Management as a process: the way in which the decision making takes place in a law firm; and
- Management as an outcome: management is often referred to as a fact, something which "made it happen", whether by a regulation, or by the "invisible hand", somehow, an organisation "was managed".

The management function, which evolves with the size of the partnership, may contribute to the administration of the firm and the controlling of financial results, and help establish guidelines for partners. The ultimate decision makers are the partners, even in very large partnerships.[19] Thus, the management function is essentially

18 Orton, J Douglas and Weick, Karl E, "Loosely Coupled Systems: A Reconceptualization", *The Academy of Management Review*, Vol 15, No 2, April 1990, pp203–223.

19 See, for instance: Empson, Laura, "Who's in Charge? Exploring Leadership Dynamics in Professional Service Firms", June 2013; Chambliss, Elizabeth, "New Sources of Managerial Authority in Large Law Firms", in *New York Law School Legal Studies Research Paper Series* 08/09 No 28.

weak, and its role in the formulation of strategy is therefore not that important, as suggested in Greenwood *et al*'s Propositions 1, 5 and 6 above.

For a better understanding of the role and function of management, we should differentiate law firms according to size.

Smaller law firms with up to seven partners tend to organise the management by delegating tasks to each partner, such as marketing, finance, IT, human resources, etc. The partners take over these jobs on a voluntary basis, often in line with personal preferences and knowledge. They thus contribute as a collective group of 'managers', and they struggle when conflict with their roles as owners arises. For instance: while the need to invest in IT might be obvious, older partners might resist it since they fear a diminution of their profit, whereas the benefits would accrue for those who stay longer in the firm.

Once the partnership increases to more than seven partners, we find that a group of usually three partners are tasked with the management of the rest of the firm, with more or less clear instructions on how to manage and how to make decisions. Hence some partners manage others – a challenging situation as conflicts may occur at every corner. This proves most difficult for those partners excluded from the daily management since they do not understand and respect the decisions taken by some. The latter is because they are used to joint decision making or, at least, to being as well-informed as those with the information. Thus we find boards which basically avoid taking decisions, those which are always asking their fellow partners to monthly, sometimes even weekly, meetings, and those which are more eager to take decisions up to a certain threshold of importance. It should be noted that monthly meetings of all partners, however, is the rule rather the exception in this size of firm. The influence on strategic decision making is, therefore, very limited.

Once the group of partners exceeds the number of 16 partners,[20] we very often found law firms changing management again, now instituting a committee of usually around three partners to look after the main management tasks, such as marketing, finances and human resources. The remainder of the management items are delegated to employed staff with specialised knowledge. These boards usually do

---

20 This is an observation made at the T-Group research in United Kingdom; also confirmed by Patrick McKenna in www.patrickmckenna.com/pdfs/Big%20 Industry%20Groups%20Suck.pdf.

not have any formal decision-making power, and are more often than not limited in regard to, for example, spending or hiring decisions, either by express limitations in the statutes or by being asked to refer to the partnership for formal decision making. Very often, there is no formal planning; there are no budgets, so that even minor spending decisions must have a formal approval by the whole partnership (we found stipulations in partnership deeds that a vote of the whole partnership should be taken when the decision exceeds the value of as little as, say, €5,000). This limits, of course, the ability to take decisions and manage, let alone to change direction or the strategies of the firm. Moreover, internal guidelines – such as tracking bills, time recording, client intake, etc – are often not handled by the management. Nonetheless, the partners active in these fields are aware of the respective information and know that the firm needs to act in certain areas. In brief: partners are and remain supreme, and the ownership role they enjoy also plays a role in everyday tasks and decisions.

Only when a law firm has around 40 or more partners, we observe that a single managing partner is elected to administer the whole firm. This does not mean that he or she enjoys more decision-making power; very often, the managing partner is surrounded by a committee of sorts which helps him or her to make the decisions, but at least there is a single point of authority for the employees of the firm. Partners do still enjoy a large degree of autonomy, even if they pretend, in their public statements, that a strategy is in place. Very often, there is not.

Even larger law firms tend to become what has been termed 'managed professional businesses' as opposed to 'professional partnerships'. This archetype change has consequences both for strategy formulation and execution, and this type is the one which is usually referred to when academics (not most consultants) speak about "law firm strategy".[21]

However, whenever the partnership is sitting together (eg, on weekend retreats), the group dynamic of these meetings largely decides the outcome. And this means that it is not a structured, disciplined exchange of views and sharing wisdom but rather an unstructured discussion of the same topics every year. The repetition of identical themes – mainly the contribution of partners to the success, and the distribution of the resulting profits – is

---

21 But not yet in regard to strategy formulation in 2003: See Pinnington and Morris, "Archetype Change in Professional Organizations: Survey Evidence from Large Law Firms", *British Journal of Management*, Vol 14, 2003.

characteristic of these meetings. Occasionally, questions about partner promotions are also of importance, as well as people policies etc. Consensus building in the sense of stopping diverging views from being voiced is the primary focus of this exercise (see Greenwood *et al*'s Proposition 5 above). Hardly ever are there discussions about strategies as the markets served are too diverse, and the interests of partners too divergent.

Budget meetings happen only in larger firms, with more than, say, 20 partners, and these are based on the previous year's numbers, not economic considerations about the best use of resources, new pricing mechanisms or clever project management tools. Thus, general market controls (not key performance indicators) are still the rule rather than the exception (as stated in Greenwood *et al*'s Proposition 4 above).

2.8 Legal tech and legal process optimisation as part of emerging strategies in midsize and larger law firms

Introducing better service inside a law firm might have an impact on its strategy. On the one hand, it alters the offering, thus making it more attractive for certain types of cases by certain types of clients. It also introduces a combination of legal, technological and process know-how, often in the hands not of lawyers but of specialised co-workers. The introduction of these qualifications alters the cost base and over time the business model of a law firm, as it tries to stay in a market, although at more competitive delivery practices (speed and costs).

It is still too early to predict the impact of these new processes and technologies in the market place, but they are assumed to be a game changer – at least in market segments where repeated, standardised demand needs to be met by standardised legal offerings at a cheaper price and quicker speed than today's solutions.[22] We find arguments for both cases.[23]

The question for a law firm to answer, however, is if it wants to compete in these markets or look beyond these market segments; that is, if it can escape this trend. At the time of publication of this book, we do not see legal tech having a major impact on law firm strategy or business. This change, if it comes, will affect the fringes of the market rather than the core. It is difficult to predict

22 Beaton, George and Kaschner, Imme, *Remaking Law Firms: Why and How*, 2016.

23 See: matter management, assisted by legal tech, as described by Felix Dette; and legal project management, as described by Ignaz Fuesgen.

when change will happen and new competitors, often with a different business model, organisation, ownership structure and business proposition, might enter the field. They will build their own market, battle among themselves, and will need to look at their own strategic repertoire. It is highly speculative to predict that these service providers will change the legal market.

2.9 Ethics as a boundary to strategy formulation

We observe that ethics is a cultural boundary for the formulation of strategies (see also Greenwood *et al*'s Proposition 2 above). The ethical boundaries of the profession demand not only that the core principles of the profession are preserved but also that the dilemma between economic imperatives and legal requirements is always dissolved in favour of the latter, in addition to a number of more or less clearly defined codes of conduct (eg, Bar rules). Tomasz Wardyński argues in his chapter how important that is both for the individual lawyer and the industry itself.

In small law firms, we often find a policy in place whereby partners are accepting nearly every client seeking legal advice. While this makes it difficult to specialise, or to earn the fees needed to run the practice, it is important to the partners; to question it because of simple economic considerations is sometimes considered a 'breach of ethical rules'. The impact on strategy is obvious.

Similarly, midsize law firms often have ethical considerations in place which forbid one client to pay, for instance, more than 5% of turnover. This restriction is in aid of the goal of staying independent. Sometimes we also find ethical limitations on certain client interactions, in addition to what might be written in codes of conduct or what is expected from a lawyer as part of the organisation administering justice.

In larger law firms, the ethical boundaries are increasingly blurred.[24] Economic imperatives dominate. This goes hand in hand with a tendency to prefer merit-based profit-sharing models,

---

24 See, for instance: Parker, Christine E, Rosen, Robert Eli, Lehmann Nielsen, Vibeke, "The Two Faces of Lawyers: Professional Ethics and Business Compliance with Regulation", *The Georgetown Journal of Legal Ethics*, Vol 22:201; Galanter, Marc S, Henderson, William D, "The Elastic Tournament: The Second Transformation of the Big Law Firm", *Stanford Law Review*, Vol 60, 2008; Kirkland, Kimberly, *Ethics in Large Law Firms: The Principle of Pragmatism*, 2008; Kirkland, Kimberly, "Ethics in Large Law Firms: The Principle of Pragmatism", *The University of Memphis Law Review*, Vol 4, 2005; Parker, Christine, *Peering Over the Ethical Precipice: Incorporation, Listing and the Ethical Responsibilities of Law Firms*, 2008; Regan, Jr, Milton C and Bauman, Jeffrey D, *On principles: Legal Ethics And Corporate Practice*, 2005.

whereby the individual partner, not the group, takes responsibility, and whereby the decreasing commitment towards the profession in general, and the group in particular, diminishes. Whether this represents a major threat to law firms in this segment remains to be seen. Recent examples include the ENRON scandal, in which the lawyers of a large US firm, Vilkins & Elkins, were involved and the CumEx scandal, which involved Magic Circle firm Freshfields, among others. While individual lawyers were prosecuted in the end, the firms as such had been responsible for allowing this to happen; in the case of Freshfields, the company accepted having to pay a fine of some €50 million in Germany alone – which it surely would not have done without admitting some major malfunction at play.

Another issue is the discussion about the introduction of 'Chinese walls': it stands in direct contradiction to the rule that a law firm shall not represent two parties in the same legal issue. Large law firms argued that they were merely trying to offer their services to more than just a single client, as in procurement processes. However, there are serious doubts if the introduction of Chinese walls is working, requiring the individual lawyer to become a social 'hero'[25] in the traditional sense of the word. However, the self-regulation of law firms by the Bar failed in this respect, and the strategic implications are clear.

3. Market side

Looking at the market side of the business of law, we look at clients, markets and services. These are subject to the dynamics of competition, thus opportunities and limitations which law firms find when trying to strategically position their services.

What we can observe is that the current legal model of most law firms in basically all jurisdictions in the developed world delivers services addressing most diverse legal needs. As of today, it delivers:

- a high degree of service mentality, ethos and dedication;
- a worldwide 24/7 service to all kinds of businesses and most kinds of private client issues;
- specialisations on every legal issue/industry problem etc;
- a high degree of standardised legal procedures applied by every lawyer around the globe, with a basic understanding of the legal issues at stake and a willingness and ability to overcome them to the advantage of clients;

25 Lazega, Emmanuel, "Time to Shrink to Greatness? Networks and Conflicts of Interests in Large Professional Firms", *Revue für postheroisches Management* I, Heft 10, 2012.

- a close collaboration of lawyers around the globe in every aspect of the law in each jurisdiction;
- at a price which is generally in line with needs (otherwise it would not be used); and
- with a financial output for partners commensurate with the high workload, the entrepreneurial risks and a service mentality which comes with it (not taking into account 50 to 60 work hours a week, much more than the usual co-worker in other industries is able and willing to provide).

Such a collaboration can be provided by few, if any, professions across the world. Chartered accountants or tax advisers may approach the level of cohesion, and medical professionals might be considered as well. Consultants fall far short, as theirs is an unregulated profession.

Traditional law firm partnerships cannot compete in every aspect with other business models; they offer specialised services, not standardised, automated solutions to standard problems. But we would suggest that, in general, the strategies of all law firms combined are able to address most of the demand side of the market and provide services. We accept that some segments are underserved due to the pricing model, but we would suggest that this is a 'public policy issue', not a problem which the legal market must solve by itself, as long as it is public policy to require lawyers to propose their services for freely set fees.

We suggest looking at those elements of the market side of their business strategy which deal with the offering of law firms. In that respect, it should be considered which strategies are available to the firms to adapt to changing needs or a changing competitive landscape. In addition, we propose that the size of the law firm should once more serve as a determinant for the kind of strategy formulation and strategy execution available to the companies.

It is useful to investigate the structures of the demand side before venturing into possible strategies. Unfortunately, very few existing studies have considered the demand side.[26]

---

26 For instance, in the United Kingdom see: Pleasence, Professor Pascoe and Balmer, Dr Nigel J, *In Need of Advice? Findings of a Small Business Legal Needs Benchmarking Survey*, Cambridge, April, 2013; "Legal Services Market Study Part 3", *Law Society*, 2012; in Germany see: *Der Rechtsdienstleistungsmarkt 2030, Eine Zukunftsstudie für die deutsche Anwaltschaft*, edited by Deutscher Anwaltverein, 2013.

When reviewing the legal market, we can observe a very high degree of core strategic advantages of the current strategies in place. It remains to be seen when, how and where the much heralded end of lawyers' traditional organisation of their business (as P2) and their defined strategies will come.

3.1 Main decision: decide which markets to serve

One of the choices a business may take is which kind of clients to serve, and which ones to exclude.

For instance, one of the most basic strategic choices for lawyers, and law firms, is whether to serve private clients or businesses – one of the main divides of the demand side of the market. If a law firm fails to respond to this question, those lawyers serving business in such an undecided law firm partnership will quite soon find themselves in a position where they need better services, a higher-quality system, and nicer offices than those serving private clients. A failure to address this issue will result in a discussion about service standards now requiring an answer. If this strategy debate ever concludes, a strategic choice is made, allowing for the streamlining of the operation towards the targeted clientele.

However, while this is clearly a very important strategic decision, you rarely find law firms making clear-cut statements about which clients not to serve in the future, because, very often, some partners' business cases depend on serving these clients. It would amount to asking partners to leave – something which rarely happens. Even very large law firms, such as Eversheds, had to make this decision rather late in its development (in 2003).[27]

Law firms which had built a reputation among certain clients, like banks, were forced to decide if they would be able to cater to the needs of the typical clients of banks as well, such as larger lenders, or rather avoid a potential conflict of interest by not taking on these clients. Smaller law firms rarely face a concentration of clients from the same industry or with similar interests, allowing them to avoid this dilemma for the most part.

3.2 Growth strategies

Law firms understand that they need to grow in order to be able to handle different matters, in particular when working for businesses. (Private client law firms do not experience this kind of pressure to

---

27 See www.thelawyer.com/issues/8-december-2003/eversheds-axes-london-private-client-business/.

grow, as the areas of law which they need to cover are simply fewer and less complex; such as family law, inheritance law, neighbour law, building law, administrative law, and the like.)

One traditional way of doing so is to build specialisations in certain areas of law. This enables the individual lawyer to provide higher quality and easier standardisation.

In smaller law firms, specialisation is available only if there is an agreement in place to respect this choice and to deal with the economic consequences. For instance, if a lawyer agrees to work only in family law, while another focuses on commercial litigation, the financial contribution of the latter might be higher. So, these two need to discuss costs and/or profit sharing if they wish to provide both specialisations to the marketplace.

In midsize law firms, this question has usually been dealt with, and thus specialisation is existent and respected. However, the kind of client acceptable to the partnership is very often an area of strategic debate, as, for instance, the question of whether to serve private or corporate clients. They may then discuss whether to practise through practice groups. Inside these practice groups, a law firm can build more capacity and cover more specialities within one area of law, but individual partners need to agree on organisational and leadership issues.

Specialisation in terms of industry specialisation is practised only in larger law firms, except where the whole firm is focused on one industry, usually defined as a 'niche' firm. Very few law firms have a clear strategic objective – for example, "to serve the top 100 financial institutions in the world". (This actually was an objective of, but not followed through by, one of the Magic Circle firms at the beginning of 2000.) Such clarity of aim contradicts the other elements in strategy, as mentioned above.

As a result, there is a need for collaboration in larger law firms which tend to build silos either by office or by practice group. This may be surprising since the partners as owners are supposed to have all the same interests in full use of the resources, but as Heidi Gardner demonstrates, with data from very large law firms and Big 4 accountancy firms, there are huge potentials left on the table.[28] This internal competition is not yet fully explored, just as group dynamics as one of the main characteristics inside partnerships have not been sufficiently understood and described.

---

28 Gardner, Heidi K and Matviak, Ivan, *Implementing A Smart Collaboration Strategy*. See also Heidi K Gardner and Ivan Matviak's chapter in this book.

3.3 Geographic coverage

Increasing geographic coverage has always been one of the main growth strategies of law firms. Starting in the 1960s, with the first alliances such as Baker McKenzie being founded, we now have over 200 networks offering local or national law firms a hub for their activities. Larger law firms have tried heading this way either through merger or by organising Swiss verein structures allowing for closer cooperation below full integration.[29]

Larger firms have traditionally merged with other firms to 'grow'. This has resulted, for the most part, only in the law firm being able to offer its services with more capacity and/or other locations and, to a certain degree, greater experience and skills. Nevertheless, mergers have not produced anything radically new to the market. Rather, the experience could be called "the same, but somewhere else". The geographic dimension of the offering (see Robert C Bata's chapter) is important, but might have lesser impact than other strategies (see below).

3.4 Changes on the demand side

A law firm constantly looks at the demand side of the market, trying to find new legal questions to address. While they mostly do not advertise their service aggressively (except for some very niche segments, such as personal injury cases in the United Kingdom and the United States), lawyers learn from each case and build on their experience. Two major trends have emerged in general, impacting the strategic choices of law firms.

- *Private clients:* The increasing information available to private clients in the information age has given them the ability to select and choose different service providers, including alternative legal service providers (ALSPs). Local reputation will be of lesser importance if the offering of an ALSP is cheaper and quicker. The transaction costs for visiting a lawyer are high (eg, making appointments, taking the time, explaining sometimes difficult issues, or feeling inferior to the lawyer in terms of language, relatively high prices for services). This renders alternatives attractive for issues of lesser importance.

29 McGarry, Steven, *The Handbook*: *Law and Accounting Networks and Associations*, 2019, updated each year, to be downloaded at: www.managingpartnerforum.org/tasks/sites/mpf/assets/image/MPF%20FEATURED%20RESOURCE%20-%20Handbook-Law%20&%20Accounting%20Networks%20-%20McGARRY%20-%2011.1.19.pdf.

- *Business clients:* The insourcing of legal work[30] has led to a changing relationship between inhouse lawyers and external law firms, including the need to better organise the processes of collaboration (see Ignaz Fuesgen's chapter). Still, most law firms (and thus lawyers) have a way to go to sell their services.

In each jurisdiction and the respective legal issues, these trends play out differently, but these forces are here to stay and will continue to impact law firms. Reacting to the changes in the demand side of the market is one of the most challenging for law firms, as they do not operate on data (see Greenwood *et al*'s Proposition 5, above), but rather each partner looks into his or her market, trying to find new opportunities. Except for the UK study cited above, we have never seen detailed data about the demand side of the legal market. This implies that law firms simply rely on the partner's ability to find new clients or sell something different to existing clients, if he or she wants to stay in the firm, rather than having any kind of rational decision making based on data to decide whether to go into new markets or not.

3.5 Merging and lateral hiring: their impact on the business strategies of law firms

Often raised when speaking about changing the profile of a law firm, the idea of simply hiring partners has its limitations, not just in larger law firms.[31] Retaining laterals is the greatest problem.[32] In smaller law firms, we rarely see examples of lateral hiring, or merging, leading to a better market position. Exceptions prove the rule, and therefore, such moves will always happen as one answer to changing local market conditions. Midsize law firms currently active in the market are usually the results of mergers between smaller firms, just as most larger firms are a result of rather recent mergers, starting in the 1990s (see Lisa R Smith's chapter).

In jurisdictions such as Switzerland or Austria, where no larger international law firms are present, there is basically no market for lateral partner moves. Even the top national law firms do not

30 Schwarcz, Steven L, *To Make or to Buy: In-House Lawyering and Value Creation*, 2006.

31 DeStefano Beardslee, Michele, Coates IV, John C, Nanda, Ashish and Wilkins, David B, *Hiring Teams from Rivals: Theory and Evidence on the Evolving Relationships in the Corporate Legal Market*, Revised: 21 February 2010.

32 "Lateral Partner Retention – Exit Signs", *The Lawyer*, 14 February 2011.

aggressively hire lateral partners. The few partner defections which have happened are due to internal conflicts, and the changes are based on existing relationships, without external help or consulting services.

The inability of larger commercial law firms to compete with the companies traditionally seen as the top law firms in each market, such as the Magic Circle firms in the United Kingdom, is mostly due to the reputation the latter enjoy. Thus, merging may make a law firm larger, but not necessarily more competitive. In our research of key performance indicators of the top 100 law firms in Germany, for instance, we see that larger international commercial firms (as opposed to the global elite of firms) are only able to generate the same amount per fee earner as national law firms, whether generalists or focused firms.[33] Thus, except for size, it seems that there is no financial advantage to merge or join a large firm, and we expect to see a re-evaluation of these kinds of merger in the near future, as they do offer only limited advantages over the competition.

3.6 Innovation

Some uncertainty revolves around the question to which degree innovation will impact the legal market as a whole. (Specific market segments or processes being affected have a limited impact.)

We can observe that some market segments are already reacting, and the question is not yet answered if the solution will come from the existing competitors, or if new entrants will be game changers in the legal market, maybe in combination with re- or deregulation.

What seems to be clear is that the impact is not restricted to the existing strategies employed by law firms but rather concerns introducing different business models to the legal market. These would include a different method of producing profit by organising the offering to the market in partially or completely new ways.[34] In addition, the career model in large law firms is adapted to reflect the need for new ways of doing things.[35]

---

33 Vaagt, Christoph H, *Erfolgreiche Wirtschaftskanzleien*, Frankfurt 2011.

34 See Robert Millard's chapter "Business model transformation as a tool for driving strategic innovation and growth".

35 Smets, Michael, Morris, Timothy and Malhotra, Namrata, "Changing career models and capacity for innovation in professional services", *Handbook of Research on Entrepreneurship in Professional Services*, 2012.

3.7 New entrants into the profession will follow a different strategy

The regulatory landscape has not evolved as quickly as might have been assumed in 2010, when Australia and the United Kingdom had started allowing external investors in law firms. It is noted that even in markets where there had been no such barriers from the very start, such as Russia in 1990 after the fall of the Soviet Union, all law firms were created as partnerships, with the most important ones still working like this today. So there might be both a market need as well as other incentives which rather create professional partnerships as the right fit for highly qualified legal services (as opposed to standardisable, low-value, mass instructions by business or private clients). Whether law firms need to 'remake' themselves, or whether the respective prediction will only be applicable to very special markets or segments of the law remains to be seen.

The impact on the legal arms of the Big 4 remains uncertain: they are undoubtedly gaining market share, but will remain in or around 2% to 5% of the business law firm market.[36]

4. Conclusion

Law firm strategies will continue to evolve around some core considerations:

- how to learn from existing clients;
- who to make partner;
- how much do partners collaborate inside firms; and
- which clients to service and which to not.

These considerations will produce the reputation, service levels and relationships needed to compete in a sustained way.

Profit sharing will remain an important pillar for strategy development, just as ethics are important guidelines within which law firms develop. Most of the observations made by Greenwood are still valid, but they must be refined as they become more nuanced, starting at the top level of the market with the largest law firms.

---

36 Wilkins, David B and Esteban Ferrer, Maria J, "The Integration of Law into Global Business Solutions: The Rise, Transformation, and Potential Future of the Big Four Accountancy Networks in the Global Legal Services Market", *Law & Social Inquiry* 2017; Grewe, Dr Till, *Strategische Entwicklung der Big 4: Fokussierung auf Kundengruppen*, MBA, ZuB, 2007.

Strategy in law firms: what it is and why we should care

Bente R Løwendahl
BI Norwegian Business School

1. Introduction

Traditionally, in professional service firms (PSFs) in general, and law firms in particular, strategy has (at best) been implicit in the decisions made by executives (typically partners). Since clients and projects come in unpredictable streams and it is very difficult to know ex ante which of these clients and assignments are likely to be won by our firm, strategy – traditionally seen as formal planning – has often been regarded as impossible for PSFs. In addition to the fluctuating and unpredictable nature of the demand for professional services, most such firms, at least up to a certain size, have traditionally been internally owned, typically in some sort of partnership form. An interesting and not so frequently discussed characteristic of partnerships is that they typically require consensus for any major strategic decision to be made. In many partnerships it is unheard of that some partners (ie, the majority) should make decisions on behalf of the whole collegium, against the will of other partners (ie, the minority). In small firms, this dilemma typically takes one of two possible forms:

- The firm remains fragmented, with each partner taking care of his or her own practice within the firm, acquiring clients and hiring apprentices according to his or her local needs. The firm may have common policies, but sanctions reinforcing such policies are unusual, as such sanctions would require the other partners to bring a conflict out into the open, and partners who are already busy with their own portfolio are normally very reluctant to 'rock the boat'.
- The firm remains small, growth (if any) is slow, and the partners pay particular attention to attracting, retaining, and promoting new partners that share the common set of goals and values, such that consensus can more or less be taken for granted. In such firms, client acquisition is based on consensus, and recruiting is a highly prioritised process of very careful selection of people who 'fit in'.

In another chapter in this book (Harvey, Morris and Smets), the importance of building and maintaining a reputation is highlighted. I would argue that partnerships of the type discussed in the second bullet above may relatively easily develop a consistent reputation over time, whereas partnerships of the type under the first bullet are more likely to suffer from a fragmented reputation, where the different aspects of the reputation are highly dependent on the decisions, actions and reputations of each individual partner or practice manager. As I will argue further in this chapter, strategy is crucial to linking individual partner decisions and developing a consistent reputation over time, both in the client markets and in the markets for legal expertise (new hires). As pointed out by Maister (D Maister (1982) "Balancing the Professional Service Firm", *Sloan Management Review*, 24(1): 15–29), client acquisition and hiring are two sides of the same coin; if you have the best lawyers (in a given area of law), you are also likely to attract the most challenging client assignments. And if you have the most interesting set of client assignments, you are likely to be able to choose among the very best candidates in hiring new professionals into the firm. In this sense, client acquisition (and retention) and hiring (and promotion and retention) are like the chicken-and-egg problem – after the firm has been founded, typically by a few senior lawyers with a particular expertise, reputation, and relationships with (potential) clients, it is hard to know which dimension comes first and which drives the further growth of the firm.

In traditional PSFs, it has been a common view that strategy is 'redundant'. If only you have the right experts and the appropriate list of references to previously successful business with high-prestige clients, an excellent reputation will follow, and clients will more or less queue up at your door. In the past, marketing was paradoxically seen as negative and bad for reputation (see, eg, RE Sibson (1971) "Managing Professional Services Enterprises – The Neglected Business Frontier", New York, NY: Pitman) – comments were often along the lines of: 'they must be short of business, since they have to advertise for new clients'. An innocent and highly illustrative incident happened to a small IT-consulting partnership in Norway, when they decided to advertise for new partners. They placed an advertisement in Norway's biggest newspaper, in the business section, but the newspaper made a mistake and put the advertisement in a hardly visible spot elsewhere in the paper. They were highly apologetic, and without asking the partners of the consulting firm, they decided to re-run the advertisement the next day, on the front page of the newspaper. Little did they know that compensating their customer through such an expensive spot would be highly negative; the IT partnership received a lot of sceptical comments from colleagues and competitors ('are you desperate for business, since you run such an expensive advertisement?'), as well as clients ('how much profit are you really making on my assignment, when you can afford that kind of advertisement?') (BR Løwendahl (2005) *Strategic Management of Professional Service Firms*, 3rd Edition, Copenhagen: Copenhagen Business School Press, page 78).

Yet telling potential clients that the firm has unique expertise and is doing well in particular practice areas is also important to maintaining a sustainable business, as running short of sufficient 'billable hours' may be a disaster for the firm. It is not just that idle professionals turn from a revenue-generating 'asset' into a cost-generating 'liability'; another danger is, as noted by Johan Sagen, founder and previous CEO of the IKO-group (an Oslo-based management consulting firm, later merged into Cap Gemini):

> *With three or more experts idle in the office for more than a couple of days in a row, you always run the risk of the experts figuring out something else to do with their time. And that 'something' is unlikely to fit well with your own firm's strategic direction! Worst case, you not only get a 'spin-off'. you get a new competitor in the market, who also knows your own business from the inside!* (See BR Løwendahl (1992) "Global Strategies for Professional Business Service Firms", Unpublished PhD Dissertation, Philadelphia: University of Pennsylvania (Wharton); BR Løwendahl (2005) *Strategic Management of Professional Service Firms*, 3rd Edition, Copenhagen: Copenhagen Business School Press for an explanation).

Hence, it is important to know what your strategy is, both for client acquisition and retention and to know what professionals to recruit and retain.

2. Value creation in PSFs

As stated above, strategy was often rejected in traditional partnership firms, in the same way as marketing was thought to be unnecessary or even negative. Instead, firms typically advertise promotion of new partners and make large ads for new hires, as this implicitly signals growth and success? The extent to which such hires and promotions are strategic in nature, however, is more questionable.

Strategy in a PSF is not, and cannot be, about planning. As Peter Lorange, professor and former president of IMD in Switzerland, has pointed out in many of his speeches and texts, "Strategy means choice", and choice means not only what to do in the short term or long term, but also what not to do (see Løwendahl, 1992; 2005). If a firm is to achieve consistency over time and thereby build a strong favourable reputation, it needs not only to provide consistently high quality in whatever it delivers; it also needs to have a clear focus in terms of what it does and does not do for and with its clients. Elsewhere I have also argued (T Skjølsvik, BR Løwendahl, R Kvålshaugen, S and Fosstenløkken (2007), "Learning to Choose and Choosing to Learn – Strategies for Client Co-production and Knowledge Development", *California Management Review*, 49(3): 110–128) that PSFs need to have a conscious strategy of target clients and projects in order to maximise potential learning, thereby enhancing the resource base of the firm (see, eg, Gracheva, in this volume or Løwendahl, 2005 for more elaboration on this). And an improved resource base will again increase the firm's probability of winning the most interesting (and potentially profitable) client assignments in the next period of time.

Lorange and Løwendahl (in Løwendahl, 2005; Figure 3, pages 46 to 47) described this as a three-step value-creation process for PSFs:

- You need to sell a 'credible promise' (ie, convince the client that you are the right firm to solve whatever problem the client might have). Here, reputation clearly plays an important part, and may both enhance and limit the opportunities the firm has in a given market niche. In other words, firms are both supported and hindered by their past performance, as potential clients often check on reputations 'through the grapevine'. It may be very difficult to convince a new client that you are able to solve a particular legal problem that the firm has never faced before, unless the firm has been able to recruit a new senior lawyer with an established reputation in that particular area. Well-established clients who know the firm well may be more willing to 'experiment' with new service areas, but then frequently at a discounted price and an unusually low leverage (of juniors to seniors) on the project, thereby making such service area expansions expensive (but perhaps still profitable) investments.
- You need to deliver what you promised. That means not only delivering according to contract (whether formal or 'by handshake'), but managing expectations, managing the

interaction with the client's representatives, and delivering on time and on budget (or ideally below budget for within-firm costing purposes). This sounds like the easy part of value creation, but is really at the core of what the law firm is all about. An ability to define, manage and staff client assignments in the most effective (quality assuring) and efficient (cost-minimising) way is crucial to the firm's long-term success, in terms of both profits and reputation. Just as strategy cannot mean plan, the organisation of value creation cannot mean stable and strict formal structure. But somehow the staffing of the assignment needs to be managed for the benefit of both the professionals and the clients, and what we show in our 2007 article (Skjølsvik, *et al*) is that not only should firms manage each assignment as it has been won, but they should also manage the overall portfolio of projects, both for short-term efficiency and effectiveness and for long-term learning and reputational effects that reinforce the position of the firm and help it win the 'most desired' assignments in the next round of competition. The most successful firms succeed at becoming the 'preferred supplier of legal advice' for a given set of clients in a chosen set of legal services, thereby in some sense being able to avoid head-on competition for a number of important assignments. In the 'good old days', such a position was thought to come more or less automatically, if only you had the right people and provided excellent guidance. I would argue that this is less and less true, as clients become more and more sophisticated in their purchasing processes, even for professional services such as legal advice (eg, T Skjølsvik (2012) "Beyond the Trusted Advisor – The Impact of Client–Professional Relationships on the Client's Selection of Professional Service Firms", PhD Dissertation, Oslo: BI Norwegian Business School).

- The third process pointed out by Lorange and Løwendahl (in Løwendahl, 2005), and which I would argue still is under-focused in many PSFs, perhaps particularly in internally owned or partnership firms, is 'learning from the delivery'. All firms have some kind of archival system that allows them to go back to previous cases and build on previous solutions in their legal practice, and most have some kind of electronically based retrieval system which makes it easier for everyone to access previous cases independently of time and place. The quality of such archival systems, however, varies substantially, and the firm typically needs to have very clear incentives in place in order to get very busy lawyers to commit some of today's potentially billable hours to entering previous experience into an archive for further reference. Or the firm may allow juniors to participate on assignments on a non-billable basis, in order to learn from seniors. In the author's experience, most firms, regardless of PSF-industry, struggle with this problem of knowledge retention and transfer, especially in times when business cycles are at their peak. Paradoxically, it is when you have time to take care of archives and knowledge transfer that you most need access to this information firm-wide, in order to make new sales efforts as target focused as possible.

3. What is strategy?

If strategy is not plan, what is it? As mentioned above, the core of strategy is choice. It is choosing what to do, which assignments we should give the highest priority now, what we are not going to do, and what should be our primary targets in the medium to long term. In our model 'The VCPs for PSFs-framework' (BR Løwendahl, Ø Revang, and SM Fosstenløkken (2001) "Knowledge and Value Creation in Professional Service Firms: A Framework for Analysis", *Human Relations*, 54(7): 911–31), we described the value-creating processes (VCPs) by the illustration of 'three bubbles and six arrows', as shown in Figure 1.

Strategy is the top section in Figure 1, and here we define strategy as the same as 'choice of domain', which is a concept from sociology in the early 1960s (Levine and White, 1961). The choice of domain simply means: the choice of what to deliver (ie, the range of services); to whom (ie, the set of (target) clients served); and, if applicable, where (locally, from one office, from multiple offices, nationally, regionally (eg, the European Union), globally, etc?). This may sound simple but in practice often turns out to be difficult, because choosing what to do also implies choosing what not to do; choosing which clients to serve also means choosing what (types of) clients not to serve. And choosing future target practice areas inevitably also means that some seniors will not see their 'pet projects' on the priority list. Again, ownership models requiring consensus on strategic priorities are likely to lead to more difficulty when making such decisions, not less.

Figure 1. Value-creation processes in PSFs

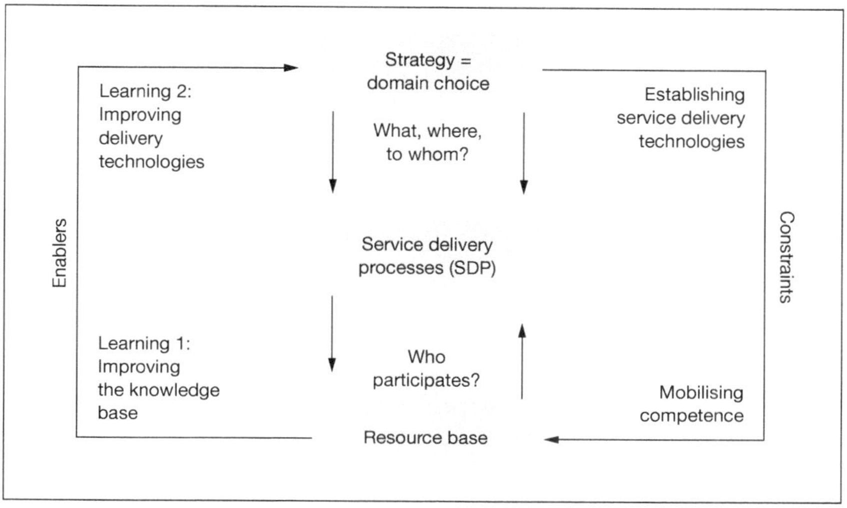

Whereas it may be easy to commit to servicing a new client in a new niche, it may be very much more difficult to get consensus on turning down an interesting assignment, or even worse, terminating a long-term relationship with a client that no longer fits within the strategic portfolio of the firm. And if one particular partner has a strong relationship with such a client, substantial resistance is likely to result.

The second section of the figure obviously represents the 'how', and is equally important for both profits, quality and learning/process development. It is not, however, as strategic in nature as the other two bubbles. The bottom section represents the resources of the firm, and although these may include both tangible resources (finances, office equipment, etc) and other intangible resources (reputation, client relationships, etc; also called relational resources in the author's book (Løwendahl, 2005)), it is obvious that the most important resources to a PSF in general and a law firm in particular, are its competences – individual as well as collective. Since individuals, especially senior professionals and experts, have not only competences but also strong opinions as to how their own resources may best be deployed, for the benefit of the clients, themselves, and the firm (typically in that order), we have drawn the two strong outer arrows in the above figure. The left-hand arrow, from resources to domain choice, indicates that the stronger your resource base and the more specialised competences you have, the more freedom you have in choosing your strategic domain. It is not, however, a question of some top management deciding on the domain, then ordering the resources into ranks and allocating them to wherever management might see fit. One good reason why so many PSFs in general and law firms in particular are internally owned is precisely that the best professionals do not take orders about domain choices. They want to be listened to and respected in these decisions, and if they fundamentally disagree and they do not expect conditions to improve in the near future, they are likely to leave for a competitor or set up their own business instead. Hence, in many ways the resource base sets the premises for what domain choices are possible (and desirable) to make. The right-hand out arrow has to do with the processes described above as 'selling a credible promise'. As pointed out by Harvey, Morris and Smets elsewhere in this book, the reputation of the firm rests fundamentally on the perceptions and evaluations of external stakeholders, and these may represent a fundamental constraint on what the PSF is allowed to do, what kind of assignments it is likely to be allowed to undertake and for which clients.

The shorter arrows in the figure pertain to learning processes, and are therefore more operational in nature. The right-hand arrows indicate that the domain choice (ie, the strategic priorities) informs and sometimes largely dictates the composition of the assignment teams and how they work together for and with the clients (the 'technology'). At the same time, the professionals have to be motivated or rather 'mobilised' to put their best effort into this particular client assignment. One important element of the delivery technology of a law firm is how the assignment team is composed and leveraged, in terms of how many senior partners are involved, how they work together, how many juniors are involved and at what stages of the process, etc. Many firms with relatively specialised practice areas have 'templates' that can be put into action very quickly, given a particular type of assignment (eg, should the firm be called in as part of a due diligence team ahead of a potential merger). This organisational template is what we call 'technology' here, in line with traditional organisational theory, and we argue that many PSFs could improve on both quality (effectiveness) and cost (efficiency) by further refining and enhancing such technology, not in terms of rigid structures, but rather in terms of a set of best practices that can be mobilised when the appropriate situation emerges.

The left-hand arrows indicate that learning takes place both within the resource section, as individuals learn and collective experience is accumulated, and as resources are combined into task forces or assignment teams for each particular client assignment. Our research has shown (eg, SM Fosstenløkken (2007) "Enhancing Intangible Resources in Professional Service Firms", PhD Dissertation, Oslo: Norwegian School of Management BI (Currently Norwegian Business School)) that the most important competence development factor in PSFs, regardless of industry, is the nature of the assignments undertaken and the role each individual is allowed to play in each assignment. Professionals learn from each other; from the clients; from working on the assignment itself; from working with the 'technology' of the assignment (especially for larger projects) from external sources when information needs to be collected or advice sought (for example, from a senior professor in that particular legal practice area) and so on (see, eg, SM Fosstenløkken, BR Løwendahl and Ø Revang (2003) "Knowledge Development through Client Interaction: A Comparative Study", Organization Studies, 24(6): 859–79 for an elaboration of these learning processes).

4. Strategy in PSFs – an oxymoron?

Is it really possible to develop a strategy for a PSF? Is it not always the client who decides what firm to work with, so that the PSF needs to be alert and flexible in order to respond to whatever needs the client might have? From the above discussion it should be clear that the author's view is that strategy is important for PSFs, and maybe even more important than it is for manufacturing firms. The typical (or rather caricatured) manufacturing firm has a set of production machinery and processes that are relatively fixed investments, and will typically strive to maintain and increase its market share based on these already well-established practices. Major strategic investments, especially those leading to diversification, are typically scrutinised in detail before the investment is made. The owners, via the board of directors, are typically involved when investments are of a large magnitude or represent a significant shift from past practices. As discussed above, PSFs very often have internal owners, and these owners – whether partners or not – are typically directly involved, not only in large and long-term financial investments of a strategic nature, but also in the everyday running of the firm. As a result, it may be very difficult to distinguish between an operational and a strategic decision, and this distinction becomes even more blurred if the strategy is not agreed upon by all key decision makers. A strategy, in terms of common goals and priorities, is crucial in order to secure consistency over time; and the more decentralised the decision making and the more autonomy individual partners have, the more important strategy is. This does not mean that every PSF should have a formal strategy document, detailing what, where, when and with whom the firm should work in the future. Here, even more than in the manufacturing firm, it is the process of coming to an agreement on strategic priorities that is of importance, not the resulting document.

The examples illustrated at the beginning of this chapter talked about the consensus-based, typically small partnership, and the fragmented one. Both of these exist in real life, in all PSF-industries, and further discussion of these will follow in the next section. In addition, there are some large, international firms, that increasingly come to resemble the structures of traditional manufacturing firms (eg, R Greenwood, and R Empson (2003) "The Professional Partnership: Relic or Exemplary Form of Governance?", *Organization Studies*, 24(6): 909–33, 2003; L Empson (2007) *Managing the Modern Law Firm*, Oxford: Oxford University Press). They have a formal hierarchy of authority, defined roles and boundaries between practice areas, clear employment contracts and training and promotion programmes, practice development departments and so on. Some of these also have external owners, who may impose further formal structures and reporting procedures on management, in order to control the return on their (capital) investment. The author's book (Løwendahl, 2005) further describes the challenges faced by these firms. They can grow very large and become global, but they need a substantial set of rules and regulations and formal procedures in order to ensure that every professional, junior as well as senior, performs up to standard and in the best interest of the owners. There is a vast literature on the challenges involved, for example, in the area of what is called 'agency theory' (see, eg, EM Eisenhardt (1989) "Agency Theory: An Assessment and Review", *Academy of Management Review*, 14(1): 57–74, for an overview), but these issues are beyond the scope of this chapter. Without having studied any such law firms in depth, however, the author would expect their strategy work to be highly professionalised, with dedicated staff at the corporate office assessing opportunities for future development, and threats from competitors and stakeholders on a regular basis. Given the formal hierarchy of authority, one might also expect most of the problems of consensus and resistance to top management decisions to be overcome by the natural subordination to common goals set by the owners. That is not to say that such large firms do not have conflicts, especially where financial and professional goals are seen to clash. Conflicts are likely to be substantial, as professional norms of conduct require that the professional puts the client's best interests first (eg, JA Raelin (1991) "The Clash of Cultures: Managers Managing Professionals", Cambridge, MA: Harvard Business School Press).

In the two types of firms described at the beginning of this chapter, strategy work may be less obvious. In the fragmented type of firm described under the first bullet point in section 1, every partner is likely to have his or her own opinions as to the priority of target clients and assignments, and the two major challenges for such firms will be:

- to achieve the necessary consistency in order to develop a common firm reputation; and
- a very strong tendency towards a myopic focus on current clients and assignments over what may be better for both learning and profits in the long run.

In the most extreme cases, one may ask why these partners have decided to establish a common firm at all, if they are not willing to give up any of their personal autonomy in order to achieve some common goals. And again, the partnership model often exacerbates these problems, especially in small firms, as every common investment, including non-billable hours to manage the common portfolio, is seen to 'come out of each partner's own pockets'. A major paradox in this respect is the fact that in order to gain the necessary respect and legitimate authority to make decisions on behalf of such a fragmented firm, it needs a very strong managing partner, who will also typically be one of the best 'rainmakers' and client advisors of the firm. And the non-billable hours of such partners are the most expensive for both the firm and the managing partner to sustain. As a result, such managing partners typically only manage part-time, and after all client matters have been dealt with. Again, in times of peak demand, setting strategic priorities will be under-prioritised, despite the fact that it is in good times that the firm can easily afford to set aside time and money for longer-term investments.

The firms described in the second bullet in section 1 traditionally operate under an implicit assumption of consensus, and as long as these areas of expertise fit well with client demand, strategy may also be implicit, yet still result in consistency in decisions and actions over time. A major issue for such firms is often how to deal with behaviours that do not conform to the implicit consensus. What should be the sanctions in such circumstances? Who monitors the work of others? What are the consequences of setting personal priorities above those of the common good of the firm? Challenges also typically arise if this firm decides to grow large and incorporate multiple practice areas, and/or if the firm decides to set up offices in multiple geographical locations. In one of the firms studied in the author's early work on PSFs, the firm ended up having more than 10 'divisions' or practice areas, and conflicts soon developed as the practice areas had different activity and profitability levels, and sometimes demand from a client would overlap several business areas, thereby leading to conflicts over billing rates and the distribution of profits. Similarly, conflicts may arise as some practice areas are more likely to require the work of many juniors, thereby resulting in high leverage and a high profit potential, relative to other practice areas where clients prefer to deal with one or two senior partners directly. On the other hand, a large number of juniors means higher fixed costs, and in times when demand is low, partners in other practice areas may be reluctant to finance the non-billable hours of juniors in other practice areas. Again, there is always the danger of the best professionals seeking to take their expertise, reputation, and client relationships elsewhere if they do not feel that their firm adequately compensates them for their efforts.

In all firms, regardless of size and agreement on common goals, the most difficult challenge seems to be to turn down interesting business from attractive clients. Yet it is impossible to develop a consistent strategy, and thereby a strong reputation, without agreeing on and sticking to a clear focus over time.

5. Why strategy is so difficult in PSFs

In addition to the above-mentioned challenges to strategy work, most PSFs face particular challenges in management as a result of their very nature as professional firms – or firms run by professionals, if you will. Most professionals are trained in a particular profession, and they are members of a professional organisation with clear rules and regulations for professional and ethical conduct. The best professionals typically thrive on challenging professional problems, and most of them dislike spending their time on non-billable managerial work. Unfortunately, most firms also struggle to compensate managerial work, not only financially, but even more so in terms of status, respect and professional development. Many firms therefore prefer some kind of part-time management, either as the managing partner also takes on client work, or as the managing partner role rotates among the senior partners. In both cases, managers reluctantly take on managerial work, and this is work that they have not been trained for. As one of the engineering firm managers in one of the author's early studies put it: "we have engineers that are jewels in the crown in engineering projects, but they are basket cases in management". In some cases, firms even run into what one of the author's colleagues termed 'the hostess's dishwashing problem'; if you are asked to assist in washing the dishes, and break one of the most expensive cups or dishes every time, you will soon be taken off dishwashing duty ... In other words, there are some perverse incentives here to perform management tasks poorly, in order to make sure you stay as short a time as possible in that unwanted position. The result, in many cases, is that not only does strategy and consistent performance suffer – typically the development of juniors becomes *ad hoc*, unfocused and dependent on the goodwill of each individual partner or practice manager taking charge of the training of juniors and keeping them 'billable' and busy with challenging assignments at all times. Again, partners who focus only on their own billable hours and relationships with clients may retain more of the profits, and therefore resist taking on juniors as long as the clients and the market allow them to do so (D Maister (2006a) Strategy Means Saying "No". http://davidmaister.com/articles/4/95/1/).

6. Conclusions

Strategy is critically important to PSFs in general and to law firms in particular – perhaps even more so than for manufacturing firms. Its importance has increased over recent decades, and is likely to continue increasing, as both clients and professionals become more sophisticated in choosing the best firm with which to collaborate. Hiring professionals and acquiring client assignments are crucial for the development of a PSF. These two key processes represent a chicken-and-egg problem, in that hiring and retaining the best professionals is a prerequisite for winning the most challenging and interesting (and profitable?) assignments; and winning the most prestigious client assignments over time is a necessary condition for recruiting, developing, and retaining the best professional experts. Developing a strong reputation requires consistency in both hiring and choice of client assignments over time. The courage to turn down business that falls outside of the strategic areas of priority is crucial. Unfortunately, such strategic consistency is unlikely to emerge without a managerial commitment of senior, non-billable time. This is a constraint that may explain – but not justify – why so many firms still hope that strategy will emerge out of high-quality daily operations. That may have been the case in the 1960s and 1970s, but is not likely to be a viable approach in the years to come.

Bente R Løwendahl sadly passed away on 11 March 2017 and the publisher sends its sincerest condolences to her family, friends and colleagues. This chapter remains the same as published in the previous edition.

Drivers of change – driving strategy in law firms

Mats Anderson
Supreme Administrative Court (Sweden)

1. Introduction

In my old firm we waited for the telephone to ring. If the matter in any way could be described as business law, we took it on. In the new firm we decide what kind of work we want and then we go out and try to get it.

This quote is not from a deeper thinker than myself. It is a simple way of describing change. This chapter deals with the issue of how to manage change and how to drive strategy in a law firm from the perspective of a practitioner. To put it simply, the chapter seeks to describe how to get from the first to the last sentence in the quote.

We have only just seen the start of globalisation. Information technology will develop further. What we have today will look like the Stone Age in just a couple of years. It is easy to say that these will be the major drivers of change for law firms in the future, because this will probably be true for all industries. Sometimes, political decisions affect an industry. Many years ago, there were limits in England on how many partners there could be in a law firm (at least if it was organised as a partnership, which most law firms are). Partners in a firm which now has some 400 partners have told me that they remember times when all the partners in the firm could meet to have lunch in a small dining room. It is ironic that at the time of writing, there are discussions in my home country, Sweden, regarding a proposed amendment to the tax rules, which would mean that law firms will effectively not be able to have more than 25 partners.

We could also look at some other drivers of change. For many years, law firms have heard – to the extent that they have been prepared to listen – that clients want more for less. For a long time nothing happened. When we discussed different ways to compete in an exercise in my old Swedish firm some 20 years ago, I suggested that price was one way to compete. The senior partner who was leading the exercise looked at me as if I was something the cat had dragged into the room. Price competition is here now. The days when you just started working, did the job, looked at how much was on the clock and sent invoices to the client are gone. Now you have to give an estimate or agree on a price before you start working. If you get the job.

Globalisation, development of technology, political decisions and price pressure are of course general factors that can drive change. Then there are other kinds of drivers of change; those that you as a firm can to some extent control. You might want to improve your market position, be a 'market leader'. You might want to have a larger home market (ie, expand into new markets). You might simply be less happy with what you are and try to improve your business.

Diversity – in particular gender aspects – is in my opinion not given the priority it should have in the context discussed here. Regardless of whether you look at larger international law firms, regional firms or national firms, the picture is the same. Less than 20% of partners are women. In Sweden, the larger firms have hired more female lawyers than male lawyers for at least 20 years; but very little has happened. It was true decades ago that women often left the firm after two to four years. And it is the same now. This picture is probably true in most countries in the Western world. From my perspective it is not very productive to discuss diversity or gender as a discrimination issue. The better view is that almost half the population is a resource and talent pool and it is time to make better use of it, in order to improve our business.

On to the subject of this chapter, it is not to describe what drivers of change there might be for different firms. They will often be a combination of the above factors. What I am going to address is, as stated above, rather how to drive the strategy of a firm specifically in management of change situations.

I have had the privilege to be involved in this kind of exercise in two different capacities, as a partner in a law firm and as a law firm consultant. I think it will be easier for the reader to relate to the points I will make as regards driving strategy if I very briefly provide some examples of projects in which I have been involved. It should be noted that the type of law firms I have in mind when I share my thoughts and experience in the following are business law firms which are owned in the traditional way (ie, partnerships). The cases discussed in sections 2.1 and 2.2 are two real projects I have experienced, while the case in section 2.3 is not. It rather describes types of projects I have experienced.

2. The cases

2.1 The first case

The L firm had for decades been the leading firm in its jurisdiction.

The 1980s saw a string of mergers among law firms in the country. In 1990 three leading firms had been formed. These firms were roughly the same size (whether measured by turnover or headcount). Their geographical coverage was identical; they had offices in the three major cities in the country. And they all had the same strategy – or perhaps, rather they shared the same lack of strategy.

In the 1990s the firms fared differently. One of them was the success story of the decade. Those who had heard about the firm in the late 1980s associated its name with a family law firm. A decade later the firm was a household name, at least among those dealing with business law firms in the region. The third firm saw a steady development of its business and it gradually strengthened its position further among blue chip clients.

The L firm did not fare so well. In 1992, a group of partners left the L firm. In 1997, another group left. In the following year, the firm joined the International Firm & Alliance and in September 2001, the L firm merged into the International Firm.

This project is an exercise where a leading national firm is transformed into an office and a part of a leading international firm.

2.2 The second case

Mergers in Western Europe and a few other places had taken place. Business was coming back in the beginning of the 2000s. In the different offices of the International Firm referred to above, partners and local managers were busy trying to adapt to the strategy. People were generally happy; but not central management. In their view, the firm should not just be a leading firm; it should be the leading firm.

2.3 The third case

This concerns a national business law firm. It is doing alright. It is a top or second-tier firm, but only in its country or region. The firm's partners feel that the firm is losing ground to its competitors and needs to improve its market position, but they are not sure exactly how this should be done.

3. Driving a strategy

3.1 Perspectives of strategy

My proposition is that as a partner in a modern law firm you should be able to bring in clients and matters, carry out the work and see to it that money comes in, develop your people and develop your business. I appreciate that very few people are star performers in all these areas, but my view is that in a modern law firm you should strive to perform in four areas: acquisition, financials, leadership and business development.

I apply the same perspectives when looking at a firm, an office or a department. It is a simple way of looking at it, but simplicity is a virtue here and it helps you to be consistent when you are looking at the various parts of your business and its people. I apply this perspective, regardless of whether I am hiring young associates, other staff (this is a terrible expression, as it reflects the view that there are two kinds of people in this world, lawyers and non-lawyers), electing new partners or drawing up next year's business plan etc. I believe that this helps me to take a consistent approach (holistic, if you like) when seeking to drive the strategy of the firm. Thus, much of what I say below is influenced by this 'credo' and structured on the basis of: acquisition, financials, leadership and business development. Most of the discussion below is within the fields of leadership and financials. Initially, however, I would like to make some general points and observations.

3.2 The experience industry and a clear strategy

Law firms are in the experience industry. It is simply not possible to say that one firm is 'better' than another, because we cannot measure what is 'good' or 'better', even if we have agreed what qualities we should appreciate. But some firms have such standing that clients think they are receiving Rolls Royce service when a matter is handled by a given firm. Or the legal counsel of a corporate thinks that if I retain this firm, nobody will ever criticise me for having done so (except perhaps on grounds of cost). While it is very difficult, perhaps even impossible, to explain why certain firms have achieved such a position in the market, I think that there is one thing such firms have in common. A very clear strategy.

The clearer the strategy, the better. Truly successful firms are those where the partners, associates and other staff share a view with the outside world of what the firm is and what it stands for. When the client thinks that this matter is one where we should go with firm X, and the people of firm X agree that yes, this is really our business, then there is something that perhaps best can be described as trust. The clients trust that this is a matter that is best handled by firm X and the people in firm X trust that clients come to them for this kind of matter.

Another aspect of a clear strategy is guiding your people (ie, partner appraisal, or partner development as I prefer to call it). If the firm does not have a clear strategy, it is doubtful whether you should spend resources on a partner development programme, as such a programme among other things is an instrument to help partners understand what is required of them in order to contribute to what the firm wants to achieve. If the firm cannot clearly express what it wants to achieve, it will be very difficult to provide any guidance to partners about what they should and should not do (eg, what kind of clients and matters they should take on).

3.3 User friendliness

This issue applies in many areas – time recording, the structure for contributing to the know-how system, the drafting of business plans and so on. Whatever it is that you want people to do, you must see to it that it is as simple and user friendly as possible. If one always seeks to have the things functioning perfectly on day one, not much will happen. It is better to get things started and to adjust later than to seek perfection from the outset. (See, for example, section 4.3 on partner development programmes.)

3.4 Discipline and repetition

It is important to have discipline in the firm, particularly when you are trying to implement a new or revised strategy. Actions should be taken and sessions held within an agreed time frame. People must be held accountable for what they have done or for what they have not done. Too many partners in too many law firms have experienced too many partners' meetings where people have agreed to do various good things and nothing has ever happened.

In a law firm, the clients come first. If the client has an important and urgent matter then your partner should go and see the client rather than attend to internal meetings. (Whether matters are always so urgent is a different discussion, but let us just say that it is the client's privilege to decide on this – see section 3.2 on the experience industry.) In my view, best practice for handling this is to be very consistent, perhaps to the point of being stubborn. If, for example, the department you are working in has not had weekly meetings before, it is my experience that it will take quite some time to get it into everybody's mind that you actually have these meetings. If you are consistent, and hold the meetings at the same time every week or month, it will eventually be in people's minds and they will show up. If you are flexible and shuffle your meeting times around, this will never happen.

4. Leadership

4.1 Buy-in from partners

It is fundamentally important that partners buy in to the firm's strategy. The firm's strategy is not what management or a majority at a partners' meeting has decided. Rather, it is what the partners do in the daily struggle in the office. If the management says that the strategy of the firm is to act for large, international clients in cross-border deals, but partners are more preoccupied with acting for closely held companies in local deals, then it is the latter that is the strategy of the firm. Though this is not the main subject of this chapter, it is important to touch upon the issue of how you get buy-in from partners for a strategy, especially if you want to get yourself a new strategy. There are different techniques that one can imagine to achieve buy-in. But in my experience the only way that really works is to convince the really influential partners of the firm that this is the right way to go. The project referred in section 2.2 is a situation where this particular skill of the leaders of the firm was really tested. The reason for this was probably that, as opposed to the normal course of events, this project could not be driven on the back of discontent among people in the firm.

4.2 Listen to people

When I am involved in projects as a consultant, I seek at an early stage to carry out one-to-one interviews with partners and other people who carry the values of the firm. There are a number of reasons for this. One is, of course, that I as an outsider will get a better understanding of the firm and its people. Moreover, it is a way of opening up channels of communication. In my experience, people find it hard to resist the temptation to speak their mind for an hour or two, when confronted by somebody who is sitting there taking notes. A few common themes will always emerge from these interviews. Such themes can be good things, such as what it is that I appreciate and am proud of in my firm. But in the context of a strategy exercise, it is more the issues in the firm that need to be addressed that are of interest. I have carried out this kind of exercise in different countries and cultures. In each and every one of these cases, three to five issues have emerged as common themes. When I say common, I really mean common. Practically 100% of interviewees observe these common themes and describe them as issues that need to be addressed.

Interviews of this kind are very useful, particularly in an exercise such as section 2.3. They help you articulate what the issues really are and what it is that needs to be done. I have often found that what you can bring to the table as an outside counsel is the ability to identify an issue and describe how it can be addressed and handled.

So listen to people. But do not fool yourself and think that they will do as you say, just because you can present some good arguments. If you are in the business of managing change, you will find that people will only change and do things that they really believe in. It is, of course, better still if they think it was their idea in the first place!

4.3 Follow up what individuals do

I strongly believe in partner assessment programmes. They have been around in UK firms for many years now, but are still a relatively new feature in many other countries. In order to make it clear that it is not just a one-way exercise where the firm tells the partner what to do, but a process of two-way communication, I refer to this kind of tool as a partner development programme.

From the perspective of the individual partner, the programme will help him or her to understand what is expected by the firm on a detailed and concrete level. Being a partner in today's law firm is a much more complex challenge than in the past. It is no longer sufficient to bring in work and execute it well. In addition, a partner is expected to bring in the right kind of work, manage people and actively take part in the development of the firm. The programme should focus on areas where the individual partner could or should improve. As noted above, this is not a one-way process of communication. While feedback is given to the partner in the programme, it also provides an opportunity for the partner to express his or her opinions and expectations.

From the firm's perspective, it is a tool designed to ensure that the individual partner is actually doing what can reasonably be expected in order to assure the success of the firm. What can be expected varies with the strategy and culture of the firm.

The partner development programme also eases tension between partners or groups of partners. It seems almost inevitable that there are built-in tensions in partnerships. Junior partners often take the view that older partners do not work as hard as they should (lockstep firms), or that they watch their contacts jealously (performance-based firms). A properly conducted partner development programme makes partners more confident that such issues are handled by the firm. The partner development programme should be straightforward. The procedure, therefore, should be so framed that it takes a minimum of partners' time to prepare; questionnaires should be uncomplicated and easy to fill in, and input data from the financial system must be presented in such a way that it is easy to understand etc.

The parameters (ie, the areas covered in the partner development programme) should also be easy to understand. This will not usually be a problem as far as 'hard factors' such as acquisition and financials are concerned (see section 3.1). 'Soft factors', such as business development and leadership, are typically dealt with in a 360-degree feedback. But you cannot run before you walk. If you have not previously run programmes of this type, there is a risk with going directly into a fully fledged 360-degree exercise. It may take up too much of people's time and energy, so that they will feel limited enthusiasm for repeating the exercise. One alternative is to carry out this part of the programme in a simplified way the first time it is carried out. Instead of sending questionnaires around, the appraiser and appraisee sit down and go through the questions that you would typically have in a 360-degree questionnaire. It is important that the questions are straightforward and do not allow much room for individual interpretation. If you go to a 360-degree feedback, it is important to remember that all those taking part will need some introduction and education on how to handle this tool.

In summary, a partner development programme typically serves the following purposes:

- It helps the partner understand what it is the firm expects from him or her.
- It is a tool to let the individual partner know what he or she is doing well and what areas should be improved.
- It helps the partner articulate his or her wishes and expectations.
- It is a forum for the partner and the firm to agree on necessary actions.

- It is a part of the profit-sharing system. In performance-based firms it helps the firm to come to a fair decision on profit sharing. In a lockstep firm it serves the purpose of checking that the partner is pulling his or her weight.

4.4 Appointing the leadership

I shall not elaborate further here on how the management or governance of the firm should best be structured, or what the partnership agreement should say on, for instance, the balance of powers between the firm and the individual partner. However, it is worth making just one observation on how the leadership of the firm is appointed. If you want to bring about change in a firm which traditionally is not very managed (if I can use that expression), one thing you should consider is how you appoint the central management of the firm, and typically the managing partner. You will get a stronger management if you do it through elections, and particularly where you have two candidates standing against each other. The drawback of elections of this type is that it is often the most successful partners who throw their hats in the ring and someone inevitably has to lose. You run the risk that the loser will then leave the firm.

5. Financials

5.1 Figures make people tick

I often do benchmarking studies. I compare a firm's performance measured as turnover and profitability (using the 'classical' profit per equity partner as profitability measure) over time compared to its peer firms or other comparable players. This is a very powerful instrument. It is a guaranteed trigger for discussion and can often serve as an effective tool to make people take action.

There might be various reasons for this. One is that some markets are more transparent than others. In the United Kingdom and the United States, for instance, markets are very transparent in this field. For many years, it has been easy to follow how UK and US firms develop in terms of turnover and profitability. That is not the case in many countries in continental Europe. Moreover, it can differ a lot within a region. If you look at the Nordic region, Finland, Norway and Sweden are transparent in the sense that firms in these countries publish their turnover; but this is not the case in Denmark. However, this openness relates only to turnover, and profitability has to be figured out. So, often people simply do not have a clue as to how their firm is doing compared to their peers. But I think that to a large extent it is the comparison in itself that triggers people.

5.2 Figures when driving change

My experience is that figures are equally effective as a tool when you are working on the integration of businesses and offices. The projects referred to in sections 2.1 and 2.2 were largely about integration. We had numerous management group meetings and exchanged information regarding best practice in the areas of marketing, know-how and recruiting etc. However, it was not until we started to look at figures that things really started to happen. It was when you understood how much another office billed its major clients, what the utilisation of another group or its average turnover per fee earner were, that you could relate to your own group or office and understand the synergies from which you could benefit.

Looking at figures can, however, also be counterproductive. In my practice as a law firm consultant, the kind of assignment that has come up most frequently has been looking at and attempting to improve profit-sharing systems. This is a topic you could probably spend a lifetime discussing. (Although there are only a few basic profit-sharing concepts such as lockstep, total contribution and eat what you kill, the variations seem endless.) Profit sharing is something you must handle with extra care, especially when you are in the business of managing change. When you are doing a merger (see section 2.1), you often simply have to introduce a new profit- sharing system for parts of the new firm. Normally, it is the smaller firm and its partners that have to accept the system of the larger firm (which is usually the surviving firm in the merger). But if you are not forced to change the profit-sharing system, for instance when you seek to improve the business of a 'stand-alone' firm (see section 2.3) and are not involved in a merger, my experience is that you should consider waiting before changing the profit-sharing system, and look at other things first.

I appreciate that the suggestion to hold back on the issue of profit sharing when you are trying to achieve change might sound like nonsense. Nowadays, people like me emphasise that the law firm must be more effective as a business organisation and one ingredient of this is that the partners should strive for a common goal. It then seems logical that if the firm has an 'old fashioned' eat what you kill system – which induces people to work hard as individuals but typically does not reward them for contributing to the firm – then you start your change management exercise by looking at the profit-sharing system. This sounds logical, but my experience is the opposite. If you want things done, do not start with the profit-sharing system unless you have to.

Key performance indicators (KPIs) are tools that you cannot do without if you try to run a law firm. A senior partner in my firm once said that running a law firm is a high income, high-cost business. While people nowadays (after Lehman) pay much more attention to the cost side, I believe that this is still true. Naturally, you must control your costs; but the really material costs are salary, rent and (to a lesser but growing extent) IT. It is also true that you must see to it that you send out your invoices and ensure that they are paid. But I still think that it is the KPIs on the income side that are of interest.

I am happy to admit that I am almost obsessed when it comes to figures and law firms. I have mentioned traditional benchmarking above. But I have also spent many hours looking at other things, such as gearing (financial), where in the world a firm has its offices (if it is an international firm), the average value of corporate deals the firm is involved in, turnover per fee earner, the firm's ranking in certain league tables etc. And I have tried to cross-compare these parameters with each other. Before going into the KPIs that are more closely linked to the daily life of the firm, I would therefore like to touch upon some more general measurements.

We have already mentioned profit per equity partner (PEP). This is of course the classical measure of a law firm's profitability and it has been much criticised, especially in recent years. It is true that you can manipulate the PEP figure without really improving your business, for example simply by removing partners. But PEP has been around for many years, it is easy to understand, and in most markets, firms that have the highest reputation (in leagues tables etc) also show a high PEP relative to their competitors. I think it is here to stay for the foreseeable future.

The more I have looked at different indicators, the more convinced I am that the best measure of the quality of the work of a law firm (at least an international firm) is the income per fee earner figure.

Let us go back to the KPIs in the context of the daily struggle. One has to appreciate that one places more focus on different indicators in different firms and at different times. In a downturn for instance, it is critical that you invoice your work in a timely fashion and get the cash in. I would like to limit myself to what I think are the most important aspects to look at for most firms. In order to serve as efficient tools, your KPIs must be simple (ie, simple to understand and simple to apply). In one firm we had an interesting KPI – the gross margin per partner hour (GMPPH). I think that the idea behind it was that the only resource in the firm which was not endless was partners' time. So the more work the firm could carry out and get paid for, for each time unit spent by the partner, the better. I can understand that. I think. So if you as a partner have a number of matters in which you have recorded only a few minutes and other fee earners hundreds of hours, your GMPPH will look great. The problem was that no one really understood what we should do with the GMPPH figures.

The indicators that I think are 'must haves' if you try to run a law firm, are utilisation, notional billing rate and average billing rate.

Utilisation is often expressed in relative terms and seeks to describe what you get out of your people in terms of billable hours. If you choose to assume that eight billable hours per day equals 100% and associate X has produced eight billable hours one day, then the utilisation figure for associate X that day was 100%. The utilisation figure is useful because it provides you with adequate information on how you make use of your workforce. It is easy for everybody to understand and it prompts you to take action quickly when it is going the wrong way. It is also relevant to apply on all levels, be it at firm, office, group or individual level. As firms compute utilisation differently (eg, in the above example an eight-hour basis was used, while another firm might perhaps use a 10-hour basis), one should think twice before using this measurement in benchmarking exercises.

The notional billing rate (NBR) is an important tool, especially when you are trying to change your business, because it is through this tool you can clearly express internally what kind of business it is that you really want. If you manage to push the NBR up in your business plans and budgets, then this is a signal to your partners that they must go after better-paid work. The average billing rate then serves as a reality check.

6. Conclusion

At the outset, the working title of this chapter was "Driving strategy in changing market conditions". Initially, I mentioned some factors that I believe will be significant drivers of change in the future. Looking at historical, changing market conditions, I have in my professional life experienced the booming 1980s, financial crisis and recession in the early 1990s, the dot-com boom which saw the bubble burst in 2000, the years from around 2004 to 2008 – which was probably a golden age for business law firms – and now since 2008, the post-Lehman era where market conditions can at best be described as uncertain. It is, of course, true that when driving strategy and change you put emphasis on different aspects depending on whether times are booming or you are in a downturn. In the golden age, the credo was that partners should sell and look after relationships with the clients; and senior associates would manage projects. In the aftermath of Lehman, the emphasis is on bringing cash in, with partners having to dig into files rather than do client entertaining. But I believe that what works and what does not work when you are driving a strategy in a law firm is much the same, regardless of whether you are in a bear or bull market; and this is what I have tried to address in this chapter.

This chapter remains the same as published in the previous edition.

How to drive change in a partnership setting

Wolf-Peter Gross
Law Firm Change Consultants

Professional service firms are basically subject to the same change dynamics as other companies. At the same time, they have significant special particularities. These are essentially the result of the singular professional self-image and the variety of roles ranging from co-owner on the one hand to professional on the other. These must be considered in change processes if they are to be successful.

1. Change in general

Change is easy if "the old comes in the garment of the new".[1] Dealing with the resistance of individuals as well as organisations is the linchpin of change projects. Generally, humans find it difficult to change something in their lives. We already know what provides us with a feeling of familiarity and security – even if we can cognitively grasp the price we pay for remaining in a familiar situation. The known seems to be better than the unknown. In trusted environments we know our way around, have learned our survival techniques – and no one can truly guarantee that the new will be better; it could be worse! Humans tend to imagine the worst. We are very good at anticipating and preparing for risks and dangers. Decision psychology has shown in impressive experiments that we are more susceptible to losses than to gains. The strategy of staying with the tried and tested seems to be deeply rooted in our developmental history. Clinging to what is familiar offers more advantages for survival than taking risks.

As brain research shows, there is a range of individual willingness to change, which is partly genetically predetermined and partly strengthened by socialisation. Accordingly, several groups of people can be observed in change projects, which can be divided into 10%–15% drivers, 35%–40% passive protagonists, 35%–40%

1 Based on Elfriede Jellinek in: *Am Königsweg* (textbook 2017).

wait-and-see sceptics, and 10%–15% refusers, according to the Gaussian formula of normal distribution. In professional service firms, experience reveals a somewhat higher percentage of sceptics, which can be attributed to the professional socialisation of this group. Lawyers, accountants or tax advisers are in a unique position when identifying risks and developing strategies to avoid them.

Another characteristic of the change process is that every person experiences emotional phases which are defined by corresponding behavioural patterns.

It is fundamental to recognise and accept these emotional phases, which have been researched by sociologists. Professionals tend to seek out the factual level and repress the emotional side. In their own affairs, however (ie, when it comes to their own change), emotions play the central role. It is important to work with these emotions in order to implement change projects successfully. There are two pieces of bad news: there is no shortcut from the state of denial to that of positive acceptance; and the change curve occurs in organisations with a time lag – typically, the masterminds and initiators of change are emotionally in a different phase than the circle of early initiates and even more remote from the rest of the partnership. This has implications for the communication and design of the change process. People accept and adapt to it at their own pace. Understanding and agreeing takes time, and even if the

Figure 1. Change curve

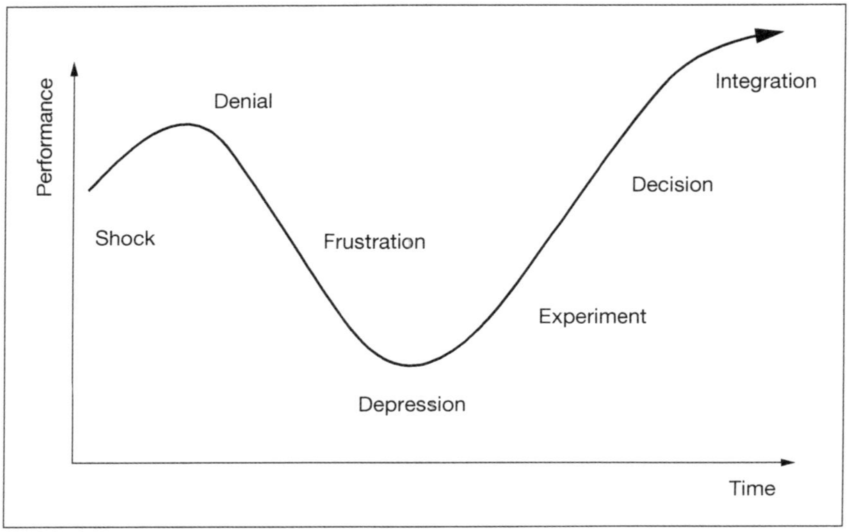

change protagonists wish otherwise, a "once and done" approach is counterproductive. The duration depends on various factors such as the degree of need for change, the attractiveness of the goal, the extent and impact of the change, or the previous change experience of the partnership.

Another essential prerequisite for understanding the management of change projects is the change formula: $C = D \times V \times F > R$.[2] The natural resistance to change is so great that the product of the necessity of change, times its objective, times the first steps in the desired direction must be greater than the resistance.

The process of change only comes into operation when the why and the purpose of the change are clear. The why results from the initial situation and corresponds to the "dissatisfaction" factor in the change formula. The target needs to answer the meaningful question of what the purpose of the change is. There is a natural gap between the initial situation and the target of the change, which needs to be bridged. The description of the task packages and the change process (ie, the architecture of involvement and participation), as well as the first quick wins, are the necessary stabilisers that every change project requires in order to become viable. Ideally, the project should have a motto that inspires and strengthens the sense of unity.

These basic logics of change management apply equally to professional service firms. However, there are further special characteristics to be considered.

2. Change in professional service firms

The professions of lawyers, auditors and tax consultants are essentially liberal professions. Independence is their core element. Deeply rooted convictions and values are derived from their professional autonomy, which shape their self-perception as well as influence the structures, behaviour, governance and processes in law firms. Professionals, most of whom claim to have the authority to make judgements based on superior expertise and training to become judges (continental Europe), do not want to be told how to work. The argument of professional independence is standard in

---

2 C = change; D = Dissatisfaction with how things are now; V = Vision of what is possible; F = First concrete steps that can be taken towards the vision. If the product of these three factors is greater than R = Resistance, then change is possible. Because D, V and F are multiplied, if any one is absent (zero) or low, then the product will be zero or low and therefore not capable of overcoming the resistance R.

the case of changes in order to ward off supposed interventions in the *status quo*.

At the same time, a high-value orientation is evident. Especially in professional partnerships, this is expressed in a strong consensus orientation and respect for the professional spheres of the other partners. This naturally influences the breadth, depth and speed of change.

Subliminally, other interests are also involved, which are (often covertly) defended. The professionals are in internal competition and want to avoid anything that could undermine their authority, reputation and credibility in the partnership. Transparency regarding client relationships and performance standards, which could unmask their own contributions, is often avoided. This is an important obstacle, particularly in change projects designed to increase the firm's competitiveness. Arguments such as an allegedly inconsistent base of figures are typical masking tactics designed to distract from the necessity of the project. Referring to a work–life balance and denouncing inappropriate working conditions in so-called sweat shops are also part of the repertoire, especially of those who are economically rather weak and therefore assume the role of value keepers. In law firms, change is related back to one's own individual performance/willingness to perform, thus generating in change projects a subliminal fear of being squeezed out of the system.

In addition, influence plays an important role in partnerships. Partners who wish to maintain their informal power within the company are less willing to be open to change and to try a new approach if this could potentially affect their ability to exert influence "under the radar".

For all the generalisation, there are significant differences in the ability to change between the professional partnership and managed professional business archetypes. In the latter, a large part of the decision-making authority has already been delegated to management for system-related reasons, and these partnerships are usually so large that the influence of individual partners is relativised. However, even with these types of law firm, the group dynamics, which play a considerable role in any change project, must be considered.

3. Case study

A leading multidisciplinary partnership in continental Europe aimed at internationalisation. Some strategic masterminds recognised that the important clients from the upper middle class could only be retained if they were offered convincing advice along their mostly global value chain. A potential merger partner had already been identified, and initial informal discussions had taken place. The multidisciplinary partnership itself had previously been locally based with several offices, and *de facto* neither cooperated on a supra-regional level nor did it have an integrated working platform. Moreover, the range of economic contributions was very broad. It was therefore necessary to harmonise the systems and processes, to establish internal integration while at the same time shaping the merger with an international partner. A chief operating officer was hired to strengthen the platform, and a consulting process was commissioned for the integration and the merger. On the consulting side, the proposal was made to combine the topics. A steering group was formed and a process architecture developed. In a first step, the partnership was confronted with the market challenges in order to create an understanding of the necessity and to activate the partnership's energy for change, which had been very low until then. In follow-up workshops, the strategic options were elaborated and the consideration of a merger was evaluated. As expected, the reactions were very restrained, the new territory appeared too unknown, and the question of what this could mean for their own business cases, especially regarding the weaker partners, was too uncertain. These concerns were not discussed openly but rather through arguing supposed cultural differences (linguistically, in relation to the mentality and, above all, to the organisational form of the potential international merger partner, which was a managed firm). Accordingly, workshops with partners of both organisations were held in order to get to know each other, to talk about the structure of their business, possible similarities and market challenges. This led to a considerable reduction in reservations. A high level of participation was then organised in the merger roadmap through the sub-projects business integration, people integration, financial integration and merger communication. Methodically, an approach was chosen based on the logic of holistic change.

The large group of the partnership dealt with the merger and delegated the elaboration to working groups, which then brought their results back to the large group. Throughout this work, the approval rate rose continuously, so that in the end the necessary majority could be organised. Two factors were decisive. On the one hand, the partnership agreed on a common understanding: if you do not expect any comprehensible disadvantages from the merger, you will not stop the project. Secondly, the merger was negotiated

Figure 2. Work and decision-making structure[3]

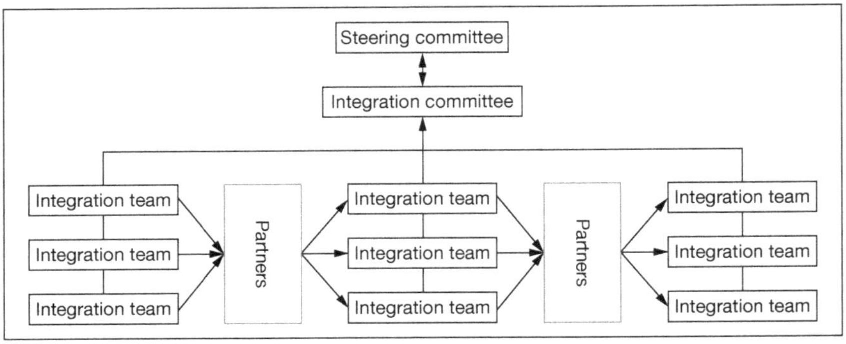

in such a way that the profits were guaranteed by the international organisation at an attractively higher level for a period. The process provided the push, the incentives created a pull effect, the participation provided security.

During the implementation of the merger, formats were continuously made available in which the departments could gain confidence, develop transnational business and align their standards and processes.

4. The change process

The change process can also be visualised in professional service firms with the help of the so-called 'House of Change': the need for change is derived from the analysis of the initial situation; the vision is elaborated in workshops with the partnership; the work packages for achieving the goals are defined; and a process architecture is developed to ensure that the partnership can make good decisions. As the supreme authority, the partnership must always have the decision power.

4.1 Starting point

The law firm industry and the legal market are constantly changing. Major triggers are: a more professional and self-confident purchasing behaviour of clients; the differentiation of panels; the reduction of leverage; the tendency to insource legal advice; the use

3 Figure is author's own creation but see also Dannemiller Tyson Associates, *Whole-Scale Change, Unleashing the Magic in Organizations*, 1 January 2000.

Figure 3. The House of Change

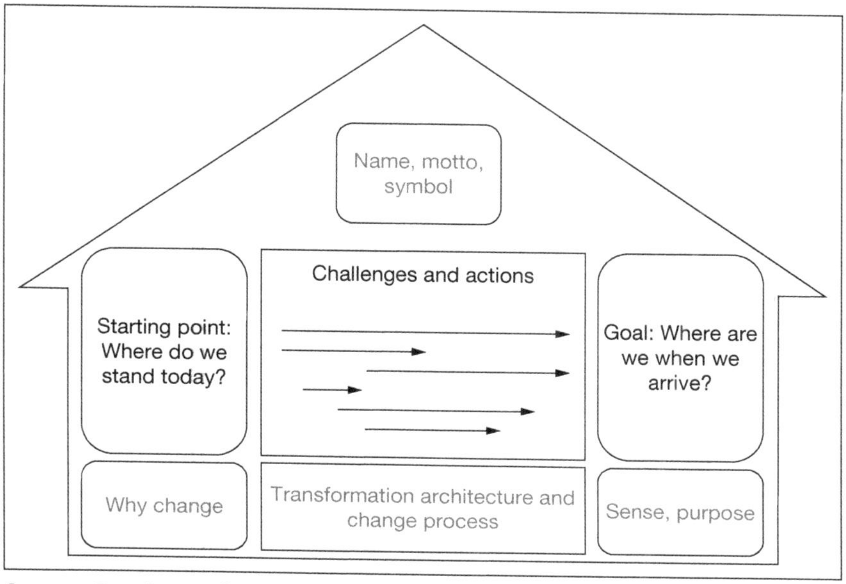

Source: Based on the model of the consulting organisation Beratergruppe Neuwaldegg.

of alternative legal service providers; and technical developments for the automated processing of standard business, etc. Other internal topics are differences in profit distribution, asymmetries in contributions and resulting conflicts, collection and cash flow bottlenecks, pressure on rates, personnel development (partner track) or succession issues.

All these challenges typically relate to people, processes or tools and can affect performance in the areas of productivity, communication, collaboration, case management and customer service, cash flow and marketing.

As a rule, law firms adapt dynamically to minor changes in their environment. An example is communication, which has evolved from dictated letters to self-written emails or smartphone communication and has become significantly faster. Increased client demands for information are answered by means of newsletters or theme events. Efficiency programmes have cushioned the margin impact of clients' demands to achieve more with less. Law firms also adapt dynamically to billing requirements or sometimes even work on their clients' databases.

In other areas, law firms find it harder to adapt to change, especially when it comes to responding appropriately to creeping or disruptive developments. The latter are rare. The former are not. They usually result from key performance indicators not being taken into account or requirements being lowered when recruiting. The latently perceived changes in revenue per professional, the hourly rates realised, the profit per partner are whitewashed, looking for excuses such as the belief that young professionals must be offered an attractive environment regarding work–life balance. This usually distracts from economic problems, initiated by the wrong choice of partners and perpetuating the pattern of "close your eyes and hope for the best".

The need for change is often seen in terms of operational issues: uniform marketing presence; better and more stringent processes; higher efficiency; improved quality standards; or a professional legal operations management. More difficult are strategic changes that affect the business model or market positioning. This is because partners tend to set their own business model as a benchmark, and criticising it means criticising the way they see themselves in relation to the freedom to exercise their profession – or simply fuelling the fear of not being able to keep up with the pace of change and becoming system losers.

The analysis of the initial situation usually requires a distanced view, putting together market positioning and the key performance indicators. This is the only way to objectify and mirror the filters of self-perception. Methodically, tools can be used to investigate the most important external and internal factors of influence of the macro-environment by means of the PESTEL analysis[4] and the SWOT[5] analysis, as well as the financial analysis, based essentially on economical evaluations, time keeping and other basic data sources.

Systematically, it is helpful to distinguish which kind of change is at stake, since this has implications for the design of the change process.

So-called learning organisations have developed a permanent and thus low-threshold mode of adapting to change based on continuous market observation and the evaluation of key

---

4 PESTEL stands for Political, Economic, Social, Technological, Environmental, Legal; variations are, for example, STEEP, PEST or PESTLIED, which include or exclude further factors.

5 SWOT stands for Strengths, Weaknesses, Opportunities, Threats.

Figure 4. Classification of change

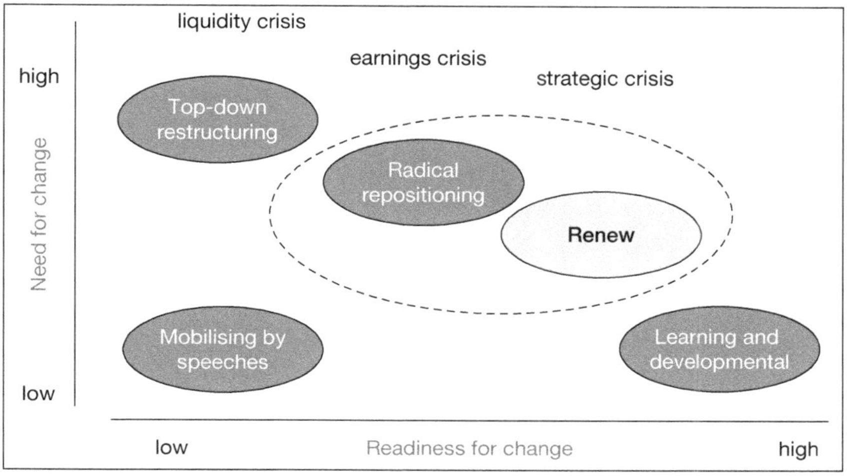

Source: Based on Barbara Heitger, Alexander Doujak, Hard cuts, new growth: The logic of emotions and the power of numbers in change management, *Frankfurt/Wien 2002.*

performance indicators. In such partnerships, the course of the firm is discussed on an ongoing basis. As a rule, they are healthy at their core; the need for change is correspondingly low, unless unforeseeable influences arise. Law firms with a high need for change and a low willingness to do so have usually systematically overlooked the warning signs and are facing insolvency – which is then almost unavoidable. In the profession's history, law firms that suffer from too much debt and a ramshackle partnership, that fail due to their aggressive growth course, that held on to personnel costs during the dot.com crisis, that failed to integrate their global offices and suffered from a number of poorly performing offices, that were strategically dependent on a client, or that relied on high-risk fee agreements have disappeared from the market time and again.

Most change projects take place in the field of strategic crises or, if these have not been dealt with, in the field of earnings crises. Strategic crises basically require a reorientation of the law firm, placing considerable demands on the partnership to learn from past mistakes, to part with beloved comfort zones, and to consistently face the market requirements. This requires an attractive, convincing vision along with a process of change that enables the partnership to reach its goal.

4.2 Goal and vision

A law firm in a strategic crisis or even an earnings crisis cannot reinvent itself overnight. It is illusory to strive for an evolutionary leap. Unlike in traditional companies, the depth and speed of change in partnerships depend on the degree of consensus orientation; this is typically higher in professional partnerships than in managed professional businesses. Against this background, it is often difficult to find a goal that is market-attractive (ie, clearly recognisable and backed up with a comprehensible, resilient value proposition). Such a quality vision, however, is a necessary basis for the possibility of generating more profitable sales.

A typical example is a medium-sized law firm with several locations, which was only loosely integrated and predominantly worked its local markets. Only in a few outstanding business areas did it have broadly based international clients with whom top-tier business was done. The consolidated key figures were below market level, and accordingly the firm was increasingly unattractive for highly qualified, ambitious professionals. In addition, major clients began to doubt whether the platform was sufficiently resilient and able to provide advice with the necessary breadth and availability. The greatest challenge in the necessary change process was to find a vision that was not only externally but also internally designed for most of the partnership to buy into. Resistance was particularly high because partners who did not find their knowledge portfolio in the focus of the vision were worried about further marginalisation. It was therefore important to underpin the vision and the goals with a business development process that offered a critical majority of partners a comprehensible and credible opportunity to gain access to new sources of income through the change.

Targets do not have to be only of an economic or strategic nature. They can also have cultural components, especially if the pressure to change results from internal tensions and conflicts. In any case, it is important that the target image provides orientation, creates identity, is SMART, and above all attractive. Methodologically helpful for this are creative techniques such as mind maps, design thinking and analogous forms of work such as the creation of collages, videos, etc, since they allow a more emotional approach and thus ensure congruent values from which the meaning of the change can be derived. The sense behind the development is just as important as the why, as this is a decisive motivational factor. This corresponds to a basic human need for our actions to have meaning and to find confirmation in them.

The sense can therefore also be described as a necessary pull factor for change projects.

4.3 Change process

Change means uncertainty. Familiar territory is abandoned while the new one is not yet "ready for occupancy". The change process creates the necessary security at various levels.

From a purely operational point of view, it is important to flesh out and agree on the work packages and measures necessary to bridge the natural tension between the initial situation and the goals. In the case of an integration of previously loosely cooperating law firm locations, for example, a bundle of implementation packages were formulated, including a uniform external image, knowledge management and product development, controlled business development and cross-selling, and harmonised personnel management and development, as well as a partner mission statement, workplace equipment, and integrated economic cycles and governance. A working group was assigned to each of these work packages, with the task to elaborate these considering the interfaces and interactions with the other work packages. The procedure was deliberately chosen. There had been unsuccessful attempts at integration in the past. One reason for failure had been the low level of understanding of law firm management in the average partnership. The aim this time was to make the partnership competent to decide on the sometimes far-reaching consequences of the integration for the firm as a whole and for one's own case. On the other hand, the energy for change was relatively low, although the analysis clearly demonstrated the why. In order to increase the commitment and the buy-in into the goals of the project, it was therefore necessary to organise the most active participation possible and to ask partners to contribute to the success of the project by taking on partial project responsibility.

The measures to be defined must be adapted to the respective project and, above all, they must be affordable. In general, a high degree of participation is helpful in partnerships, as the professionals (at least in professional partnership organisations but also in managed professional businesses) know how to avoid top-down approaches very effectively. They decide when they have understood and are convinced – and they want to have a real decision out of respect for their co-partner position. Participation also always means more work in addition to the mandate work, from which there is *de facto* no exemption for such projects.

At the process architecture level, the organisation, governance and mechanics of involvement and participation for the project are defined. This includes elements of classical project management (ie, there is a project management that coordinates the project including the sub-projects, checks the processing within the framework of time and money budgets, controls the expenditure, reflects and determines the necessary steps with regard to the further procedure in the sense of the objective, and ensures continuous communication). If there are sub-projects, they should be closely linked to the project management.

The elements of involvement and participation are to be individually tailored to the project and the law firm. In medium-sized to large professional service firms, large group formats in which all concerned parties are involved are of importance. They have decisive advantages compared to the procedure model of classical management consultancies, the result of which is usually an externally formulated recommendation for action (although certainly tailored to the advised company). This is like a foreign body that is often rejected by the organisation and has no real chance of becoming effective. The resistance to change is too great. Large group methodologies, on the other hand, are the most efficient way of working with precisely this resistance, using their energy to work out the best solution for the firm. Organisational conferences of this kind are much more than workshops, which are rather small settings and only allow a sequential approach. Large conferences drastically shorten the decision-making and information procedures through the simultaneity of information, processing and decisions. At the same time, the quality of the solutions is usually increased.

Change projects in professional service firms are often complex, as they usually have a cultural dimension in addition to the strategic and structural dimension. Trivialisation or quick solutions do not really help here either; rather, issues with conflicting interests require different perspectives, experiences, competencies and ideas to achieve appropriate solutions. Large group settings are the appropriate form of work for this. These settings are often unfamiliar to professionals and are sometimes viewed suspiciously at first; secretly, a loss of control is probably feared, or it is suspected that individual interests cannot be enforced one-to-one in large group formats. Experience shows, however, that this suspicion quickly evaporates as soon as the participants learn how intensively they can involve their thoughts and ideas in the process. The consequence is that decisions that are jointly worked out and made by the partnership have a completely different kind of binding force, thus increasing the probability of implementation exponentially.

The basic idea is to bring the whole system into one space and to work with it in such a way that change happens from the very beginning (so-called real-time strategic change). As described in the case study, the process architecture for larger change projects involves several large conferences, typically preceded by an evaluation (eg, in the form of structured interviews) and an analysis. One can start, for example, with a future conference, which is particularly suitable for designing the common future with a large group and already planning it concretely.[6] Future conferences create a sense of community, a spirit of optimism and a high degree of motivation. The participants gain an understanding of their past, clearly recognise their present situation and develop a common picture of the future. In the end, action plans for the unanimously chosen future are created. The action plans are then commonly deepened in smaller groups and brought back into the partnership in the form of soundings, where they are enriched (methodically, for example, in the form of a World Café or marketplaces) and worked out by smaller working groups until a decision is ready. Depending on the project, this may require several sequences in order to enable the partnership to become familiar with the change and actually adopt it.

It is very helpful when the first wins and successes are achieved quickly, because they yield the confidence that the desired goal can be achieved. In the case study, success stories of joint pitches, cross-national product developments, cross-selling successes and so on were an elementary component of the large group conferences. They were presented by senior associates or partner teams and generated enormous positive energy, contributing significantly to the project.

Change usually requires different behaviour than before. This does not happen automatically upon a decision of the partners' meeting, but needs a longer period in which the partnership reflects again and again whether said change in behaviour can be observed in the desired clarity. Some partners will be able to implement this better than others and, if necessary, support may be provided through individual coaching. The change process will only be successful when the results of the implementation have solidified in a resilient manner.

---

6 On future conferences, see Marvin Weisbord, *Was ist eine Zukunftskonferenz?* 1996.

5. Leadership

Change projects place high demands on the management of the law firm. The leadership has the task of initiating changes, defining the decision-making framework for the change project, winning powerful or dynamic partners for the project, negotiating and enforcing budgets, organising the process until it is commissioned by the partnership, and dealing with resistance in the initial phase so that it does not nip the process in the bud.

In reality, the power spectrum of management is often weak. This is a proven strategy to maintain the *status quo* or to be able to claim a veto right at any time. Of particular interest in such a marginalisation of management are those partners who are particular profiteers of the existing system, either because they are economically very successful in it (the "sinners") or, at the other end, despite weak contributions, are protected by it (the "saints").

When professional service firms get into trouble, it is up to leadership to put the firm in the forefront and make sure that it is not taken hostage by sinners or saints out of self-interest, as they

Figure 5. Performance levels in professional service firms

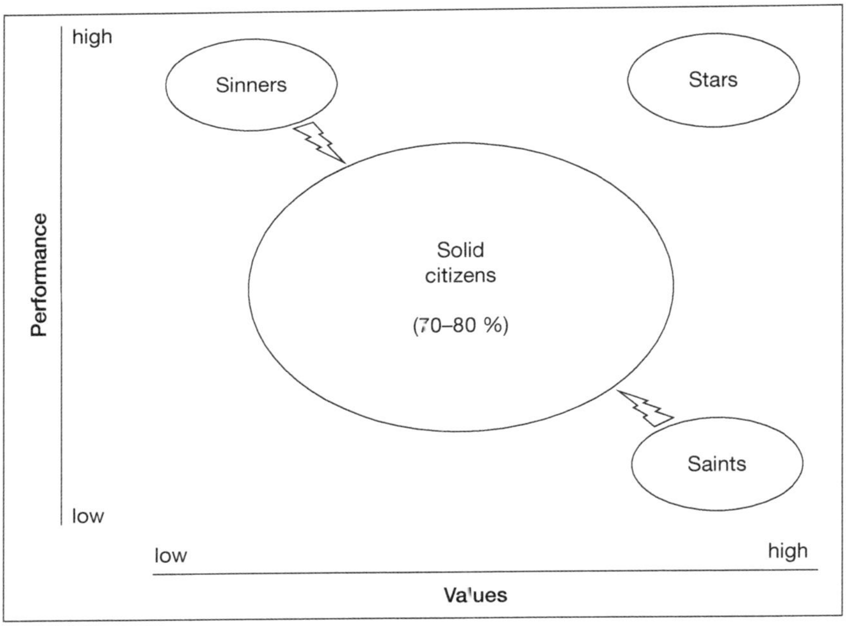

are always an absolute minority in terms of numbers. Otherwise the price will be paid by the "solid citizens". If the firm's management is too weak, the informally powerful partners often take over this task; usually these are the "stars" who enjoy a high internal reputation for their integrity and entrepreneurial drive.

In these constellations, it makes sense to strengthen the formal management in a targeted manner (eg, through mentoring or coaching), making it more capable of acting and effectively available for the change project.

6. Conclusion

Professional service firms are generally very capable of reacting quickly and flexibly to low-threshold adaptation and development requirements. If undesirable economic developments are systematically overlooked or early warning signs are not taken into consideration, partnerships find it increasingly difficult to change course. Patterns of conflict avoidance, consensus orientation or the self-conception of individual freedom of professional practice are too deeply ingrained. Change only has a chance to be successful if the project is embedded in a binding process. This requires a kind of "initial spark" either from the firm's management or from informally powerful partners who feel responsible for the firm as an organisation or who are strategic masterminds. At the beginning of the change process, the persistence tendencies are particularly high in professional service firms. Professionals are only prepared to support change if they understand the necessity and the goal (ie, the why and the wherefore), and have translated this into their own business case. Looking at the partnership structure of professional service firms, it is particularly important to enable the partners to negotiate the new *status quo*. Partnerships are communities of values that share certain basic ideas about the way they do business and changing them is like changing the basis of a business, which must be discussed and agreed upon accordingly. Top-down approaches or externally developed solution concepts therefore have a hard time getting into the implementation phase at all. In contrast, integration and participation formats such as large conferences are particularly effective methods that help the partnership to understand the starting position, develop a common goal and operationalise the need for change. The phases of change processes can essentially be categorised as follows: the phase up to the commissioning of the change project by the partnership; the development of answers and solutions to the challenges which require a response; and, last but not least, the implementation phase, in which behavioural changes are practised, consolidated and secured. In each of these phases, the partnership plays an essential role that must be taken into account in change projects if they are to be successful.

Resource-based approach to strategy: what makes your law firm unique today and tomorrow?

Dina Gracheva
Independent strategy consultant

1. Introduction

Legal business has always been seen as a special case. With strict restriction allowing only lawyers to own law firms and regulations that to a certain extent limited competition, partners managed their law firms in a very traditional way. There were only slight differences in the organisational structures of firms and in the ways of managing and allocating resources. The legal profession has been slow to innovate and there was a widely held opinion that law firms do not "do" strategy.

That is already all in the past. The 21st century brought a new reality to the legal world: digital technologies enabled new ways of delivering legal advice; and fierce competition and the constant appearance of new players in the field pushed firms to reinvent their traditional thinking and models. We live in a world that is fast, ambiguous and highly technological; a world where change is the new norm, where unique capabilities that made firms successful in the past can very quickly become "out of fashion". In this new reality law firm partners and senior leaders need to be and act as the best corporate business leaders and ensure that strategic thinking is embedded in management of their resources.

2. Available resources

What exactly are the resources of a business in which people sell their knowledge to other people? Managing partners of the top-tier firms usually mention brand/reputation, individuals and a track record of major deals as the most important key success factors for their firms. Are these the only resources available for lawyers? And how can we build unique and successful strategy based on such resources?

First, let us look at the resources available for law firms. Yes, reputation, individuals (lawyers/partners) and track record are extremely important for winning clients; however, the differentiation in the legal business and the clients' long-term loyalty is based on many more important factors (and the unique mix of such factors). Based on the degree of ownership of and control over the business resources, they can be classified into the following three categories (see Table 1).[1]

Prahalad and Hamel,[2] who contributed to the development of the concept of a resource-based approach, compare a corporation to a large tree, where (putting it into a legal business environment) the services and expertise are the leaves, flowers and fruits, but the root system that provides nourishment, sustenance and stability is the core competence. The main benefit of the resources is their long-term nature and a high degree of plasticity when they can be adapted to changing markets.

The core of the strategy in the resource-based approach lies in the ability to identify and effectively deploy and develop the right resources, find the capabilities that can become a competitive advantage for the firm and then manage and develop these capabilities. In a professional services environment, where most of the resources are rented rather than owned by firms, this task becomes even more important.

3. Identifying resources

3.1 Step one: analyse the resources

Not all resources qualify for being used for creating competitive advantage. The value of resources is determined in the interplay with market forces, and research on strategy suggests several 'tests' for evaluating resources and their ability to create core competences. The real value is created when the resource has one or more of the following characteristics.

- *Market demand:* This is quite an obvious test, and if you really know your clients it should not be difficult to assess whether the resource is in demand. Do your clients need your office or your network connections in a particular country? Do they value your ability to organise effective cross-country teams?

---

1 Framework is inspired by the work of Bente R Løwendahl, *Strategic Management of Professional Service Firms.*

2 Prahalad, CK and Hamel, G, *The Core Competence of the Corporation.*

Table 1. Ownership and control of resources

Organisationally owned resources	Individually owned resources	Controlled by external stakeholders
Information (client-specific information, industry knowledge, databases, etc) Firm's 'past' (track record of deals, past rankings, awards, etc) Organisational culture Management procedures (firm governance structure, project management standards, various routines, methods and management processes) The most important management processes for the law firm: • Talent acquisition and management • Customer relationship management • Innovation capabilities	Individual competences (knowledge, project management skills, client relationships skills, special talents) Individual reputation and access to certain markets/ clients	Brand of law firm Individual reputation Clients' loyalty to the firm and individuals Connections and networks Rankings and recommendations

Or cross-disciplinary teams? Whom/what do they consult with before making their choice of law firm? What are the criteria for selecting the panel of legal advisers? Do they value the diversity in your teams? Questioning the market demand for resources is a good place to start when assessing whether the capabilities already owned by the firm are still corresponding to the clients' needs.

- *Scarcity:* Is the resource unique, rare and hard to copy? The resource that brings competitive advantage is not easily available for other market players. Uniqueness of resource gives companies the opportunity to sell value generated by it at a price higher than that of competition.
  - Physical uniqueness is one of the most common reasons for a valuable resource to be inimitable. Resources such as a firm's partners with their individual mix of knowledge, skills, talents and connections are physically unique.
  - Path dependency is another source of scarcity. Resources such as a track record of deals, past experience with a client or brand awareness require significant time to copy and thus give firms a competitive advantage. Such resources constitute a firm's 'past'.
  - Casual ambiguity is the unique recipe for "how" the firm can generate value for its customers. It is the complex combination of people and processes used to produce the output. Organisational culture and an ability to innovate are clear examples of such competences that act as a key differentiator. While competitors may develop the same technologies and skills, the combination of relevant organisational learnings and coordination processes cannot be easily replicated.
- *Appropriability:* Is the value created by a resource captured by the firm? This seems to be one of the most critical questions for professional service firms, where the individual capabilities of firm partners play an essential role not only in production and delivery of the services, but also in management of the business. In a professional services environment it is inevitable that individual resources will be used to create competitiveness. Partners and consultants 'deliver' the brand, they 'own' client relations and can also 'hold' the track record of deals. Therefore it is particularly important that firms create a healthy mix of resources as a basis for their strategy – with a good portion of those resources being controlled by the firm itself.

3.2 Step two: shift the control

Business-minded managing partners should also look for resources within the firm which will not only be unique and valuable, but also appropriable – that is, fully controlled by the firm. Such resources lie in organisational capabilities and include information management, project management, the internal organisation of the firm, its unique corporate culture and its managerial competences (in talent management, marketing, strategy, finance, etc).

The nature of the legal business will always save room for a 'personalised' element, so the role of partners will always be strong. However, by developing organisational capabilities firms will be able to shift the power of control from individual level to firm level, and therefore create a more sustainable basis for the future.

One of the 'winning' approaches for the future is increasing control over valuable and unique organisational competences without reducing the absolute value of individually controlled resources. Investing in core competences, along with developing organisational capabilities out of individual ones and professionalising the management of the law firm, becomes the key area of focus for managing partners. This task can be summarised as 'shifting the control', as depicted in Figure 1.

Take the example of big consulting firms. While having strong individuals (consultants and partners), those companies also developed an array of internal processes and frameworks that on the one hand ensure the delivery of the highest quality results, but at the same time protect the firm from losing the appropriability of the resources. If all consultants and partners leave a firm's office, it will be able to redeploy resources from other offices that will deliver the same quality results. This is possible because these companies constantly transform individual knowledge and skills into organisational capabilities and distribute this organisational knowledge throughout the firm. It is therefore the primary task of law firm leaders to strengthen the organisational capabilities of their firms in both transforming individual knowledge into organisational knowledge and developing the resources that the organisation owns and controls.

3.3 Step three: nurture and strengthen organisational competences

Understanding the sources of competitive advantage in a firm's capabilities and nurturing and growing these competences across organisational boundaries become the most important management

Figure 1. Shifting the control of resources

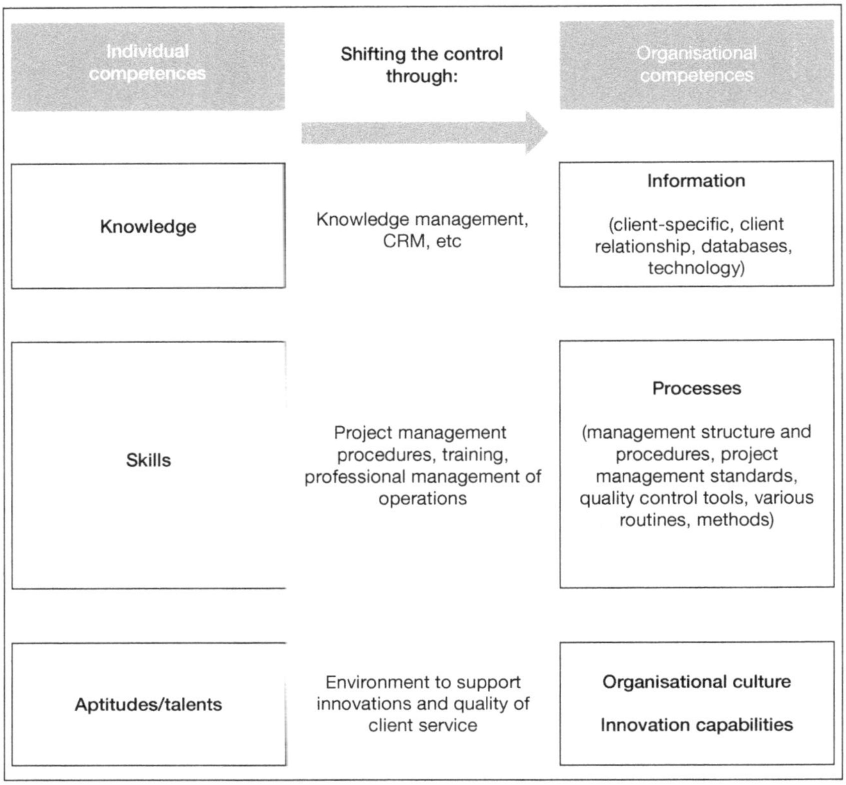

objectives. Strategy is not a one-time exercise. To be successful, firms need to live their strategy and continuously strengthen important organisational resources such as talent management, organisational culture and innovation capability.

(a) Firm's culture

There has been extensive research on culture in the legal business, with some even positioning culture as more important than strategy. Without disputes, strategy and culture go hand in hand. Culture can support or limit the strategy, strategic changes can reshape the culture, and vice versa; both culture and strategy change over time and it is important to continuously ensure that these changes are towards the same direction.

Organisational culture should be viewed not only as a set of core values written in a firm's guiding document, but also as a real tool and component that is vital in building the strategy. If you imagine your firm 20 or 30 years from today, in the time horizon that is impossible to plan, what are the key characteristics of your firm? These are the dimensions of the culture, of the core behaviours that you need to succeed sustainably. And these behaviours should be aligned and already nurtured today so that the culture can shift over time towards what the strategy requires.

(b) Innovation

In a rapidly changing environment, it is important for law firm managing partners to constantly look inside the firm and ask themselves: what were our core competences that brought our business to success? Are these resources still in demand? How can we modify them to serve emerging clients' needs? What new resources should we develop?

Here the innovation capability comes into play and helps management to disaggregate the resources and pick up and develop those that would help to achieve competitive superiority that answers the demands of tomorrow's world.

Launching activities aimed at innovative problem solving is a tricky task for companies, and this initiative has no room for a top-down approach. The culture of innovative thinking must be carefully cultivated in the organisation, and the very first steps from management can be crucially important for the success of the venture. Innovation, both in groundbreaking work and in the delivery of services, is part of the strategies of many successful law firms. It is supported on the highest level by all partners and senior leaders, but the key element in becoming successful in innovation is the special culture that management is able to create and develop.

There are several management approaches that have proved to be successful in other businesses and can be implemented in the law firm environment, bearing in mind the specifics of structure, operations and established management systems of law firms.

- *Time allocation:* Inviting employees to participate in the work of one or several innovation initiatives, management should allocate time that employees can use for these projects. Investing non-billable hours in participation in innovation task forces should be supported by the firm's management.
- *Flat structure:* Creativity needs freedom. Open interaction and idea exchange are facilitated in a flat, non-hierarchical structure (not what is usually the case in law firms). Hence, it is important to avoid the formal roles and positions when it comes to innovation task forces.

- *Commitments, not assignments:* Participation in the groups is based on the principle of commitments rather than assignments. Employees are free to choose the group that corresponds to their interests and beliefs. The role of leaders therefore is to encourage people to participate, rather than to allocate the resources.
- *Efficient communication:* Individuals at each level should be able to come up with ideas and discuss them openly with peers. The firm, on the other hand, needs to create procedures and tools to be able to capture the ideas. To be effective, this should be an ongoing dialogue rather than random brainstorming sessions. Interaction in smaller teams, as well as use of the firm's intranet to capture ideas, can be effective communication tools.
- *Broad networking:* There are plenty of ideas from outside the firm and the industry that can be sourced. And as law firms are naturally very active in networking, these activities can be used not only for business development, but also for unearthing new ideas.
- *Peer review:* Peer review of participation in the task force rather than formal evaluation will encourage and motivate employees and firm partners to bring the idea when it brings value.

Companies that are willing to step on the track of innovating and changing the landscape, whose management is eager to empower its employees, and that clearly see the long-term values of innovation will have more market power, will be able to predict changes, and will be able to develop those resources that will enable a strategy that delivers sustainable success and growth.

The role of professional ethics in shaping law firms' strategy

Tomasz Wardyński
Wardyński & Partners

Preface to the second edition

This chapter was written in 2013. The world has changed ever since. Just as the first 15 years of the 20th century were characterised by the inertia of the 19th century, the first 15 years of the 21st century were powered by the flywheel of the 20th century. Reality is changing constantly in a way that is hardly noticeable in the present. We realise only later that the world has changed in every possible dimension. Until then, we continue to use with foolish confidence all the definitions and notions we know from the past. This continues until we finally realise that those terms and concepts are no longer adequate and do not fit.

Today this is happening with even greater speed and bewilderment. Such terms as 'post-politics', 'post-truth' and 'disruption' are used to describe and name phenomena that confront us and catch us off-guard, leaving us shocked or disappointed. Technology has changed culture and relations between people. Social development has broken cultural taboos. The speed of the changes has wiped reflection and critical thinking from social life. Emotions, mostly negative ones, have become the main fuel for decision making in society. And political leaders have perfected the skill of manipulating those emotions in collaboration with bad-faith media and rogue capitalists. All this happened before we noticed what was happening and before we could realise the lethal threat to the traditional institutions of our civil society. Only one thing has remained stable and constant in this world of volatility, uncertainty, complexity and ambiguity: fundamental ethics and principles. Professional ethics continue to play the role of a gyroscope and a compass, helping the profession stand straight and navigate towards the good while avoiding the evil. And this role of ethics is only increasing.

In this new reality, the legal profession's responsibility to secure the harmonious functioning of society has become both particularly vital and difficult. Its task in the 21st century is to understand and explain how evergreen fundamental principles must be practically applied in Economy 4.0, where old concepts and terms are no longer adequate.

Learning fast is a challenge for the legal profession in this reality. Without this skill, decrypting new forms of abuses and providing effective protection against them will not be possible. But maintaining the trust of society, which is always a function of the profession's adherence to ethics, is even more important and challenging.

The omnipresence and omnipotence of the new and ever-changing media is a practical challenge for lawyers' practices, which must ensure protection of clients' legitimate rights against abuses of an entirely new kind, scale and intensity, in a system of justice unable to keep pace with technology. But it is an even greater challenge from the viewpoint of protecting the goodwill of the bar and its members and assuring public trust in the profession: first, because like all members of society lawyers too fall prey to surveillance capitalism; and secondly, because the "jurisdiction" claimed by the "court of public opinion" is expanding exponentially with new media, and advocates may have to resort to the media if they want to practise effective advocacy. But this is an unimaginably treacherous territory for a lawyer.

At the same time, erosion of trust and engagement in political processes is met with the decline of the rule of law and manifest abuses of legal positivism and literal, cynical interpretation of *lex* coupled with disregard and contempt for the *ius.* As a result, encroachments on the space for civil society and its freedoms can be observed everywhere. The explanation given to the public is that this is a necessary price society must pay to gain security. It is up to lawyers to unmask the improper purpose and disproportionality of the measures used by populist authorities, and ultimately their illegality. This will inevitably raise questions about boundaries between law and politics, and place lawyers under scrutiny similar to that to which politicians are accustomed. From the beginning of world history, those in power have always had the tendency to abuse it, and when the legal profession stood up against these abuses they would turn to tactics undermining the credibility of the bar – most often alleging unethical conduct. It is therefore of utmost importance that lawyers do not provide grounds for such allegations, but maintain the trust of society. Ethics will therefore be even more in demand in the era of the Fourth Industrial Revolution.

1. Introduction

Among jokes circulated at social events, those about lawyers elicit ripples of laughter. A popular anecdote quoting a client saying "When I see my lawyer on the street I quickly cross to the other side, because if he greets me, the next day I will be billed 500 dollars" amuses everyone – except lawyers.

Why is it that the legal profession, and especially the vocation of a business lawyer, does not arouse positive feelings, but is often treated with dislike and distrust?

This chapter does not aim at a detailed and exhaustive analysis of society's negative perception of the legal profession. However, it attempts to explain how the commercialisation of legal services poses a challenge to preserving the proper attitude of the public *vis-à-vis* law firms and consequently the legal profession as a whole, and how this must be taken into account in law firms' strategies. This has a direct bearing not only on the prospects for success of individual law firms, but on the condition of the legal profession as such and its ability to exercise its vested function and role within the system of the rule of law.

2. The significance of trust in the legal profession

The role of the bar was defined by the experiences of the 20th century which shaped the conception of a democratic society based on the rule of law. The bar, as an institution entrusted with the protection of the rights of citizens against abuses by the authorities and other persons, is an important element of this conception.

The abuse of power or rights, especially by the ruling class, is a natural tendency of human nature against which we should constantly struggle. The rule of law and the state governed by law is the only mechanism which has proved capable of preventing such abuses. The legal profession is one of the fundamental pillars of this mechanism. Effective performance of their function by lawyers and by the bar is impossible unless the particular lawyers and the institution as such enjoy the trust of the public and their respective clients. In social relations, trust constitutes the very fabric, the foundation of a civil society, and enables its proper functioning. This trust takes on a special importance in relations between the legal profession and society. It is an informal 'power of attorney' accorded to the bar by society to represent it in relations with the state and other institutions of power.

Trust means a conviction on the part of clients that the actions of professional institutions and their members (ie, individual advocates and legal advisers) are subordinated first and solely to the justified interests of their clients. Trust in the profession in general, and in each member of the profession in particular, is the fundamental basis for the existence of proper representation and the proper functioning of the relationship under which we are retained to provide legal assistance. It rests on strict compliance with and respect for certain core values, by the institution of the bar as a whole and by individual lawyers as members of the profession.

3. The genesis of the law firm as an enterprise and the danger posed by this phenomenon

Preservation of the profession's core values and the trust vested in the institution of the bar by society have posed various challenges throughout the profession's development. This development has been particularly dynamic over recent decades. The worldwide economic boom over the past 30 years has been accompanied by the rapid growth of law firms. This is because law firms play a vital role in the process of economic globalisation. They have assisted their clients in carrying out projects around the world by adapting the forms and methods by which their clients pursue their initiatives to suit the requirements of the relevant local jurisdictions.

The scale and nature of such undertakings has required the formation of teams of specialists working together to implement projects. These teams have evolved into firms which often operate across numerous countries representing various types of legal systems. Law firms are therefore institutions where partners and their associates practise the legal profession collectively and therefore should always be looked at as groups of professionals fulfilling a role vested in the bars and law societies and as an element of the mechanism of the rule of law.

The role of law firms in forging the image of the legal profession cannot be underestimated, even though the bulk of legal assistance is still rendered by sole practitioners and small partnerships, which constitute the basic structure of national bars. Law firms work for big commercial clients on matters often covered by the media. They are attractive to young lawyers because they offer the experience of working on commercial projects which would not be available to them in other segments of the profession. Young lawyers are given this opportunity without having to bear the financial risk related to such work; furthermore, they are offered financial stability. Finally, law firms build up professional goodwill from which coming generations of lawyers can benefit. They transfer this goodwill to younger lawyers, thus securing its sustainability, which ultimately constitutes the law firm's reputation in the eyes of the public.

However, the need to maintain large teams has required, and will continue to require, the assumption of the significant risk of financing them. This risk is tied to the fact that there are no guarantees of a steady flow of an appropriate number of matters generating fees sufficient to cover the costs of the existence of such teams. In assuming this risk, law firms have joined the ranks of numerous other enterprises operating on the market for services. As a result, business plans, budgets, financial targets and efficiency rates influence relations within the firm and with its clients. The pressure to achieve profit targets has become a particularly important driver for law firms' activity. In other words, law firms – apart from being groupings of legal professionals fulfilling their function in civil society – have become enterprises fully dependent on the laws of the marketplace and competition.

4. Risks associated with commercialisation

This dual dimension of law firms' operations poses particular challenges to the need to protect the trust which the bar and individual lawyers should enjoy from their clients and from society as a whole. As stated above, cultivation of this trust depends on the fulfilment of certain core principles. Strict compliance with these principles may, however, appear at first sight to be a burden, impeding the firm's growth in a competitive market and putting it on a worse footing than those who are less scrupulous in respecting them.

The rules of economics require market players to maximise their profits by charging the highest possible prices, subject only to the laws of supply and demand. Those who do not move forward are moving backwards. Competitive pressure forces firms to expand their market share by accepting all possible matters and meeting all existing demand. On a competitive market, a player who refuses to serve a willing client risks not only the loss of the profit which this client could bring, but a deterioration of market share and – consequently – economic extinction. Competitors are required to advertise themselves, demonstrate superiority over other players, and disclose details of their experiences and references from satisfied clients.

This has eroded the lawyer's relationship with the client. Legal assistance, which is primarily based on intellectual and human values, has been reduced to a commodity, and the methods for earning legal fees have come to resemble the manner in which fees are charged on the marketplace by other service industries.

The pressure to achieve profit targets has led firms to charge excessive fees and not pay enough attention to what is most important in the lawyer's profession: a genuine intention to help the client. The need to remain competitive and retain 'market share' pushes firms into accepting as many matters as possible. As a result, the rule prohibiting lawyers from acting for clients with conflicting interests is increasingly compromised. Immediate economic efficiency and the clients' consent become final arguments in favour of accepting such instructions, and the need to preserve a certain image and prevent any suspicions on the part of the public is marginalised. Some law firms are increasingly hesitant to refuse assistance in matters that display the hallmarks of abuses of rights, arguing inconsistent legal positions depending on what a particular client demands. They eagerly help their clients to disguise their abusive conduct as formal legitimate activity. It also happens that in their relations with the media, some law firms reveal, without any moderation, confidential information relating to their clientele and the cases they handle, with a view to building up the image of celebrities for themselves, their partners and associates. All this is always excused by the argument that the economic interest of the law firm and the rules of competition require such behaviour. In general, an opinion prevails that such are the requirements of the market, and law firms have to proceed with this kind of conduct if they want to survive as economic entities.

As a result, lawyers are perceived as yet another category of service providers who, merely by virtue of some incomprehensible tradition, enjoy privileges which they exploit to extort high fees from clients. This exposes the legal profession to action by competition authorities, mainly within the European Union, which have conducted research resulting in the Clementi report in the United Kingdom[1] and the Monti report in the European Union.[2] The research analysed legal services purely from an economic viewpoint. As a consequence of this process, there is a shortage of trust in law firms. This deficit deprives the entire profession of the necessary mandate to fulfil its function, thus undermining the rule of law and the foundations of civil society.

1 Sir David Clementi, "Review of the Regulatory Framework for Legal Services in England and Wales: Final Report", December 2004.

2 Mario Monti, "A New Strategy for the Single Market at the Service of Europe's Economy and Society: Report to the President of the European Commission, José Manuel Barroso", 9 May 2010.

5. Influence of commercialisation on law firms' strategies

Paradoxically, although commercialisation of the profession can be seen as a reason behind degradation of the lawyer–client relationship and erosion of social trust in the bar, the laws of the market can contribute to the process of regaining the profession's role and position in the system of the rule of law.

Building trust in the law firm among its current and potential clients should be the most urgent business task of every lawyer in the firm and the common denominator for each law firm's entire strategy. This is not only in the interest of the profession as a whole, but in the best economic interest of each individual law firm. There will always be a compelling demand on the market for lawyers who provide honest assistance to their clients and whose trustworthiness in the eyes of the courts, administrative authorities and market participants is uncompromised. If there is a shortage of such law firms today, it can only increase the benefits for those who are the first to fill it.

Therefore, when defining their firm's growth strategy, lawyers must remember that all of their decisions should first and foremost be a function of the principles of professional ethics. To put it provocatively, one can say that the best way to secure a law firm's financial success and stability is not to pay too much attention to its finances. This does not mean that a law firm should neglect to secure the resources necessary for its operations. We must remember that our business costs and investments in the systems in operation at the firm are also our obligation, as alongside our earnest, personal, professional efforts, they also determine the quality of the assistance we are able to provide and will continue to provide for our clients. Nor can we forget about the firm itself, which is the basic instrument that enables us to perform our professional duties. However, the basis for the success of each individual law firm as well as the profession as a whole is the client's confidence in the firm's brand – that is, the belief that the firm's sole motivation is an authentic concern for the good of the client and the client's interests.

This must have a direct bearing on the firm's pricing strategy. Lawyers cannot forget that in the process of exercising their rights, citizens fully depend on their assistance. The complicated nature of legal systems, which are becoming more and more regulated, makes it difficult for the public to comprehend the purpose of legal provisions. In addition, the threat of abuse by the authorities and other players on the market makes clients vulnerable. In this context, the need for legal assistance is perceived as something they simply cannot avoid. Hence, the public perception is that it is not a service but paid help granted to those who cannot do without it. This particular combination of necessity on one hand and the inability of self-assistance on the other provides lawyers with work. This relationship of dependence gives legal fees an ethical dimension; hence the lawyer's need for scrupulous compliance with the ethical obligations which are a condition for the client's trust in the legal profession.

The fee must always correspond to the real intellectual value of the service rendered and may not be excessive. Above all, it cannot be ruthlessly charged to a client when his or her legitimate rights are being violated and he or she suffers objective damage from the point of view of a social sense of justice. Very often lawyers and law firms should get engaged in defending clients' interests almost on a *pro bono* basis, because, in effect, such a defence is not only in the interest of the client but also of society as a whole and the rule of law in particular. In such circumstances, an exacting expectation of a legal fee for every six-minute time unit, as applied in many law firms, makes clients feel blackmailed and abused. Consequently, they have a feeling that the profession is totally commercialised and bereft of moral values. When this feeling is shared by many clients who then exchange their views among themselves and publicly articulate negative opinions about the profession, then it is not only the profession that suffers but the whole of civil society because, as stated above, trust in the profession disappears and the public mandate to the profession ceases to exist. As a result, lawyers cannot expect appropriate respect from society, the public administration and decision makers, and the danger is that they then become an ineffective element of the mechanism of the rule of law.

In gaining a reputation for uncompromising integrity and trustworthiness, a law firm must be prepared to reject potential instructions if so required by ethical norms. In the concrete measures undertaken by a lawyer or a law firm under instructions from individual clients, the aim of legal assistance is to prevent future abuse or to eliminate present abuses. This is so, irrespective of whether the lawyer represents the client before a court, during negotiations, or when drawing up measures the client plans to implement. Such representation must always take place within the framework of the existing legal system. It is also vital to understand that for the sake of upholding the values of civil society, lawyers should abstain from collaborating with clients who aim at abusing power or want to act to the detriment of civil society – or the other party – even at the cost of losing the revenue which such a client could generate. It is therefore vital to understand while building a firm's strategy that there are limits to the interest of the law firm as an undertaking and that financial objectives cannot compromise the role of the lawyer within the society.

For the same reasons, a law firm should act with utmost prudence when accepting instructions from clients who may have conflicting interests. 'Chinese walls' can do more to harm a law firm's image than the firm may be able to gain from using them. A reputation for unwillingness to engage in any activities which could cast doubt on the firm's adherence to the principle of eschewing any conflict of interests is hard to overvalue, but very easy to lose.

In its dealings with the media, a law firm must always have in mind that confidentiality is more important than the celebrity image of the firm and its lawyers. The doubtful benefits of disclosing to the public impressive details of cases or transactions handled by the firm cannot outweigh the benefits of a reputation for discretion and absolute respect for the principle of confidentiality of the client's affairs.

6. Conclusions

The dual nature of legal services and the legal profession has been clear for many years, and it is no great revelation to state that lawyers perform a service. Given its purpose, however, this service holds a special place defined by the architecture of the system. It is this service that enables implementation of the principles of due process and other fundamental rights. This has to do not only with proceedings seeking to defend or establish rights, but also ordinary advice, which helps a client take decisions that are consistent with the legal order. In consequence, the sum total of all legal services provided by the bar within the global community, and the voice of the bar in the dialogue with authority for the purpose of compelling respect for the rights of a civil society, is one of the most important foundations of a democracy under the rule of law. The tendency towards the abuse of power, by act or omission, is after all a psychological trait of practically every person, and will almost always manifest itself when external conditions allow. Proper performance of legal services has an impact on the decisions taken by clients to act in compliance with the legal order and with respect for the rights of others. Of course, instances do occur in which the profession is misused for purposes inconsistent with its guiding principles. In an age of commercialisation and mercantilisation of life, examples of such abuses are frequent.

While defending the rights of a client, a lawyer also performs a service. That is a truism. Owing to their dependence on cash flows, law firms are subject to the rules of the market. One of them is that an undertaking selling a service on the market should always accept clients and deliver a service the client wants. Thus, it may seem that when a law firm refuses to accommodate a prospective client whose interests conflict with those of another of the firm's clients, and the prospective client must go elsewhere, the firm as a market vehicle will suffer a loss. Or it may seem that the rules of the market require a law firm to spread information about the success it has achieved for clients in other cases, or even reveal certain information which ultimately, under the rules of professional conduct, is confidential. In the same way, building up a celebrity image of a law firm and its lawyers may be considered necessary under the rules of the market. From this point of view, many are of the opinion that professional ethics constitute an unnecessary burden on a law firm which hampers the firm's competitiveness and thus has a negative effect on its financial results. In our view, this is only an apparent contradiction.

A basic rule of the market is that undertakings who survive, especially in times of crisis, are those selling products which are in short supply. In our view, the main shortages on the current legal market, thanks to the commercialisation of the profession, are decency, fairness and honesty. In the view of the authors of this publication, no legal service can be provided to clients unless it carries these three fundamental human values. With a view for the public to be able to make a proper judgement as to whether a law firm secures these values, it will be necessary to know whether the firm fulfils the appropriate ethical standards. With this in mind, we have a strong conviction that even though at first sight ethics may seem to require special effort, ultimately they constitute an essential element of a law firm's strategy.

In developing strategies for their firms, lawyers cannot forget the obligation to provide their firms with the necessary cash flows for their existence. It is also in the best interest of their clients. In drafting financial plans, however, a law firm must not forget that much work that would usually have been charged to clients over the last 30 years will have to be offered either for free or at cost, and also that there may be a lot of work offered to existing and potential clients on a *pro bono* basis because it will be related to problems of clients fighting for basic justice. This is why lawyers today must be prepared to act often with no regard for their immediate financial interest. That is the only way to secure public trust in a law firm's brand. Moderation and modesty in building up the firm's reputation should always be in mind when it comes to the firm's presence in the media.

Recent publications on the legal profession underline the necessity of investing in upgrading the firm's capabilities and efficiency in delivering legal assistance. All these publications are quite right in pointing out the extent to which technical development, especially in IT and communications, should change lawyers' way of thinking and imagination in inventing new, more effective ways of bringing reasonable value and effective solutions to clients' problems. We could not agree more with the conclusions drawn by Richard Susskind in his books.[3] We think, however, that the basis for effectiveness is not the free market economy and its mechanisms, but first and foremost the honesty and loyalty which lawyers owe to their clients and that the legal profession owes to society. This brings us back to the fundamental truth underlying the nature of legal assistance, which is that it is rendered not for the sake of earning money but with a view to protecting the rule of law and the legitimate interests of our clients. In this sense, this particular philosophy must be implemented and enforced at all levels of a law firm. It should underlie the behaviour not only of partners and associates, but also the entire staff of the firm, through all stages of dealings with existing and potential clients. Everyone in a law firm must always remember that the firm is there to perform the constitutionally defined role of providing legal protection to citizens by complying with the statutory duty to provide legal assistance to those who need it and who are not in a position to protect their rights on their own.

The law firm as an institution is an undertaking and as such is vulnerable to commercialisation. If the commercial side of the law firm is overemphasised, the image of the profession suffers, and in consequence the public no longer understands the role of the profession within the mechanism of the rule of law. It may thus be stated that a law firm is a special type of enterprise whose economic

---

3 Richard Susskind, *The End of Lawyers? Rethinking the Nature of Legal Services* (Oxford University Press, 2008); *Transforming the Law: Essays on Technology, Justice, and the Legal Marketplace* (Oxford University Press, 2003); *The Future of Law: Facing the Challenges of Information Technology* (Oxford University Press, 1996).

interests are always subordinated to the purpose and function of the bar as established by law. When selecting the profession of a lawyer, we must be aware of what this profession is truly about. An awareness of the social role and true nature of the profession enables us to take proper decisions in compliance with our temperament and our internal conviction that the mission of the profession is identical to our own personal mission.

Implementing a smart collaboration strategy

Heidi K Gardner
Harvard Law School
Ivan Matviak
Gardner & Co

1. Introduction

By now, most law firm leaders have got the message: they can better meet – and exceed – their clients' expectations when their partners collaborate across organisational silos to provide more holistic, tailored, joined-up advice. Clients demand that their external counsel not only help to solve strictly legal problems, but also add value by delivering holistic and contextualised solutions to the wider business problems. Ideally, outside lawyers will anticipate clients' potential problems and use their perspectives from across client matters proactively to surface issues and lead the client toward solutions. This type of superior client service requires teams of lawyers to integrate their expertise across disciplines and geographic divides. We call it 'smart collaboration'.

Although many firm leaders have intuitively recognised the power of collaboration for improving client service – and, consequently, profitability – our research at Harvard University over the last decade has substantiated those beliefs with the hard evidence law firm leaders need to convince their powerful partners to incorporate collaboration into their firm's strategy. Using robust analytics on millions of data (eg, timesheet, personnel and financial records) from dozens of professional service firms, we have empirically demonstrated that firms engaging in smart collaboration boost revenues and profits and increase client satisfaction and loyalty.[1]

Our research, consistent with other scholarship in related areas, shows that firms engaging in smart collaboration are far better at

1 Gardner, Dr Heidi K, *Smart Collaboration: How Professionals and Their Firms Succeed by Breaking Down Silos*, Harvard Business Press, 2017; Gardner, Dr Heidi K and Lobb, Annelena, "Collaborating for Growth: Duane Morris in a Turbulent Legal Sector Case Solution & Answer", Harvard Business School, 26 July 2013; Gardner, Dr Heidi K, "When and Why Clients Want You to Collaborate", *The American Lawyer*, 28 June 2016.

attracting, engaging and retaining top talent. For example, our research uncovered a structured approach that law firms can use to improve the success rate in integrating laterally hired partners. By rapidly engaging the new partner in collaborative opportunities with their colleagues, and holding the hiring partner accountable for the newcomer's integration, firms benefit from remarkably better success rates than firms where the lateral hiring process fails to focus on collaboration.[2] Increasingly, research also clearly links collaboration with personal health and wellbeing.[3]

By our estimation, more than 70% of forward-thinking law firms have now incorporated collaboration as a core pillar of their strategy.[4] The major question on the table: how to implement a strategy of smart collaboration. A strategy is only good if it is put into practice.

This chapter lays out a research-based, practical approach for law firms to turn their collaboration strategy into a living, breathing part of daily life. Given most firms' culture of high autonomy and decentralisation, they will need to drive it both from top down and bottom up. First, we propose a way to get started: conduct a diagnosis to uncover specific barriers, build commitment and plan for change: this step is essential to make sure you are solving the root-cause problem(s), rather than the superficial symptoms. We then introduce three different interventions that firms can use, depending on what collaboration-related issues they are trying to resolve.

2. The case for change: understanding barriers and quantifying upside

Even when partners accept the importance of a strategy entailing smart collaboration, their intellectual buy-in often fails to translate into behavioural change. Many leaders have a set of hypotheses or

---

2 Gardner, Dr Heidi K and Gillespie, Anusia E, *Smart Collaboration for Lateral Hiring*, Globe Law and Business, October 2018.

3 Gardner, Heidi K, "Smart Collaboration for Greater Wellbeing", *The Best Lawyer You Can Be: A Guide to Physical, Mental, Emotional, and Spiritual Wellness*, 1st Edition, Levine, Stewart L (Editor), American Bar Association 2019; Lieberman, Matthew D, *Social: Why Our Brains Are Wired to Connect*, Crown Publishing Corp, 2013; Richard, Dr Larry, "Wellness is the Cake, Not the Icing", *PD Quarterly*, November 2018.

4 Not all firms use the term 'collaboration'. Some instead mention 'cross-selling' – which is unfortunate terminology because many clients and partners despise crass, self-serving up-selling. For more on this distinction, see Gardner, Heidi K, *Smart Collaboration: How Professionals and Their Firms Succeed by Breaking Down Silos*, Harvard Business Press, 2017; Maister, David, "Making Multidisciplinary Practices Work", 2005, available at https://davidmaister.com/articles/making-multidisciplinary-practices-work (accessed 4 February 2020).

assumptions about what holds the firm back. When we conduct research inside firms, however, we often find that leaders' views are only partially supported by the data.

Why are leaders' views disconnected from others'? One reason is that leaders' views are biased, merely because of their position; research in social psychology backs up the oft-observed situation whereby people's views change when they attain greater power.[5] Beyond the mere perceptions, though, leaders' experience of collaboration is often genuinely different from others in the organisation for a few reasons. First, leaders often are long tenured in that firm, meaning that they have had ample time to build broad-reaching, productive networks of colleagues inside the firm. Secondly, they were presumably elected because people trust them; as we see below, trust is a critical foundation for collaboration. Finally, few people say 'no' to a leader's request for help. All in all, people at the top actually do face fewer collaboration obstacles – the distortion between their views and others' views of collaboration is not merely one of perception. Nonetheless, getting a clear-eyed view of the firm's true readiness for implementing a collaboration-related strategy is crucial for getting started on the right path.

An objective understanding of the firm's launching point for a new or modified strategy helps the firm's leaders to pinpoint how and where to spend their energy – and, more importantly, how to direct others to do the same. Leaders must constantly reinforce that 'smart' collaboration is a means to a much larger end: providing holistic solutions to clients' complex issues. If instead the partners feel that they are being asked simply to 'collaborate more', then they are likely either to waste time and effort, or simply to ignore the mandate. A call for unfettered collaboration is irresponsible and counterproductive.

This need to pinpoint specific intervention points requires leaders to conduct a thorough diagnostic phase before trying to implement a collaboration strategy. In our experience working across multiple law firms in North and South America, Europe and Africa, we have found that this initial diagnostic phase sets up leaders for success in three ways:

- It helps them to understand the perceived and actual barriers to collaboration, ensuring that they are focused on the issues that the full partnership sees as critical;

---

5 Van Kleef, G, Oveis, C, Van der Löwe, I, LuoKogan, A, Goetz, J and Keltner, D, "Power, Distress, and Compassion: Turning a Blind Eye to the Suffering of Others", *Psychological Science*, Vol 19, No 12, 2008, pp1315–1322.

- It generates compelling evidence about the potential upside of making changes (ideally quantified in monetary terms), which is essential for motivating high-autonomy partners to even consider new ways of working; and
- It prioritises actions based on both the anticipated upside (return on investment (ROI) in financial terms, plus other benefits that are harder to quantify in the short term, such as morale) and the challenge of implementation (friction points that can hinder the capture of ROI).

2.1 Uncovering barriers to collaboration

Identifying the typical barriers to collaboration requires a two-pronged approach. First, you need broad-based inputs from across the entire partnership – not only to ensure that you are collecting and interpreting views from everyone, but also to build a sense of participation amongst the whole group of senior leaders. Research clearly shows that 'voice' is a critical element for helping people feel invested in a change effort.[6] The way to access wide input is to use surveys that ask simple, open-ended questions about partners' perceived barriers to collaboration. Ideally, a team trained in qualitative research methodology will analyse these free-text responses, separating discrete barriers that respondents had co-mingled, and assigning each to a category. Multiple people should code each response to minimise interpreter bias, and check that inter-rater reliability is high; discuss differences to get a clearer, unified interpretation. Although labour-intensive, this method preserves the integrity of people's own words and avoids the 'demand bias' problem associated with multiple-choice surveys.[7]

These are the typical barriers we have found in our work with firms:

- *Knowledge of the firm's offerings:* Since firms can vary in size and jurisdiction, it may be difficult to know who can do what, to what capacity and with what resources. This barrier is especially prevalent in firms that have grown through mergers. It is also frequently cited as a barrier in large firms with dispersed offices, although it is remarkable how little

---

6 Lines, Rune, "Influence of participation in strategic change: resistance, organizational commitment and change goal achievement", *Journal of Change Management*, 2004.

7 'Demand bias' occurs when responses appear to be influenced by the perceived purpose of the study – based on affiliation with the researcher or deduced from the survey structure.

awareness partners have of their colleagues' capabilities even in smaller firms.

- *Competence trust:* When collaborating, one needs faith in others' professionalism, skillset and capabilities – not only technical legal skills, but also client-handling ability such as responsiveness. The lack of strong trust presents a clear barrier. It shows up in quotes that may refer to "loss of quality control" or having to "prod and then being embarrassed by poor delivery". Again, this can be an issue for firms that have merged: a partner will think: "By definition, half the partners who joined from the 'other' firm are below average ... but which ones?"
- *Interpersonal trust:* Unlike competence trust, interpersonal trust pertains almost entirely to distrust in someone's character and intentions – rooted in previous observations or simply a lack of familiarity. Typically, partners who joined as lateral hires have been vetted extensively in terms of their ability, but their new colleagues will worry about their prowess in porting client relationships from one firm to another: "Are they going to steal my client next?"
- *Lack of time/inefficiency of collaboration:* The collaborative process can be logistically challenging due to different time zones and language or cultural barriers, for instance, and to the time required to explain the task to someone else. Every partner is undoubtedly busy: the real question is not whether they have time, but where they choose to spend it. We often see this barrier arise in firms where the structure (eg, incentives) and leaders fail to hold people accountable for delivering on collaborative goals.
- *Incentives and key performance indicators:* Many partners report their firm's compensation and performance management structure as barriers to collaboration. And rightly so: no perfect compensation system exists because each one has both known trade-offs and unintended consequences. Some, however, are more broken than others – especially the ones that rely strictly on formulaic calculations of individual outcomes.[8]

8 For more on this topic, please see Gardner, Dr Heidi K, Chapter 6, "Collaboration for Ringmasters" in *Smart Collaboration: How Professionals and Their Firms Succeed by Breaking Down Silos*, Harvard Business Press, 2017.

- *Selling skills and confidence:* Often it is best if partners can identify collaborative opportunities for their clients – picking up on different clues that may demonstrate additional client needs or broadening the scope of the initial pitch. This is the most under-reported barrier by partners: many do not recognise their deficiency, and even those that do are typically reluctant to admit it.

The second 'prong' of the barriers identification involves in-depth interviews and focus groups. After coding the data, quantify the relative frequency of mentioned barriers and feed this information back to a range of participants. Test your understanding of the identified barriers by interviewing a select group of partners one-on-one. When selecting interviewees, consider including thought leaders and opinion shapers; strategic selection of interviewees helps to build individual commitment to the project and organisational momentum.

2.2 Generate a compelling picture of the potential upside

This step involves two distinct kinds of analyses using (i) financial data and (ii) client inputs. The first analysis involves quantifying the 'money on the table' your firm is currently leaving behind by not serving clients with the full range of offerings. In brief, you must analyse your current client portfolio to determine the average revenues for each group of clients that are served by the same number of practice groups. In one firm, we saw that revenues were 5.7 times higher for clients served by three practice groups than by a single one. Those clients served by five practice groups generated fees 17.6 times higher than those with just one kind of service (see Figure 1).

The next step is to calculate the upside: how much is it worth if you shift just 10% of clients in each category to the next-higher category? The numbers along the solid graph line in Figure 2 show the number of clients served in each category; the ones in the circles along the dotted line show the hypothetical new portfolio if 10% of clients in each category moved one step to the right. For this firm, the incremental revenue of this shift would add up to nearly $43 million. That's an 11% increase in the firm's total revenue.[9]

9 Gardner, Dr Heidi K, "By Failing to Collaborate, Law Firms are Leaving Money on the Table", *The American Lawyer*, October 2018.

Figure 1. Revenue impact of smart collaboration at Firm X

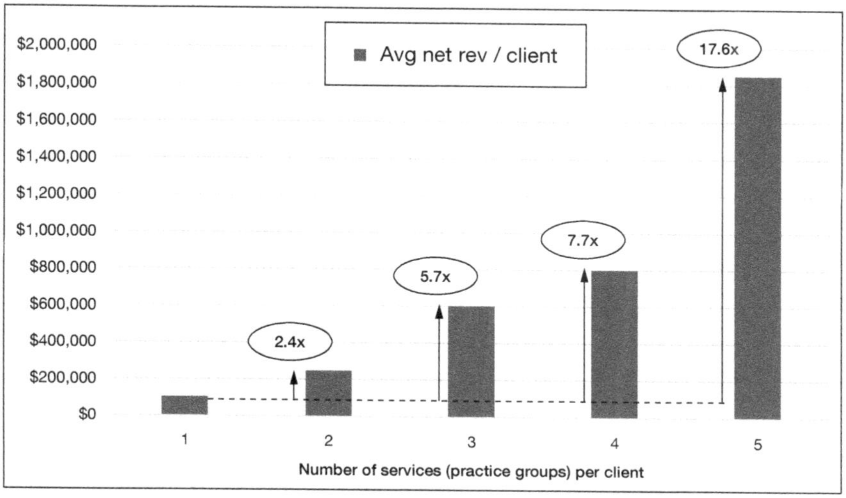

Figure 2. Firm X: Upside of shifting portfolio by 10%

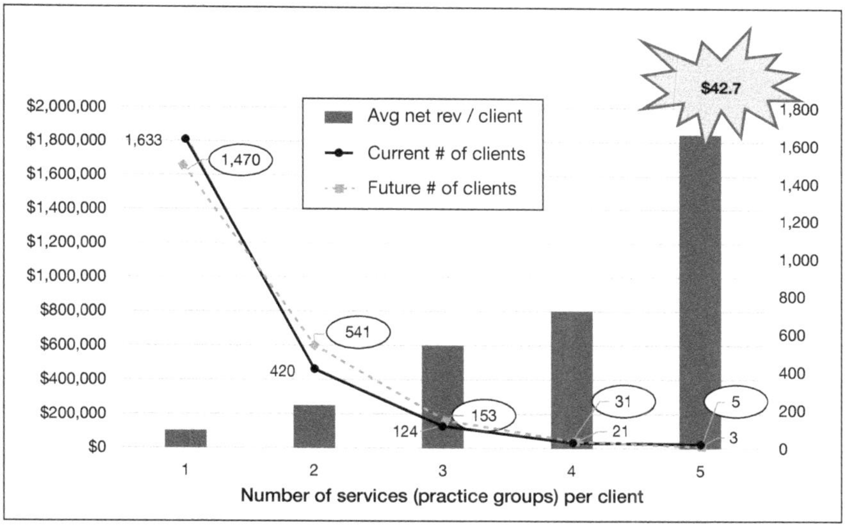

This figure is typical across the firms we studied that are collaborating well – that is, doing complex work for clients that results in appropriate levels of increased revenue. In general, firms are missing out on up to 15% of overall revenue by not figuring out how to make this shift. When you translate this into money terms – "We could gain forty million pounds of profit by collaborating better"– it tends to catch partners' attention!

The second piece of analysis for understanding the upside of collaboration involves targeted client interviews. Engage with a representative sample of key client contacts, ideally general counsel, in order to understand: What gives my firm a competitive advantage with the client, specifically related to collaboration? Where can we add more value to the client by bringing the full breadth of the firm's capabilities? Beyond providing invaluable insights, these inquiries are appreciated by the client because they signal the law firm's keen desire to serve its client better.

When using these findings to gain firm-wide commitment for a programme to advance collaboration, leaders can learn from the work of Professor Daniel Kahneman, for which he won the 2002 Nobel Prize in economics.[10] His prospect theory shows that "losses loom larger than gains". To increase partners' sense of urgency, leaders can frame the outcome of increased collaboration as avoiding a loss – that is, "money left behind" – rather than revenue gained, which according to prospect theory is less powerful.

3. Goals and accountability: using technology to turn service gaps into delivered targets

Despite the large proportion of law firms today that include collaboration-related goals in their strategic plans, many lack a solid understanding of exactly where collaboration may have the most impact and how much it could help them achieve. As a result, these firms lack the ability to tie collaboration to performance outcomes.

Simply put, firms cannot just state that collaboration matters and hope lawyers change their behaviour. You need to set specific objectives, based on a deep understanding of your data and its implications, and then hold people accountable for delivering.

Research in social psychology shows that people's motivation to perform is significantly stronger when given specific, measurable goals rather than being told to 'do your best'.[11] This finding runs counter to many law firm leaders' assumptions that highly autonomous partners operate best when they set their own goals. But in fact, lawyers are most engaged and productive when they have

---

10 Kahneman, D and Tversky, A, "Prospect Theory: An Analysis of Decision Under Risk", *Econometrica*, 47, 1979, pp263–291.

11 Locke, Edwin A, "Motivation Through Conscious Goal Setting", *Applied & Preventive Psychology*, Cambridge University Press, 1996.

a clear sense of direction aligned with the firm's strategy, which also enables them to discriminate between higher-value and lesser-value work. This approach holds true provided that lawyers understand the rationale behind the targets and have had the ability to accept or modify the proposed goals.[12]

With this psychological underpinning and a deep understanding of the typical barriers to collaboration in law firms, my team has worked with a technology company to develop a data-driven software tool that uses machine learning to identify, prioritise and quantify the highest-value collaboration opportunities across the firm. It also leverages timesheet data and other records to reveal which lawyer in the firm is best placed to act on the opportunity. Whether you are using this tool, called WhiteSpace, or a homegrown solution, here are the elements that distinguish an excellent solution from the typical 'gap analysis' that law firms have long attempted – and often abandoned – during strategic planning:[13]

- *Analyse and quantify collaboration successes and opportunities:* Using the full range of data on your current client portfolio, determine where cross-practice service provides the most value to similar sets of clients (eg, average collected fees across the retail banks or biotech companies you serve). The purpose is not simply to see where gaps exist and try to plug them (which would result in the client-abhorrent cross-selling); instead the analysis should turn up clusters of services that some clients already benefit from. By benchmarking like-to-like clients, the analysis will then quantify the 'size of the prize' if lawyers can team up to bring insights from those clustered offerings to benefit more of your client base. This step addresses the typical barrier, "What is the full range of services my firm offers?" for harried lawyers who do not have time to study their firm's online directory or knowledge management database.
- *Prioritise options:* The first step could turn up many thousands of opportunities, so this is where technology is essential: use algorithms to rank those choices based on inputs that are critical for your firm. For example, weight choices by the profitability of the account (no point trying to sell holistic solutions to clients that unrealistically squeeze your margin), history of client loyalty, depth and breadth of current engagement, and

12 Locke, Edwin A, *A Theory of Goal Setting & Task Performance*, Pearson College Div, 1990.
13 For an overview of this tool, see www.whitespacesoftware.com/.

other factors. Although most finance departments could do this step manually, it would take hundreds of hours; software should be able to do it in seconds.

- *Match trusted experts with opportunities:* For each high-priority area, mine your data from billing records, timesheets and other archives to figure out: (i) who has worked on similar issues – ideally both in terms of content and the client's sector – and therefore has the right expertise to pursue the new offering; and (ii) who has prior experience working with the existing client team members. Then develop a shortlist of potential partners to execute on the opportunity. A data-driven shortlist promotes competence trust by signalling someone's credentials, and interpersonal trust by ensuring that at least some existing client team members are familiar with the proposed new team member. It thus helps to overcome efficiently the barrier that many partners report: "I don't know who does this kind of work – or whether I can trust them." Smartly designed software can also promote a firm's diversity and inclusion goals by ensuring that each proposed 'slate of options' includes a mix of people, rather than simply the 'usual suspects'. Overall, this step is almost impossible to perform efficiently and accurately unless you are using a technology solution that leverages artificial intelligence.
- *Convert goals into accountability:* Once the right potential team has been targeted at the best opportunity, partners need to collaborate to bring the plan to life. Here, technology is useful because it creates an electronic 'paper trail' to allow the firm to view who is accountable for an identified goal and monitor progress against the objective. For example, a transportation sector leader could see that the client lead partner for a specific airline client had set the goal of expanding the firm's data privacy services with that airline by X amount, and that the client lead partner had asked a particular partner in the data privacy practice to join the team and help achieve that goal. A software tool can automatically propose options for partners in the data privacy practice (to the lead client relationship partner), and prompt him or her to select an individual or decline them for a specific reason. If the tool uses machine learning, it will 'learn' over time which client opportunities are most relevant for each particular partner and adjust automatically. Accepted goals

can be converted into specific, quantified objectives that leaders can use to establish accountability – in ways that are far more transparent than traditional strategic planning and performance management.

A typical lawyer's strong sense of urgency means that most partners are unwilling to wait for the data, and instead simply use intuition to prioritise their business development efforts. If a firm wants to use a data-driven approach, leaders need to acknowledge that manual analysis is likely to be too slow to meet partners' needs. A software solution such as WhiteSpace should not replace business development or finance professionals, but rather augment their ability to add value by removing the drudge work and inherent biases, and then focusing them on the most important opportunities.

Implementing any strategy requires a leader to translate firm-wide aims into on-the-ground actions; a collaboration-related strategy demands even more attention because it requires significant coordination across individual partners. By leveraging technology to help develop data-based goals, leaders can better harness the full range of their existing data and translate it into specific, measurable objectives that allow them to hold specific individuals and teams accountable for delivery.

4. Upgrading partners' collaborative business development capabilities

For most law firms implementing smart collaboration, their primary goal is to enhance their client service, leading to higher revenues and profit. Lawyers achieve these outcomes by collaborating across silos to address their clients' VUCA (volatile, uncertain, complex, ambiguous) problems. After all, these are the challenges that can have the biggest impact on the client, require a range of specialised skills across service offerings and tend to be the least fee sensitive.

Unfortunately, however, many lawyers lack the advanced business development skills and confidence to pursue smart collaboration. Adding to the challenge, our research shows that this lack of confidence and skills is one of the most under-reported barriers to collaboration within firms. Perhaps this is because most lawyers have been trained to think that delivering technically excellent legal advice is the sole criterion for pleasing their clients; some have no idea what it means to truly deliver value-added, proactive client service. Others might be aware of the need to do so but lack the know-how for engaging in the kinds of relationship-building activities that unearth those opportunities. Still others are unwilling to admit that their deficiency is the cause of the problem. As a result, many firms fail to address their partners' capability gaps and miss many business growth opportunities.

The obvious answer to addressing this lack of collaborative business development capabilities is to invest in targeted professional development, but traditional training approaches need to be seriously revamped in order to achieve the kind of ROI that is possible.

4.1 Maximising professional development ROI: seven essential principles

Unlike knowledge development on domain expertise (eg, regulatory changes), skills training in areas such as business development, leadership and talent management is – regrettably – often viewed as a 'soft skill' and is undervalued in law firms. In our work with firms, we see two reasons why this misperception is so prevalent. First, training is often delivered as a one-off event. The content is treated as stand-alone material rather than embedded in lawyers' daily work or clearly linked to outcomes that they value. In the end, the impact is minimal because partners revert to their usual routines as soon as they are back at their desks. Secondly, even if a programme is structured to reinforce the learnings over time, nearly all professional development departments lack the statistical and analytical capability to rigorously quantify and monitor the outcomes. Without an understanding of the training's ROI, sceptical partners fail to see its value to the firm, and professional development leaders struggle to legitimise the programme as essential rather than 'soft'.

These problems with traditional training are hardly unique to law firms: research shows that much of conventional corporate training is ineffective. For example, a McKinsey survey found that only 12% of employees apply new skills learned in learning and development programmes to their jobs, and only 25% of respondents believed that training had a measurable impact on performance. Fewer than 50% of companies surveyed even keep track of participants' feedback about the training, let alone measure the impact on performance.[14]

14 DeSmet, Aron, McGurk, Monica and Schwartz, Elizabeth, "Getting More From Your Training Programs", *McKinsey Quarterly*, October 2010.

Moreover, many training programmes focus on individual learning; at worst, this approach risks reinforcing lone-wolf behaviours and mindsets like over-confidence in one's own individualistic ability. Instead, to expand lawyers' ability to engage in collaborative business development and address client's most VUCA challenges, a programme needs to embed the following principles:

- *Immediately relevant content:* Focus on applying concepts that can be immediately applied to clients and pending matters.
- *Live simulations:* Run simulations (and do not call them 'role plays') so that participants are not only exposed to concepts but also engage in real work. Would you rather fly with an airline where the pilots were lectured on how to fly, or where they practised using flight simulators?
- *Aligned to goals:* Link content to outcomes that are valued by the participant and their organisation. Ideally the curriculum is tied to key performance metrics; themselves tied to a firm's strategic plan.
- *Group learning:* Participants not only learn the content, but also enhance the skills needed to work in teams (eg, leading without authority, holding difficult conversations). Ideally, participants are selected so that their bonds formed during professional development will carry over to real work.
- *Video-based feedback:* When people can see their own performance on video and self-diagnose issues, they are much more receptive to making changes. Access to the videos after the session allows people to review – in a gripping way – the kinds of behavioural changes they need to make, and why.
- *Reinforce over time:* Apply continuous learning and guided learning principles to help reinforce the concepts and encourage the participant to embed the skills over time. Ideally, programme coaches provide 12 months of ongoing support.
- *Personalised:* Design and deliver the training based on the individual's needs, ideally measured using a psychometrically validated test so that each participant can benchmark him or herself against known population.

4.2 Case study: Advanced Business Development for Partners programme

A case study of a collaborative business development programme that embodies these principles is the Advanced Business Development for Partners (ABDP) programme by Cochran Client Development. We selected this programme to study because it embeds all seven principles listed above. By using advanced statistical techniques that replicate experimental conditions, we have been able to quantify its financial impact in ensuing years.

(a) *Overview and objectives of the programme*

The Cochran ABDP programme aims to increase the participants' skills in developing new business from prospective and existing clients. Two of its key content areas help to build strong collaboration skills:

- *Unearthing collaborative VUCA opportunities:* The challenge is to unearth the VUCA issues that are critical to the client and will lead to genuine collaboration opportunities within the firm. Lawyers are taught to bring their industry insight to bear by asking questions and listening until they recognise a potential need, which is – to many lawyers' surprise – a completely different capability than projecting expertise in a domain. The learning is embedded through simulations with mock clients (retired general counsel).
- *Key client management:* Lawyers learn how to engage with a team of peers to develop multiple relationships in complex clients that have many influencers and decision-makers. They learn how collaborating across multiple practices and offices allows them to address a client's most challenging objectives, in part by leveraging the full force of their firm's offerings and experiences.

Because the training is done in a group, it also addresses other barriers to collaboration by deepening knowledge of the firm's array of offerings, enhancing interpersonal trust and building the participants' competence trustworthiness in the eyes of other partners.

(b) *Quantifying the ROI of the programme*

To study the financial return on investment of the ABDP programme, we collected data from a large (AmLaw 50) law firm that had trained multiple cohorts of partners. To estimate the ROI, we treated participants as 'subjects' in an experiment and compared their outcomes to those of a matched sample of partners who did not get the training.[15]

---

15 The sample of peers was matched based on demographic and professional characteristics (eg, practice group, gender, tenure at this firm), and on their origination levels at the time the ABDP programme launched. For robustness, we computed two different matched samples and statistical results were highly similar.

Figure 3. Financial impact of trained partners vs control group

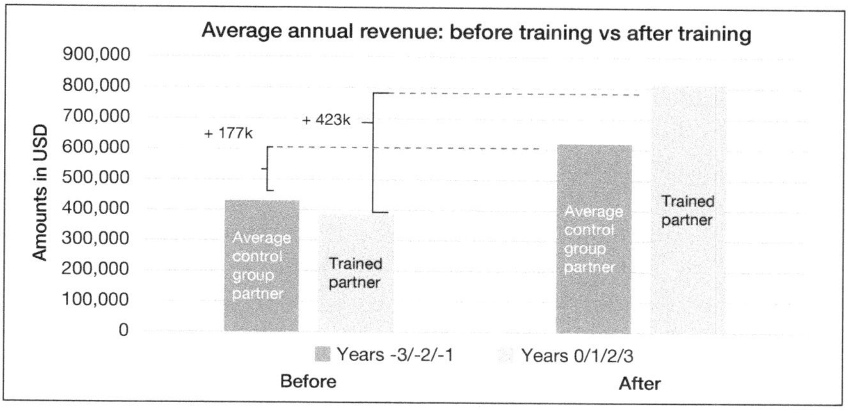

Our analysis showed a dramatic effect on participants' success in generating client revenue for the firm (see Figure 3). In the three years prior to training, participants originated slightly less, on average, than their peer control group. Over the three years after the ABDP programme, however, trained participants' origination levels climbed by an incremental $423,000 per year, whereas their untrained peers' levels climbed by $177,000 per year. That means that the annual financial impact of the training was $246,000 per participant delivering a three-year ROI of nearly 30X.

In sum, our research demonstrates that partners can significantly improve their collaborative business development capabilities – and thereby generate very significant financial returns – if the professional development programme embeds the seven essential principles outlined above.

5. Optimising individuals' and leaders' collaborative behaviours

Leading an organisation toward enhanced collaboration requires more than organisation-level strategy. As covered above, our research in law firms uncovers individual-level barriers that firms need to mitigate in order to foster bottom-up support for collaboration. To drive toward a more collaborative firm, individuals need to understand their own starting point on collaborative skills and tendencies, and learn how to leverage those tendencies to create more effective teams.

Each person has the potential to enhance collaboration at the team and organisational level by deploying their unique combination of strengths in conjunction with the diverse strengths of others in the group. Smart collaboration at the organisational level hinges on team diversity – effectively deploying the group's broad set of behavioural tendencies and skills to maximise the benefits of collaboration. By becoming aware of your natural tendencies and making deliberate choices about how to behave in a team setting, you have the power to help the group collaborate more effectively.

For example, one behavioural tendency we have uncovered is called 'risk spotting'. If you are strong on this tendency, you will be acutely aware of potential risks. You can use this ability to help groups avoid falling prey to 'group-think' and ensure a diversity of views, including dissenting opinions, are heard. In contrast, people with the 'risk seeking' tendency are relatively quick to identify opportunities. This tendency is valuable in surfacing new and potentially bold ideas. At the same time, a watch-out for risk seekers is your potential for over-optimism, even in the face of critical challenges.

Both behavioural tendencies (risk seeking and risk spotting) can thus be valuable depending on the context, and they will be more valuable if used intentionally and in balance with tendencies of other group members. More generally, because no single behaviour is optimal across varying situations, individuals, leaders and teams need to understand how to use those tendencies effectively and flexibly.

This capacity starts with people understanding their own behavioural tendencies and preferences, as well as the natural tendencies of those they work with.

5.1 Methodology to develop a tool for optimising individuals' collaborative behaviours

Many people have, to some degree, an intuitive sense of their behavioural tendencies. However, this can lead to an overreliance on those strengths, emphasising them even in sub-optimal situations, and blind spots. People need an unbiased view of their tendencies so that they can choose how to respond in any given situation and thereby increase their ability to create the outcomes they want at work or at home. This objective view can be gained through psychometric tests.

Psychometric tests are a standard and scientific method used to measure individuals' psychological characteristics and behavioural tendencies.[16] A robust and scientifically developed psychometric test which follows prescribed standards will be rigorously evaluated for validity, reliability/errors of measurement and fairness in testing.[17] These tests can be helpful tools to understand more deeply your behavioural tendencies so that you can be more deliberate in how you use them.

We have conducted empirical research with multiple law firms to identify specific behavioural tendencies closely aligned with smart collaboration. For example, our research measured the results of partners' actual collaborative actions, such as expanding a client relationship across practice groups, and studied the behavioural tendencies associated with those successful collaborative outcomes. We distilled these behavioural tendencies into seven dimensions of smart collaboration, as outlined below.

5.2 Individuals' use of a behavioural-based psychometric tool

As noted above, one major imperative in implementing a strategy of smart collaboration is helping partners, other fee-earning staff and allied business professionals to understand how their own behaviour contributes to – or undermines – effective collaboration across the firm. This is where it is crucial to use a psychometric self-assessment, based on psychological traits that research shows to predict collaborative behaviour at work and in groups. According to our studies in law firms, the seven dimensions include areas such as the following:

- *Individual vs group:* our tendency to engage in collaborative work. In general, would you rather work on your own or in a team?
- *Close vs distant communication:* our preference for the frequency of interactions, and comfort with revealing personal information. Do you talk about your outside relationships and interests with colleagues, or keep that side of your life private?
- *Wary vs trusting:* the base level of trust we are likely to feel for our colleagues. Do we inherently trust others, or wait for them to prove themselves?

16 Ziegler, M and Brunner, M, "Test Standards and Psychometric Modeling" in Lipnevich A, Preckel F and Roberts R (eds), *Psychosocial Skills and School Systems in the 21st Century*, The Springer Series on Human Exceptionality, Springer, Cham, 2016.

17 Furnham, Adrian, "The Great Divide: Academic Versus Practitioner Criteria for Psychometric Test Choice", *Journal of Personality Assessment*, Vol 100, No 5, 2018, pp498–506.

Once people get an objective view of their own position on each dimension, they can learn how to use their own tendencies as a strength.[18] This is critical: rather than try to change an individual's preferences, the objective should be to help a person maximise their effectiveness by being mindful of when and how to use those tendencies.

Turning insights into action requires practical, personalised guidance. For example, a 'distant' communicator: requires less frequent communication; minimises small talk and pleasantries; prefers to get straight to business; keeps their private life separate from their professional one; and is comfortable with remote working. A 'distant' communicator can leverage their behavioural tendencies to the benefit of the team by:

- Sharing the limelight and giving others – especially introverts – the time and space they need to contribute fully;
- Empowering others to take initiative on team communications;
- Keeping the team focused on what needs to be done; setting clear agendas and bringing meandering discussions back on point; helping streamline written work products; and
- Creating a shared vision so that the team understands the business priorities even with infrequent communication.

Research also shows that change occurs over time and requires deliberate, repetitive effort. Doing so – especially getting time-starved lawyers and staff to focus on collaboration – means that people will need to receive periodic prompts over time to help them focus on the most high-impact practical actions they can take to engage in smart collaboration.

5.3 Leaders' benefits from a behavioural-based psychometric tool

Leaders need access to their team's psychometric test results (collectively; not attributed to any specific individual). With insights from these findings, leaders can better understand, manage and motivate their teams to engage in enhanced collaboration within the group, with other parts of the firm and with clients.[19]

---

18 We have developed a set of technologically enabled, psychometrically validated tools based on these ideas. See https://smartcollaborationaccelerator.com/.

19 For a technical treatment of different compositional effects of personality on group outcomes, see Moynihan, Lisa M and Peterson, Randall S, "A Contingent Configuration Approach To Understanding The Role Of Personality In Organizational Groups", *Research In Organizational Behavior*, Vol 23, 2001, pp327–378.

For example, imagine that you lead a team with a high proportion of people with a 'concrete' tendency (ie, behavioural preference for tackling pragmatic issues rather than ambiguous or complex ones). Your team overall may struggle to understand and lean into ill-defined problems. By identifying the few team members with a preference for the 'complex' (ie, those that are attracted to complicated, ambiguous and uncertain issues and innovation), you can leverage them to help the group define a problem – that is, break it down into comprehensible pieces and create a 'mental map' that facilitates a common understanding. As the group moves toward a clearer view of the challenge and requirements, the majority members who prefer the 'concrete' can focus on developing execution plans.

By understanding the behavioural tendencies and skills within the team, the leader can identify potential barriers to effective collaboration and intentionally deploy the needed skills to drive the team forward.

6. Conclusion

When law firms can encourage their partners to engage in smart collaboration, they boost their revenues and profits, increase client satisfaction and loyalty, improve the success rate of lateral hires, and improve their ability to attract, retain and engage talent. Not surprisingly then, a majority of major firms around the world have included the tenets of smart collaboration in their firm's formal strategic plan.

Turning this plan into action requires an investment – and some innovation. To implement a strategy based on smart collaboration, the best firms will engage in the following kind of steps: (i) understand the current barriers to collaboration within the firm and quantify the potential upside of mitigating those obstacles; (ii) use AI-driven (artificial intelligence) technology to identify, prioritise and track progress against opportunities to address the client's most VUCA challenges; (iii) enhance partners' skills in collaborative business development; and (iv) deepen individuals' and leaders' understanding of their own collaborative tendencies and equip them with tools to help them embed routines that build on their strengths. Firms that invest in these approaches stand a much stronger chance of creating distinctive competitive advantage by becoming their client's strategic partner through smart collaboration.

Business model transformation as a tool for driving strategic innovation and growth

Robert Millard
Cambridge Strategy Group

1. Introduction

Will leading law firms in the future have radically different business models to those of today's leading firms? How will emerging digital technologies impact the practice and business of law? Will client needs be radically different and, if so, how? How will the needs of the people working in these law firms, and in client organisations, be different? Will the legal service providers of the future even be law "firms" as we currently understand them, or will clients purchase their legal advisory services from radically different kinds of service providers?

For today's law firm leaders these are existentially important questions. On their answers depend the strategies that their firms will need to develop and implement, and the business models that they will need to build, to optimise their performance over the coming years.

The business model used by many large law firms today is still essentially the same 'Tournament of Lawyers' model described by Galanter and Pallay in 1990.[1] Admittedly, it has been modified somewhat and law firms today are quite different in scale and in their use of technology, compared to 1990. Although less rigid than the pure hierarchies (Figure 1), nonetheless these structures remain essentially flattened pyramids of people, founded upon the billable hour (Figure 2).

Discussions about innovation and change involving business models frequently use trendy terms such as 'digital transformation' and 'disruption', and 'agile' and 'lean six sigma'. These can create the illusion that change is something new, or that we are in a 'pre-transformation' stage and once certain steps are taken, we will find

1 Galanter, M and Palay, T, *Tournament of Lawyers: The Transformation of the Big Law Firm*, 1991, University of Chicago Press.

Figure 1. A strict hierarchical organisational structure, typical of organisations where members of the organisation are tightly bound by a system of strict seniority, with minimal discretion allowed on the part of individuals to control their own work or collaborate outside of their sub-unit

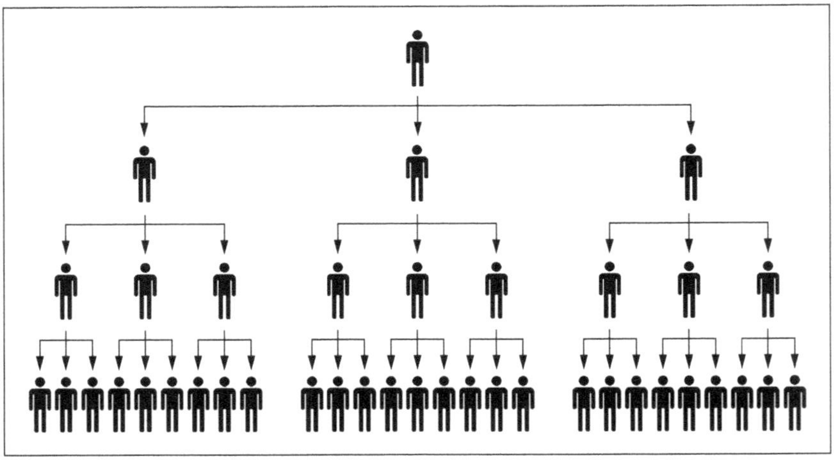

Source: Author.

Figure 2. A flattened hierarchical structure, similar to the strict hierarchical structure but with lateral collaboration across peer levels encouraged and more individual discretion to control one's own work at the more senior levels

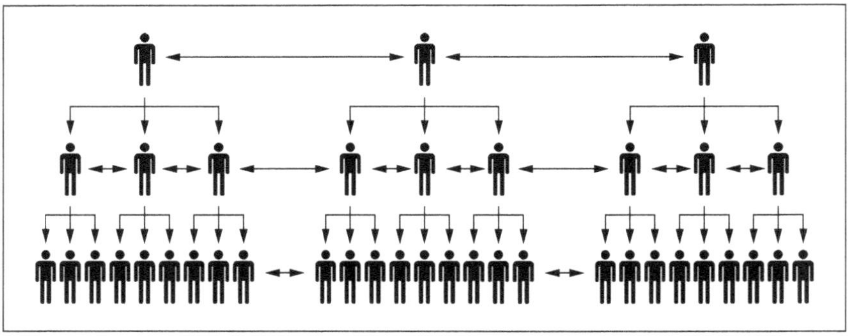

Source: Author.

ourselves in a new state of dynamic equilibrium with our markets with no need for further change – at least for a while. Neither is true. Most of these new terms describe things that have been studied for many decades and about which a solid foundation of well-proven theory exists – that is, how organisations respond to changes in their external environment. To understand how business models of law firms specifically are evolving, it is useful to go back to these basics.

In this chapter, we will focus on that underlying core of theory to explore:

- how a firm's business model is different to strategy and why that matters;
- the essential elements of a modern law firm business model;
- the options available to law firm leaders to transform their business models; and
- generic business models that might become more prominent in the future.

2. How a firm's business model is different to its strategy

The distinction between 'strategy' and 'business model' may seem superficially obvious, but both terms have been so widely interpreted over the years that overlap is inevitable. Writing in 1994, Peter Drucker described the core issue of what we now call 'business models' (he used the term 'theory of the business' instead) coming under pressure and evolving over time as follows:

> *The story is a familiar one: a company that was a superstar only yesterday finds itself stagnating and frustrated, in trouble and, often, in a seemingly unmanageable crisis ... The root cause of nearly every one of these crises is not that things are being done poorly. It is not even that the wrong things are being done. Indeed, in most cases, the right things are being done – but fruitlessly. What accounts for this apparent paradox? The assumptions on which the organization has been built and is being run no longer fit reality.*[2]

To reiterate: Drucker writes that it is not the firm's strategy that is wrong. It is not even that the strategy is right but poorly implemented, although this is often blamed. It is that the firm's business model is no longer a proper "fit with reality". This poor fit then becomes an obstacle to the firm achieving its strategic objectives, even when its systems and processes are working superbly well. Paradoxically, it is when those systems and processes are working superbly well that this can be an especially formidable obstacle, because the conflict between strategy and business model becomes that much more pronounced.

---

2 Drucker, PF, "The Theory of the Business", *Harvard Business Review*, September–October 1994.

2.1 What is strategy?

Strategy is the long-term intent of the firm, usually reduced to the mix of clients, services and markets which it chooses to prioritise. It is reflected not in a dusty document on the managing partner's bookshelf, but in the firm's major everyday decisions. Some of these decisions are the product of a predetermined plan (deliberate strategy). Others are triggered by unanticipated changes in the firm, its clients or its markets (emergent strategy). In a 'volatile, uncertain, complex, ambiguous' (VUCA) world such as today's is frequently described, it is not unusual for emergent strategy to overwhelm deliberate strategy. Organisation resilience and agility are then as crucial to the firm's long-term success as a clear view of what the firm seeks to achieve. A solid body of theory also underpins these points, going back at least to Henry Mintzberg's 1985 article "Of strategies, deliberate and emergent".[3]

2.2 What then, by comparison, is a business model?

By the simplest of definitions, a business model is how a firm plans to make money.[4] It is a story (sometimes but not always in narrative form) that explains how the firm works and how value is created. A good business model answers Peter Drucker's age-old questions: "Who is the customer?" and "What does the customer value?"

Writing in 2002, Joan Magretta describes business models as having two parts.[5] Paraphrased to fit the context of law firms, the first part includes all the activities associated with generating the services that are sold to clients – that is, developing the knowledge management system upon which the work product is based, implementing the technology platforms that are to be utilised, managing the firm's people, and so on. The second part includes all the activities associated with selling that service to clients – that is, finding and reaching clients, pitching to clients, engaging with clients about particular matter, developing the work product and delivering it to clients.

A more comprehensive view on business models is provided by Alex Osterwalder and Yves Pigneur, whose nine-part 'business model canvas' offers a template to develop and record assumptions

3 Mintzberg, H and Waters, JA, "Of Strategies, Deliberate and Emergent", *Strategic Management Journal*, Vol 6, No 3, July–September 1985, pp257–272.

4 Lewis, M, *The new new thing: A Silicon Valley story*, 2014, WW Norton & Company.

5 Magretta, J, "Why Business Models Matter", *Harvard Business Review*, May 2002.

not only about the firm's key resources and activities, but also its value proposition, client relationships, delivery channels, client segments, cost structures and revenue streams.[6] It provides as much a checklist to make sure that everything has been covered, as a means to compare the firm's business model with that of others.

In his 2018 book *Reinvent Your Business Model*, Mark Johnson argues that business model innovation offers a better route to transformational growth than reinventing strategy.[7] It offers scope for innovation beyond the service/product and process innovations on which almost all law firm innovation is currently focused (Figure 3). Oliver Gassman, Karolin Frankenberger and Michaela Csik (2014) furthermore show how 55 business models account for 90% of the world's most successful companies.[8] It is not necessary, in developing even radically different business models, to start with a blank slate. Almost all possible variants relevant to law firms or almost any other kind of business (even those that are highly leveraged with digital technologies) have already been invented and are available to learn from and emulate.

3. The essential elements of a modern law firm business model

When thinking about business model transformation of law firms specifically, people frequently get stuck on using the hierarchical 'Tournament of Lawyers' pyramid as a foundation, only modifying it by changing its shape and adding components (see Figure 2). This is illogical. It assumes that the value-creating processes of law firms will forever remain constructed only around hierarchies of people. A more useful approach is to consider the different components of business models generally, and how they 'fit reality' as Drucker put it – and then consider how those components need to change and what structure that suggests. In this section, covering the essential elements of the business model of a modern law firm, we use Johnson's framework for this purpose. Figure 5 on page 122 provides a thought-framework for considering the core elements of a law firm business model, and how each drives performance and strategy implementation.

---

6 Osterwalder, A and Pigneur, Y, *Business Model Generation*, 2010, Wiley.

7 Johnson, MW, *Reinvent Your Business Model: How to Seize the White Space of Transformative Growth*, 2018, Harvard Business Review Press.

8 Gassmann, O, Frankenberger, K and Csik, M, *The Business Model Navigator: 55 Models that Will Revolutionise Your Business*, 2014, FT Publishing.

Figure 3. Business model transformation allows for additional innovation potential on top of service/product and process innovation

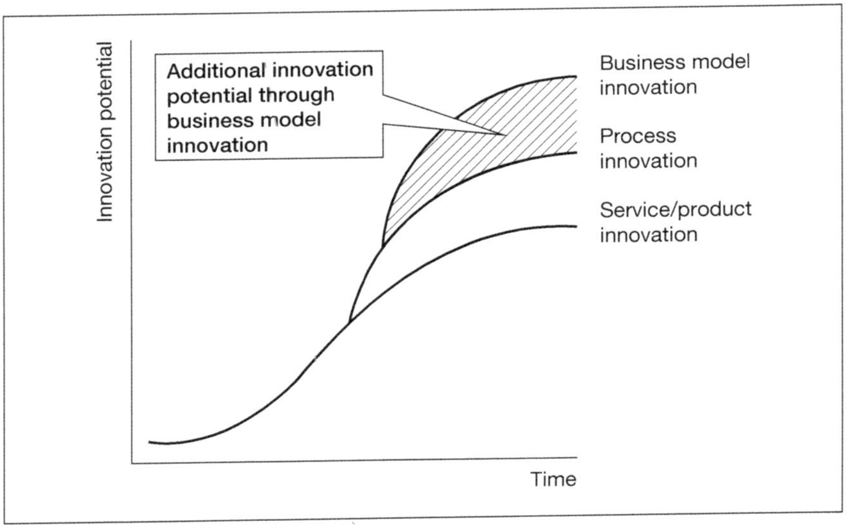

Source: Adapted from Gassmann et al, 2014.

3.1 Client value proposition

A powerful, well-articulated client value proposition (CVP) is the first cornerstone of any effective business model. It communicates to your firm's clients why they should engage with you rather than your competitors. It clearly articulates the benefits of your products or services. The best CVPs focus clearly on important client needs and propose service offerings that effectively solve those needs, at prices competitive to comparable solutions available to clients (including doing the work in-house.) They are client centric. They are not simply a list of practice/services offered by the firm, or areas in which the firm specialises.

Clearly, the first step in developing such a CVP is to understand those most important client needs both current and in the foreseeable future, and what solving them means from the client's perspective. Clients after all do not buy legal services, but solutions. As Harvard Business School professor Theodore Levitt (1925–2006) first pointed out, a customer buying a drill is really buying a hole.[9]

9 Levitt, T cited in Christensen, C, *The Clayton M Christensen Reader*, 2016, Harvard Business Review Press, p46.

Figure 4. One of the most persistent 'BigLaw' fallacies is the notion that a law firm must consist primarily of a hierarchy of people (a 'pyramid') and that any future law firm business model will necessarily be a variant of this structure

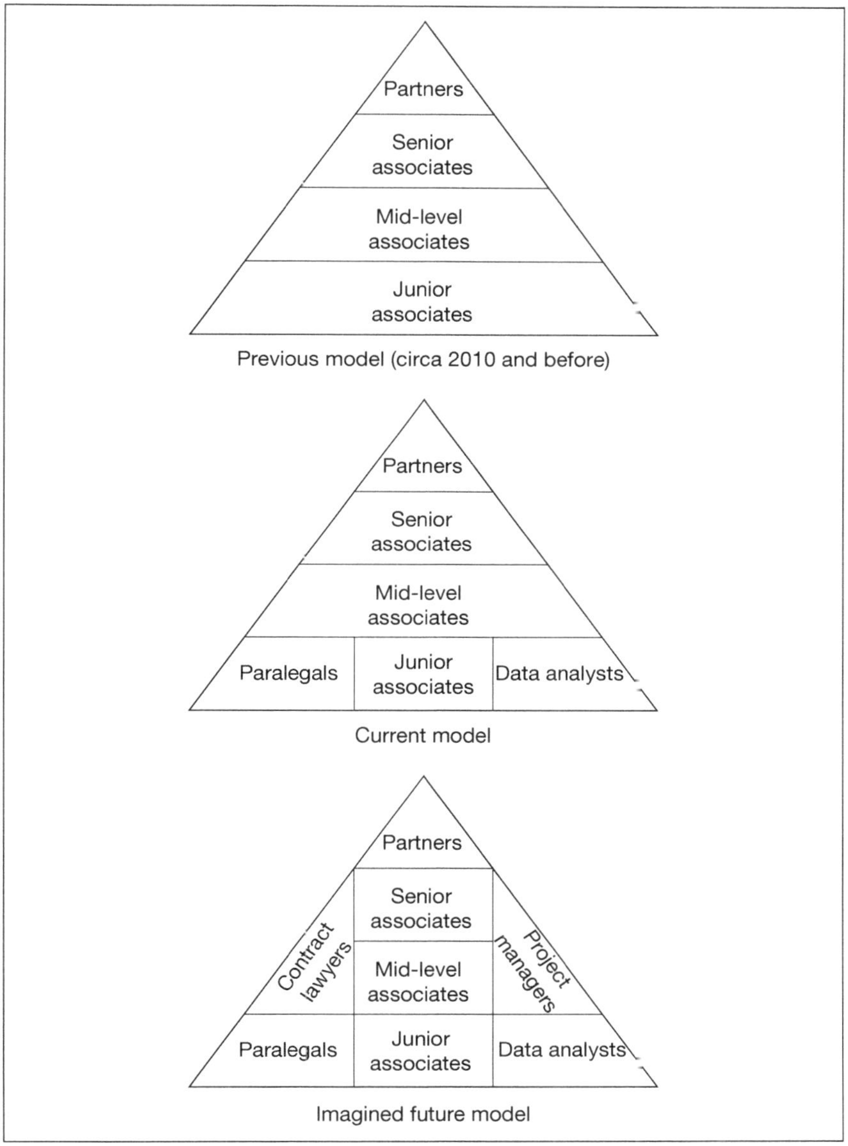

Source: Author.

Figure 5. A conceptual outline of the essential elements of a modern law firm business model

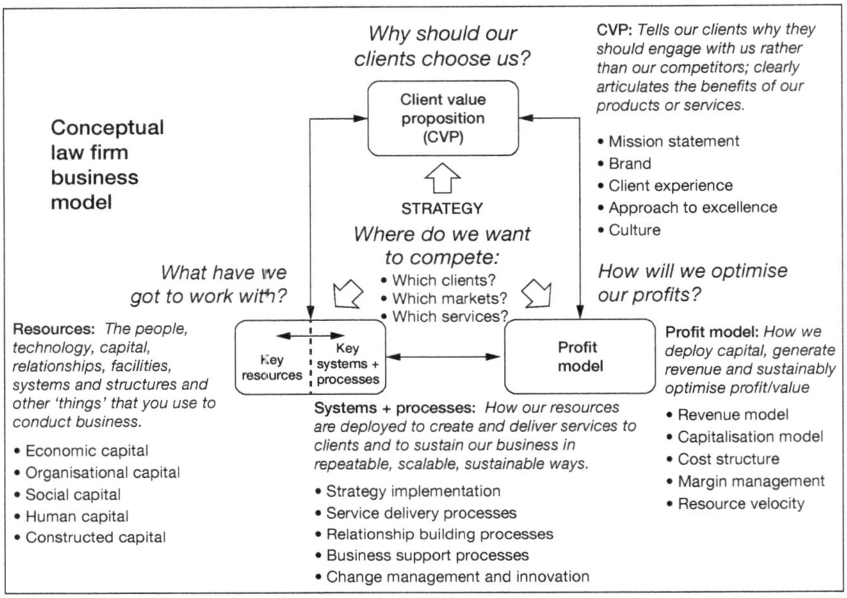

Source: Adapted from Johnson, 2018.

The drill is simply the means to achieve that. Exactly the same principle applies to clients acquiring legal services, so the best law firm CVPs focus on the 'holes' rather than on the firm's services more directly. Again, this is a point that is superficially obvious, but in-house counsel report with distressing frequency how external advisers appear to be more focused on selling them services that they have already defined, than seeking to understand what they need. Correctly diagnosing these 'holes' frequently requires careful observation, even research. 'R&D', if you like. As we discuss later in this chapter (see Figure 9), the single most significant challenge that firms face today is understanding how client legal needs are changing in response to digitalisation of their businesses. Once that has been addressed, from the client's perspective, key questions in developing the firm's CVP include:

- How important is it to the client for this particular need to be met?
- How satisfied is the client with the current solutions?
- How well does the solution proposed compare with other options available?

- What resources are needed to competitively deliver the proposed solution?
- How might the solution be priced?

Each individual need has its own solution, hence a specific CVP to be communicated. Collectively, these individual CVPs communicate a broader message to clients and the market at large about the firm as a whole. The most important facets of this collective CVP are outlined below.

(a) Mission statement

Also known variously as 'strategic intent' or 'vision' amongst other things, a mission statement is a formal outline of the values and overarching strategic objectives of the firm. As such, it falls more usually into the domain of strategy. Properly articulated, though, it also forms the framework for communicating the firm's core CVP to the market.

Many mission statements (not just in law firms) are so generic as to be meaningless. Vanilla conflations of intent to be a leading law firm with professions of excellence in client service and of attracting and retaining the best people are pointless. To be effective in communicating the firm's overarching CVP a mission statement narrative must reference, as a minimum:

- the kinds of client that your firm prioritises;
- the markets that you intend to prioritise;
- the services on which you intend to focus; and
- features that make your firm objectively unique, in ways that clients find attractive.

(b) Brand

The firm's brand is another crucial communicator of the firm's CVP to the market. It is not enough that the firm's brand be recognised in the market (although it is better for it to be at least recognised, than not). A brand is not just the firm's logo. It is not just an identity, or an aggregation of services or products. At its core, a firm's brand is demonstrated by the gut feeling invoked in a client and others about the firm and its character, services, quality and other defining characteristics. When it reflects what clients perceive to be your CVP, the two are mutually reinforcing.

(c) *Client experience*

Client or customer experience (sometimes abbreviated to 'CX') refers to the client's overall perception of a firm and its brand as a result of comprehensive interactions throughout their journey with that firm. This is different to 'client service', which is the process of supporting clients who are purchasing or using the firm's services.

A 2019 Lexis Nexis report suggests that in a market where differentiation between most large law firms is difficult to achieve, attention to client experience offers an opportunity to create real competitive advantage.[10] While this argument is superficially plausible, it seems unlikely that competitive advantage gained through focus on client experience alone will be sustainable without similar attention being paid to the other components of the firm's business model. That said, the Lexis Nexis research discovered that 90% of law firms offered only a 'modest' or 'tentative' client experience, which they defined as a mix of engagement, effective problem resolution and strategic coherence. On that basis it would appear that for most law firms, considerable scope exists for improving this aspect of their business model.

(d) *Approach to excellence*

'Excellence' means different things to different law firms and also to different clients. For some, it means the firm being able to solve the most difficult, important legal problems. For others, it means being able to deliver a high quality of service in meeting more mainstream client legal needs across multiple jurisdictions. For yet others, it means being the preeminent specialists in a particular industry sector or other specialised area of law; or, being able to deliver high-volume legal services, with optimal efficiency and a market-leading price. As an overarching theme, excellence also means the high ethical standards that society expects of law firms, and commitment to diversity, environmental and other social norms. What 'excellence' means in your firm needs to align with your strategy and CVP if your business model is to deliver optimal performance. Importantly, there is no reason why definitions of excellence should not vary across the firm's business units and other functional groups.

---

10 "Client Experience: The new differentiator for law firms", 2019, *Lexis Nexis*, London. Available at: www.lexisnexis.co.uk/blog/docs/default-source/the-future-of-law-documents/sa-0119-112-client-experience-thought-leadership-rebrand-web-9682.pdf.

(e) *Culture*

Culture is another aspect of the firm's business model that impacts its CVP, either positively or negatively, and in particular the client experience. It also impacts the firm's human and social capital by enhancing or destroying people's level of engagement with the firm, and the effectivity of the firm's systems and processes. Culture in the context of a law firm can be defined loosely as 'how things are done here' and 'what is tolerated/rewarded and what is punished'. It follows that culture is not an aspect of the firm's business model that should be allowed simply to evolve. Careful thought needs to be given to the culture that is required in order for the business model and the firm generally to operate at peak performance, and the resources and actions needed to achieve that.

3.2 Key resources

The need to deliver on the firm's CVP has obvious implications for the capabilities that the firm needs to have in place to do so. This brings us to the second cornerstone of the business model, namely its resources. A firm's resources include the people, technology, capital, relationships, facilities, systems and structures and other 'things' that it uses to conduct its business. Again, the resource-based view of the firm is a well-established theoretical concept based upon several decades of research now, dating back at least to Jay Barney's seminal 1991 article "Firm Resources and Sustained Competitive Advantage",[11] and some would say to earlier work many decades before that. There is no shortage of material to guide law firm leaders in planning and developing the range of resources required in order to design and implement an effective business model, and to evolve that model in response to ongoing market changes.

Boundaries can be quite porous between some of the categories of capital deployed during the course of its business. The categories below are presented to better understand the sources of value rather than as a definitive taxonomy.

(a) *Economic capital*

This is the value derived from financial capital (funds available, including debt and equity finance) and non-financial capital (eg, the value of the firm's brand, knowledge/know-how, reputation, ability to perform complex work).

---

11 Barney, J, "Firm Resources and Sustained Competitive Advantage", *Journal of Management*, Vol 17, No 1, 1991, pp99–120.

(b) ***Organisational capital***
This is the usually quite intangible value derived from the firm's philosophy, structures, systems and culture, which leverage the firm's capability to create and deliver services to clients.

(c) ***Social capital***
This consists of teams, networks and groups of individuals working together, and includes their shared intellectual capital. It includes relationships that the firm has with its clients, intermediaries and other stakeholders who affect its ability to create and sustain value.

(d) ***Human capital***
This is the accumulation of competencies, habits, knowledge, social and personality attributes (including creativity) present in the firm's people and available to perform work, to produce economic value for the firm.

(e) ***Constructed capital***
This consists of structures, objects, systems or processes created by humans and used by the firm in pursuit of its objectives. Constructed capital includes decision-making and management structures, knowledge management systems, offices and equipment, and digital assets. The mix varies enormously across firms. A single office and market firm, for example, would have a very different portfolio of constructed capital to a global business that offers a mix of conventional legal advisory services, managed legal services and perhaps even other kinds of professional services across multiple markets. A dispersed geographic footprint triggers a need for a level of collaborative tools, for example, that a single-market firm might not need.

All firms obviously manage their economic (financial) capital explicitly, although some arguably more effectively than others, but few are as explicit in managing their other forms of capital. As resources capable of delivering on the firm's CVP and otherwise driving performance, though, these other forms of capital can be as influential as economic capital in driving performance. Being less scrutinised, these other forms of capital also frequently offer areas for innovation that enhance the business model in ways not otherwise possible.

3.3 Key systems and processes

In answering the question: "What have we got to work with?", resources are assets that one has, and key systems and processes represent things one can do. How resources are deployed to create and deliver services to clients and to sustain your business in repeatable, scalable, sustainable ways is the third cornerstone of your firm's business model.

(a) Strategy implementation processes

At its core, strategy is not complex. It involves setting business objectives (in law firms these usually involve a mix of which clients, services and markets to prioritise and how) and making hard choices about where to invest and what other actions to take. Successfully implementing that strategy and achieving those objectives is almost entirely dependent on processes within the firm's business model. Strategic objectives need to cascade from firm-wide level to the individual business units and other functional groups (eg, practice groups, offices, client teams, industry sector groups, business service functions) and then to individual partner and other leader business plans. This involves systems and processes, whether formal or informal. When the investments and other actions align with the CVP and the systems and processes that drive the firm's performance, better results tend to be achieved. When not, it is the strategy that usually loses. One of the most famous quotes attributed to Peter Drucker (although some doubt exists as to whether he actually said it) is that "culture eats strategy for breakfast". It is in the context of the firm's business model and its ability to deliver on the firm's strategy that culture holds such power, and it does so in concert with the other aspects of the firm's business model.

(b) Service delivery processes

Digitalisation of services and the drive for efficiency and cost reduction is having a profound impact on the processes used by a law firm to deliver its services to its clients. It seems inevitable also that this will accelerate. Inseparable from its CVP and client experience, and indeed from quality generally, this involves replacement of value chains previously limited to human effort, with new ones that involve processes highly leveraged with technology. This has obvious implications for the firm's profit model, which is the fourth cornerstone of the business model. While many firms are already heavily focused on this component of business model transformation, the radically different performance drivers often involved can cause misalignment with other components.

(c) ***Relationship-building processes***

Relationship-enhancing processes involve both internal and external perspectives. Internally, they involve initiatives to enhance engagement and build collaboration. Externally, they involve mapping stakeholders who can impact the firm's performance and designing systems and processes to optimise the most important of these relationships. Examples include the alumni programmes that some firms maintain, even to the point of developing flex working capacity such as Allen & Overy's 'Peerpoint' and Linklaters' 'Re-Link' programmes, as well as systems to manage relationships with referral firms, influencers and intermediaries, suppliers and service providers.

(d) ***Business support processes***

An exhaustive overview of a law firm's business functions is beyond the scope of this chapter, but this component of the business model includes the systems and processes that drive those functions, including finance, business development and marketing, information technology, knowledge management and human resources. These are all crucial of themselves to the performance of the firm's business model, but equally important is alignment between them. It follows that innovation focused on enhancing the effectiveness of these processes (not just cost reduction and efficiency) can be a rich area for innovation aimed at business model improvement.

(e) ***Change management and innovation***

The most recent research into innovation shows that its success is of itself heavily dependent on properly designed systems and processes. Recent research into innovation focused on new product development,[12] for example, identified some 20 success drivers, grouped into three categories. Conflating new product with new service development, those categories would be:

- Success drivers of individual new product/service projects (tactical drivers that capture the characteristics of the project or the product/service itself);
- Drivers of success for the firm (including organisational and strategic factors, such as the business's innovation strategy, how it makes its R&D investment decisions, its climate and

---

12 Cooper, RG, "The Drivers of Success in New-Product Development", *Industrial Marketing Management*, Vol 76, January 2019, pp36–47.

culture, leadership, and how the firm organises for new product/service development); and
- The systems and methods the firm has in place for managing new product/service development – for example, gating systems, Agile development approaches, and ideation methods.

Also, a firm's innovation and change management processes need to focus at least as much on incubating and protecting viable innovations to maturity, as on thinking up and testing new ideas. According to Vyakarnam and Phadke, 75% of innovations that are successfully translated into prototypes or minimum viable products (or 'MVPs') fail to translate into fully formed solutions with commercially viable business plans, clearly articulated CVPs that make sense to clients and properly conceived scale-up implementation plans.[13] For emphasis: the part of the process with the greatest risk of failure (and hence the greatest opportunity for creating value by improving it) lies in developing the MVP into a fully formed solution. Solutions partway through this process can frequently resemble failures. Solutions that would deliver significant value once properly formed can then be prematurely discarded in the absence of an objective process to assess progress and potential.

3.4 Profit model

The profit model is the fourth cornerstone of a firm's business model. It forms the blueprint for how the firm creates value for itself and its owners. It covers how capital is deployed, revenue is generated, costs are allocated, and the firm optimises its profitability generally. A VUCA world can generate unprecedented opportunities to generate profit in entirely new ways, as firms that understand which CVPs will resonate best with clients can deploy the right mix of resources and process/systems.

Defining the firm's profit model goes far beyond conventional cost accounting. To optimise profit, a firm needs to take a granular view of is service lines. It needs to understand the profit drivers of each of these and, insofar as it is possible without losing strategic alignment across systems and processes, focus the business model for each service line on its own specific performance drivers. In the

---

13 Vyakarnam, S and Phadke, U, *The Scale-Up manual: Handbook for Innovators, Teams and Firms*, 2018, World Scientific.

'Tournament of Lawyers' model, the focus (irrespective of billing arrangements) remains on production through human effort, measured in increments of time.

The profit model is also inextricably intertwined with the other components of the business model. It defines the scale that a firm requires in order to optimise profits across its service lines, how investments in assets such as lateral hires and new technologies should be prioritised, the systems and structures that are most appropriate and how these should be aligned. It defines the behaviours and mindsets that are needed and how the firm's culture needs to be proactively evolved in order to support those. Ultimately, it defines the parameters within which the firm can set and implement its strategy. In a hypercompetitive, 'VUCA' world, any law firm that does not have a sophisticated and multifaceted view of profit is likely headed for trouble.

(a) Revenue model

How much revenue is the firm capable of earning, with all its resources, systems and processes optimally deployed on the best range of activities to drive revenue production? In the business models of the 20th century, this used to be simply a matter of multiplying the number of fee earners by their rates and billable hour targets, but is now more complex. An understanding of each service line's 'fully loaded' revenue generation potential, based upon solid assumptions and clear logic, is a good place to start in assessing what the firm's optimum profitability might be, and hence at what level of production the firm is operating, as a basis for setting performance targets to improve that.

(b) Capitalisation model

The manner in which both investment or long-term capital and working capital are sourced and deployed forms part of the profit model. In jurisdictions where external equity funding and fee sharing is prohibited, capital originates typically from partner equity contributions and bank debt. In jurisdictions where such prohibitions do not exist, the sources of capital are broader and, in some cases, law firms can even access public capital by listing on a stock exchange.

Firms with business models that are heavily leveraged with debt include both high- and low-performing businesses. The same is true of firms with little or no debt. Neither is, of itself, good or bad and some firms might, as part of a business model review, consider alternative capitalisation options. For assets that need to be amortised over time for tax purposes, obvious arguments exist to spread the costs through debt or leasing. Working capital is required to fund the gap between work being done and paid for by clients and paying the firm's outgoings, including advances on partner profits. Profits are distributed at year-end. Funds are required for strategic initiatives and access to funding, at least, for unforeseen circumstances.

Growth, whether through merger or lateral hiring, also brings with it the need for both investment and working capital, although not typically vast amounts.[14] Significant debt facilities are also frequently associated with covenants that have to be considered during the course of normal business activities, including minimum thresholds for the number of partners, ratio of debt to earnings, levels of work in progress and trading debtor balances.

(c) Cost structure

The cost structure is simply the combination of direct costs and overheads. In common with many other kinds of professional service firms, law firms have cost structures that are heavy on fixed costs (mostly rent and staff salaries) and relatively light on variable costs. Comparing law firms to other professions that have already been heavily disrupted by digitalisation (eg, architectural, engineering and other professions that have been disrupted by computer-aided design or 'CAD') already shows fixed cost structures with a far lower salary component and relatively higher costs for technology. While what 'computer-aided law' might look like in years to come is by no means obvious, it is clear that the cost structures of law firms are also evolving. Doing this more thoughtfully and tactically also offers scope for innovation focused on business model enhancement.

(d) Margin management

Any law firm leader would know the firm's overall profit margin. Most would also know at least in general terms which areas of the business are delivering more profit than others. Business model innovation that focuses on margin management seeks to take a far more granular and nuanced view of margin. Optimising margin management requires a clear understanding that the CVPs, the resources that are needed and the systems and processes employed to optimise

---

14 The IPO prospectus for the DWF Group, for example, which over the past few years has been a relatively prolific acquirer of other legal service providers, notes that: "The Group's historical strategic transactions have not typically required the Group to raise large amounts of capital."

performance are different across service lines – sometimes radically so. Service lines with lower inherent profit margins can deliver the same quantum of profit or more than lines with higher margins, if the volumes suffice. Yet many law firms tend to block initiatives where margins fall below the generic, firm-wide expectations, for fear of being 'profit-dilutive'. Margin needs to be considered in tandem with the other components of the profit model, in order to accurately assess its contribution to the profit model.

(e) *Resource velocity*

Resource velocity means how quickly the firm's resources need to be used in order to support the volume of production targeted. In a human pyramid model, this is usually defined in terms of utilisation (ie, hours worked.) In business models where significant value is produced through technology, the definition is more complex. Resource velocity is further not defined only by resources deployed on production itself, but on the activities that support it. In other words, it means how quickly the firm can invent, design, create, deliver and get paid for services/products across the entire value chain, for a given investment in resources over a given period.

Resource velocity answers the question: "How will we optimise the volume of services that we can produce, with existing resources?" It defines the overall capacity of the business that is available without investment in new resources.

4. Options available to law firm leaders to transform their business models

Digitalisation of legal services is a crucial aspect of business model transformation today. It is unavoidable. Yet it remains unclear what 'digitalisation of legal services' will really mean in the medium to long term, in practical terms. A survey in late 2019 of 690 lawyers across the globe to test perceptions about the impact of digital technologies on the business and practice of law revealed a great deal of diversity of views.[15] While median views were remarkably similar across ages, geographies, size of firms and other demographics, the diversity within each of those made it difficult to draw statistically valid conclusions.

What the results did reveal were slight positive correlations between beliefs that: (a) digital technologies will have a radical

---

15 Millard, RF, *Perceptions of Digitalisation of Legal Services: A Survey of IBA LFMC and Regional Forum Members*, IBA Law Firm Management Committee "Building the law firm of the future" conference (November 2019).

Figure 6. A slight positive correlation exists between perceptions that digital technologies will have a significant impact on the practice and business of law AND that client needs will be different in 2025 to what they are today, and perceptions that platforms, big international law firms and small boutiques will have the business models most attractive to clients

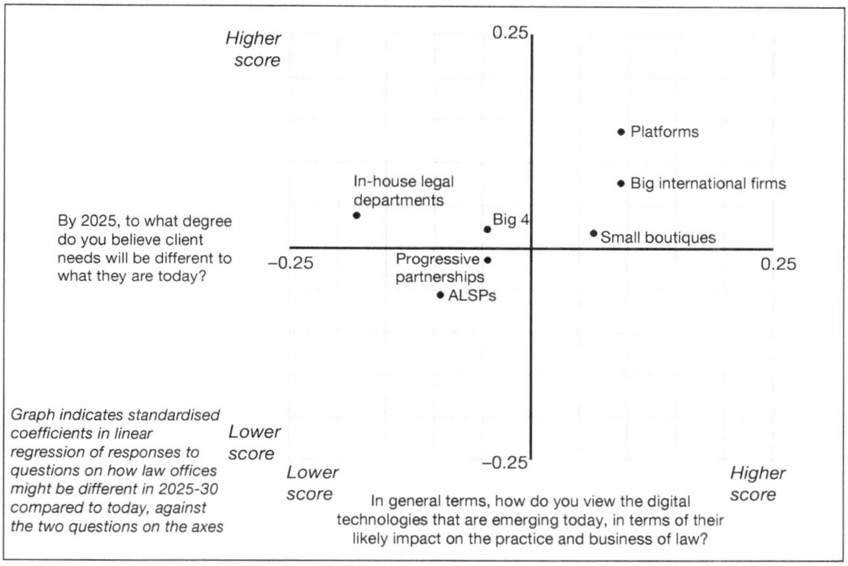

Source: Millard 2019.

impact on the business and practice of law and that (b) client needs will be significantly different in 2019, to what they are today, and that:

- platforms, the big international law firms and small, focused boutique firms will be the generic business models most likely to be attractive to clients in 2025 (Figure 6);
- remote working, more digitally delivered work and more owners of legal advisory businesses who are not lawyers will be the most likely changes in the way work is done (Figure 7); and
- distributed ledger technologies/blockchain, machine learning, robotics, cybersecurity and cloud computing will be the technologies with the greatest impact (Figure 8).

Considerably better correlation and hence statistical validity was discovered across responses to questions regarding challenges being experienced in addressing new technologies and digital

Figure 7. A slight positive correlation exists between perceptions that digital technologies will have a significant impact on the practice and business of law AND that client needs will be different in 2025 to what they are today, and perceptions that remote working, more digitally delivered work and more owners of legal advisory businesses who are not lawyers will be the most likely changes in the way work is done in law firms

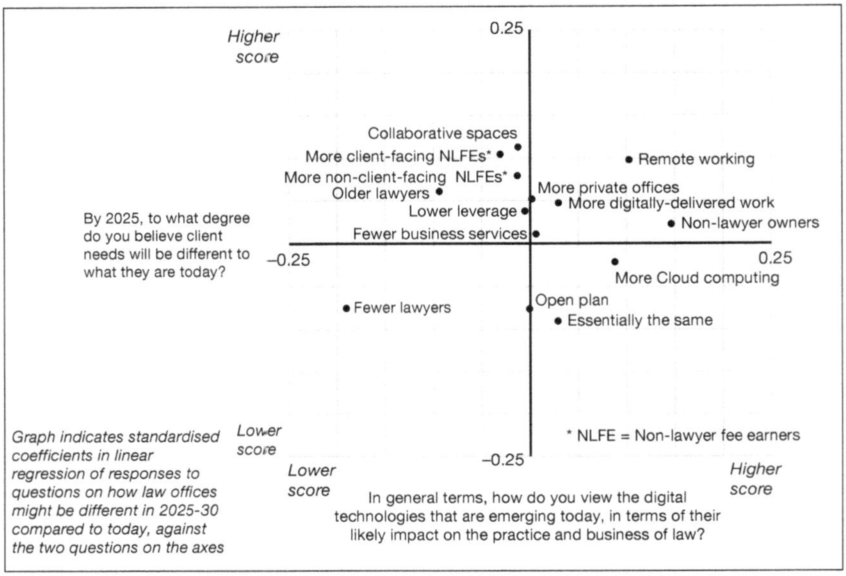

Source: Millard 2019.

transformation, with more than 50% of respondents identifying the following as the most important (see Figure 9):

- Understanding opportunities offered by new, digitally induced client legal needs;
- Costs of acquiring new technology; and
- Assessing value (separating hype from reality) with digital products on offer.

4.1 The challenges

Transforming any firm's business model is a daunting prospect, and the more successful the firm has been with its existing business model, the more difficult it is to persuade people of the need to change it. This is the essence of the 'innovator's dilemma' described by Clayton Christensen, who used it to explain why the incumbent

Figure 8. A slight positive correlation exists between perceptions that digital technologies will have a significant impact on the practice and business of law AND that client needs will be different in 2025 to what they are today, and perceptions that distributed ledger technologies/blockchain, machine learning, robotics, cybersecurity and cloud computing will be the technologies with the greatest impact

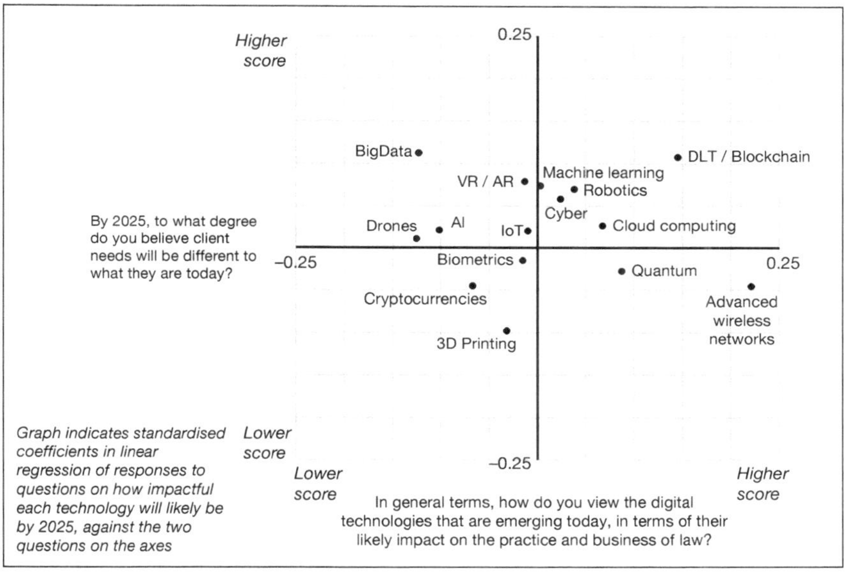

Source: Millard 2019.

leading firms in an industry fail to transform their businesses quickly enough to prevent new entrants from supplanting them.[16] Even when the firm's leadership is willing to seize the nettle of business model transformation, three challenges remain in their way.[17] These, paraphrased to fit the context of law firms, are as follows.

(a) Challenge 1: Thinking outside of the dominant 'BigLaw' logic

The logics that underpin the manner in which lawyers deliver their legal advice to clients are more structured and entrenched than those even in other professions such as medicine or architecture. The more successful a declining business model was in the past, the more

16 Christensen, CM, *The Innovator's Dilemma: When New Technologies Cause Great Firms to Fail*, 1997, Boston, MA: Harvard Business School Press.

17 Gassmann *et al*, 2014.

Figure 9. Understanding opportunities offered by new, digitally induced client legal needs was identified as the most significant challenge facing law firms considering digital transformation. Bar length indicates percentage of respondents who identified the issue as a significant challenge

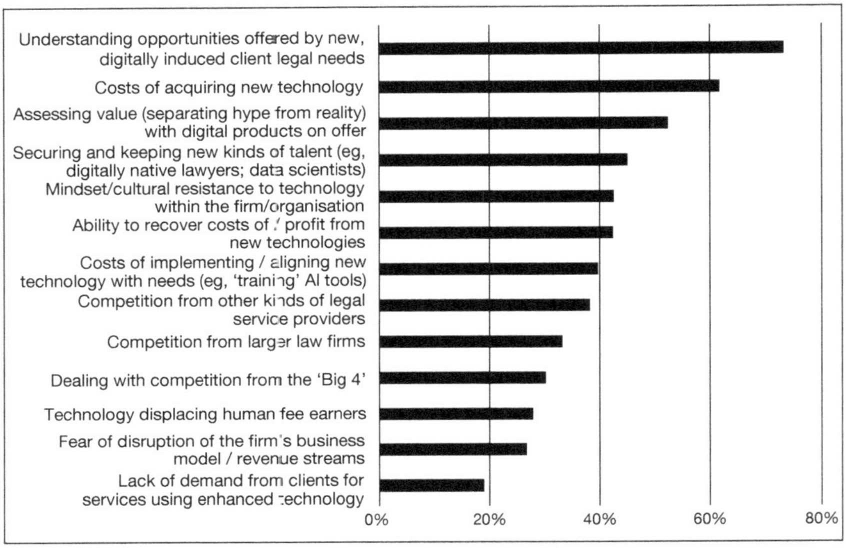

Source: Millard 2019.

compelling the arguments that will rage across the firm's leadership not to "fix what might not [yet] be broken". It is genuinely challenging for senior lawyers to think of their practices in terms other than those with which they grew up in the profession. The clinging persistence of the 'Tournament of Lawyers' model is a good example.

Younger lawyers who question the dominant logic can learn very quickly that this is not career enhancing. "The legal profession is different; sharing fees with non-lawyers might compromise a lawyer's ethical integrity and must be banned; our clients won't accept anything else" are what sociologists call 'orthodoxies', defined as shared beliefs of a group that has a long history and is opposed to changes in their logics. Entrenched orthodoxies in a firm's business model that do not align with the firm's current reality (especially as expressed by its clients) can be existentially dangerous.

(b) Challenge 2: Thinking in terms of business model rather than services and technologies

By their very nature, business models are intangible concepts. People prefer to deal with more tangible aspects of the business that are easier to 'see' and understand, and where outcomes are more obvious. For example, investing in a new piece of technology, reorganising part of the business, merging with another firm, or hiring a lateral partner or team is more tangible than rethinking a CVP, evolving the firm's culture, enhancing alignment between systems that are working at cross-purposes with each other, or finding new ways to enhance margin across multiple service lines. With the former, the outcome is also far more quickly achieved than with the latter, where benefits might take months or even years to manifest – and where recognition might not even accrue to the person responsible.

(c) Challenge 3: A lack of systematic tools

One of the great myths of innovation (not only business model innovation) is that it needs to be a chaotic process of invention undertaken by creative geniuses. Lawyers, it is said, are not innovative because they lack a 'creative mindset'. Instead, so the myth continues, they are too critical analytical, risk averse and perfectionist to be able to operate in the messy 'ready-fire-aim' world of the innovator. The fact is, though, that innovation is a discipline that needs to be managed like any other. We noted earlier the finding that 75% of innovations fail between the protype/MVP stage and fully formed solution. Success needs and depends on far more than clever ideas. Functional methods, processes and tools to assist in this process are scarce and many of the tools that have been developed are not optimised for professional service environments.

Understanding these challenges is the first step towards overcoming them though, and there is little reason to believe that lawyers find it any easier or more difficult than any other professionals who have a rich and proud tradition and play an undeniably crucial role in society.

Business models are frequently over-analysed, with too much focus on daily organisational challenges. It is far better to visualise it by taking a high-level view and better still to do that visualisation with a team representing diverse, even multidisciplinary perspectives. Not only does this provide a clearer view of the business model, but it also allows it to be critically evaluated against the backdrop of the dominant logics that drive it.

Successfully transforming a firm's business model requires a clear understanding of all the stakeholders who are affected by the firm and who can influence the success of the initiative. Trying to develop a new business model solely through internal efforts, even if combined with limited 'client listening', is unlikely to deliver the best results. Not only are clients a law firm's most important external stakeholders, but they are frequently a rich source of ideas for business model innovation. It follows that they should be included in a formal, systematic way in the firm's innovation processes.

This is doubly true when one considers that the firm's transformed business model needs to be responsive not to client needs in the present and past tense, but to their future needs which (from Figure 9) we simply do not know unless we invest in finding out. Clients are also operating in the same 'VUCA' world as law firms. They are being disrupted by the same digital and other trends that are impacting law firms. Against this lens, it makes even less sense to attempt to undertake business model innovation without close and careful collaboration with the firm's most important clients.

4.2 Seizing the white space

In today's hypercompetitive world, a firm's existing core business erodes more quickly than when markets are more stable. Some growth can usually be achieved by seeking more of that existing core business, to replace those revenues lost. This involves seeking more work with existing clients, which aligns well with the firm's existing business model. It is on this kind of growth that law firms typically focus their strategy first. It is work that is difficult to win but easy to do. Slightly more difficult both to win and to implement is exploring adjacencies. This means similar work with new clients, or servicing existing client needs in radically different ways, but that are still a good fit with the firm's existing business model. Both of these methods of growth are easy for competitors with similar business models to emulate, so are not a sustainable source of competitive advantage.

Exploring options that meet new or existing client needs in radically different ways and are a poor fit with the firm's existing business model ('white space' in Figure 10) might seem counterintuitive, but this offers the best opportunity for finding areas of real, sustainable, competitive advantage.

Doing this requires that a firm review its business model with the same proactive zeal as that which applies to its strategy. If reviewing a strategy involves reassessing priorities around markets, services and clients and how to improve the firm's market position, then reviewing the business model involves examining each of its components and benchmarking them against the firm's set of peer competitors and 'best practice' (which may be found elsewhere than amongst that set of peer competitors).

Figure 10. Business model innovation depends on which quadrant is being explored, with 'white space' offering the greatest opportunity for transformational growth by opening currently uncontested market positions

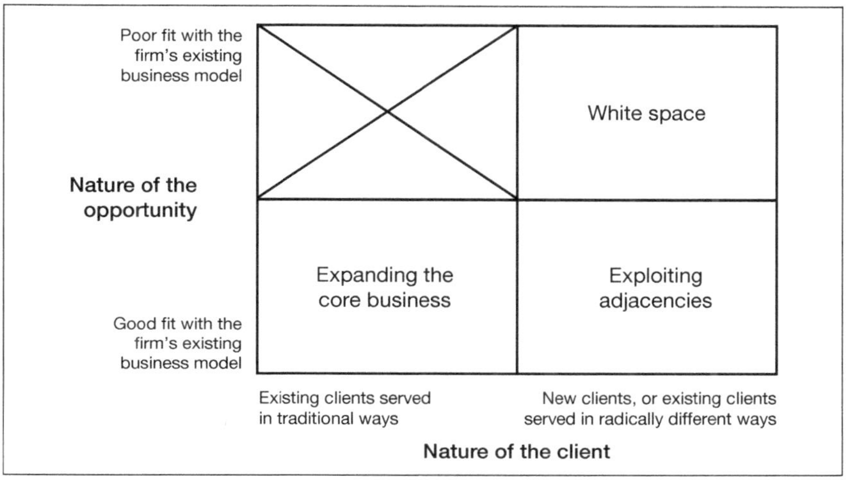

Source: Adapted from Johnson, 2018.

Benchmarking the firm's CVP needs to take a more comprehensive approach to client listening than what most firms are currently using. All the existing questions that relate to expanding the core business and exploiting adjacencies (in Figure 11) need to be asked, and client responses carefully considered. To this needs to be added new questions that can point towards the 'white space' – namely inquiring about services that the client does not believe that the firm would (or even could) offer. This involves a conversation for which neither law firm nor client might be well-enough prepared for it to be constructive.

Once the firm's CVPs have been explored with sufficient rigour to understand which opportunities need to be seized in order to exploit Johnson's 'white space', the review can move to the other three cornerstones, to examine how they might be enhanced within the context of that shift to this new, uncomfortable ground.

5. Generic business models likely to become more prominent in the future

Earlier in this chapter we debunked the myth that the business model of a modern law firm needs to be a 'people-pyramid' hierarchical structure. Some might be, but it is entirely possible that they will form a small minority. It seems also to be by no means certain that partnerships, as such, are doomed to be replaced by 'corporate' models. What are needed are partnerships that have business models that are a good fit with our current reality. Equity ownership and governance structures of a business do have a profound impact on a firm's business model, it is true, but not to the extent that partnerships are unable to transform their business models in ways described in this chapter.

Given the range of legal services that clients require from time to time, and the differing degrees to which their delivery can be leveraged with technology, it is difficult to imagine that one single preeminent business model for legal service providers will emerge for all law firms. Individual firms that follow the advice in this chapter by focusing business model innovation at the service line level might furthermore end up with multiple, rather messy business models, rather than a neat arrangement that can be elegantly reduced to a PowerPoint slide – but delivers poorer performance. Being able to articulate the firm's business model is important at least to generate clearer understanding of the performance drivers and to align

Figure 11. As the existing core business is lost to hyper-competition and commoditisation, so it needs to be replaced by finding new work in the existing or core or by exploiting adjacencies, both of which are heavily contested. Exploring 'white space', although the most difficult option, can bridge the growth gap with uncontested revenues

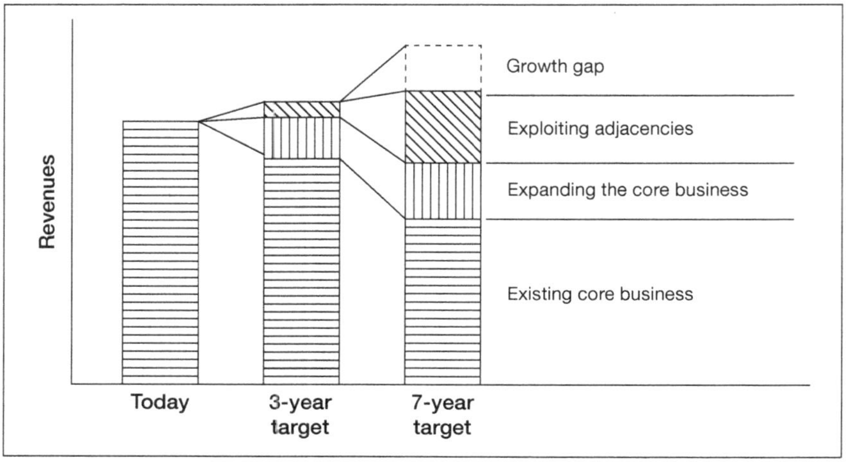

Source: Adapted from Johnson, 2018.

behaviour with these. In this final section we will therefore consider a range of business models from two perspectives, namely:

- The mix of human versus technology resource involved in value creation; and
- The nature of the professional relationships between the people.

Both have been evolving for some time and will continue to do so as the so-called '4th Industrial Revolution' unfolds.

5.1 The mix of human versus technology in value creation

Value creation and profit performance drivers vary across a continuum from where the work is done and so value delivered entirely by human effort, to where that value is delivered entirely through technology. This continuum is illustrated in Figure 12. In between are two interim models.

Figure 12. The characteristics of different business models across a continuum ranging from where work is delivered entirely by human effort, to where it is delivered entirely by a technological platform

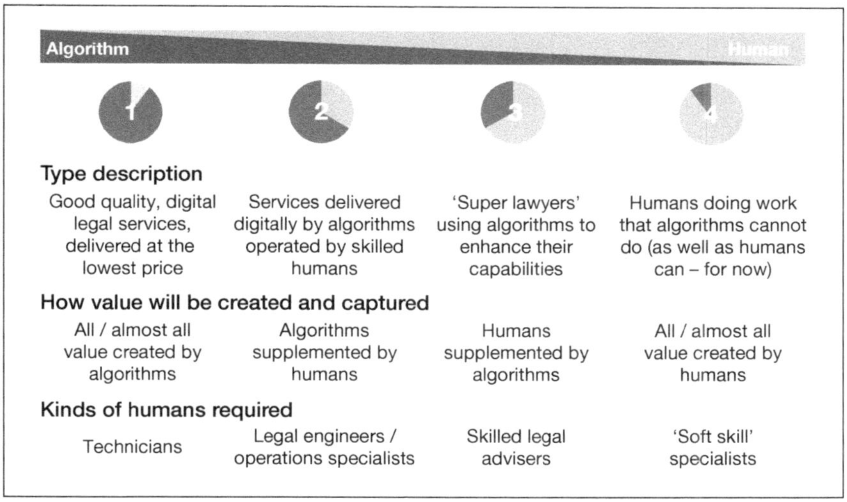

Source: adapted from Agrawal, Gans and Goldfarb, 2018[18] *and Daugherty and Wilson, 2018.*[19]

18 Agrawal, A, Gans, J and Goldfarb, A, *Prediction Machines: The Simple Economics of Artificial Intelligence*, 2018, Harvard Business School Press.

19 Daugherty, PR and Wilison, HJ, *Human + Machine: Reimagining Work in the Age of AI*, 2018, Harvard Business Review Press.

Type 4 in Figure 12 is the model that prevails in the 'Tournament of Lawyers' model. Legal work product is generated almost exclusively by human effort, either by lawyers working alone or in leveraged teams consisting of partners, associates and others. This model will likely continue to exist, but as technology becomes increasingly competent and commonplace, it will become limited to those areas of practice where the level of ambiguity and complexity makes humans better suited to the problem solving required than technology. In their 2017 paper "The Future of Employment: How Susceptible are Jobs to Computerisation?" Carl Frey and Michael Osborne[20] explored the kinds of work that are most at risk of being taken over by robotics or artificial intelligence in the next 20 years.[21] Their research concludes that the jobs least likely to be automated are those that require skills of creative intelligence, social intelligence or physical dexterity. That certainly includes a great deal of high-end legal advisory work, so it is unsurprising that Frey and Osborne regard lawyers as one of the professions least likely to be displaced by technology.

Lawyers doing that work requiring skills of creative intelligence and social intelligence (perhaps more than physical dexterity) will be required to deal with far more data in their work than before. The amount and the complexity of data involved in modern legal work involving the more difficult, important client challenges is increasing exponentially, with no indication that this trend will slow. At the same time, machine-learning technology (popularly termed artificial intelligence or 'AI') is becoming rapidly more adept at analysing vast quantities of data, accurately and efficiently, and delivering a summary of salient issues to their users. Much has been written about these technologies and their ability to enable lawyers who use them to deliver a far more valuable service to clients. In Figure 12, this falls into Type 3 – ie, 'super-lawyers' using algorithms to perform legal work of a complexity that is simply inconceivable today.

It is reasonable to expect that more and more work will move to this modality, especially high-end work. Leverage would be achieved through a combination of people and technology. A lawyer's skills would rely as much on his or her ability to use the digital tools

20 Frey, CB, *The Technology Trap: Capital, Labor and Power in the Age of Automation*, 2019, Princeton University Press.

21 Frey, C and Osborne, M, "The Future of Employment: How Susceptible are Jobs to Computerisation?", *Technological Forecasting and Social Change*, Vol 114, No 3, 2017.

effectively, as to apply his or her mind to the insights delivered by those tools. Firms would develop competitive advantage through the unique know-how developed through and within these tools, as well as the expertise of the people using them.

A point will come where it becomes difficult to distinguish between the value that is created by the lawyer versus the digital tools that the lawyer uses. The use of CAD in the architecture and engineering professions, as discussed previously, is a good parallel. The architect or engineer is still crucial to the design process, both in developing the concepts, resolving ambiguities that arise as a project unfolds and interacting with the client to ensure that the design conforms to their needs. Beyond that, the bulk of the detailed work is done by the CAD algorithms. The value generated by these algorithms forms a very significant share of the value delivered to the client. It therefore makes no sense at all to measure that value, or to bill the client, in increments of human effort. How much time the architect or engineer spends working on a design remains important, but only as one facet of how that professional delivers value.

In the Type 2 model, the value is delivered primarily by technology, but that technology is operated by humans. Machine-learning algorithms in use today arguably fall into this category, as do many of the subscription services that law firms operate, and that require frequent updating. The professionals operating the technology may be lawyers, or paralegals, but just as easily legal technologists or data scientists or even professionals from other disciplines. Because the bulk of the value is delivered by the technology, and the cost of the operators relative to the value being produced is relatively low, it makes even less sense for the work to be valued (or billed) in increments of human effort.

The Type 1 model describes where the work product is delivered entirely by the algorithm, with human input limited to initial design and development, upgrades and maintenance. Online legal service providers such as those operated by companies such as 'LegalZoom' operate within this modality, or at least at the intersection between Types 1 and 2.

Clearly, very different approaches to business model are required to extract the most value from each of the above types of work stream, for the client and also for the law firm. Few firms are doing more than dabble with legal platforms, as yet, and fewer still are exploring how they could become significant parts of their business, seeking actively to displace work currently done by lawyers or paralegals. Yet the data in Figure 6 suggests that within the next five to six years, platforms will be one of the most attractive legal service delivery models to clients.

There is no doubt that many of the tasks previously performed by lawyers (eg, sifting through millions of pages of documents) are already better done by technology. As more data and better algorithms become available, so the range of these tasks will no doubt expand. Artificial intelligence is set to move from mere 'machine-learning' to 'deep-learning' algorithms. The latter is effectively a subset of the former, the differences being:

- Machine learning uses algorithms to parse data, learn from that and make decisions based upon that learning; and
- Deep-learning structures use algorithms in layers to create an "artificial neural network" that learns, makes intelligent decisions and even self-corrects errors on its own.

A great deal of disagreement exists between experts about the limits of what deep learning might be able to achieve within a reasonable strategic horizon (say, three to five years). It is facile to suggest that deep learning is without demonstrable limits and, if simply given more time and data, it would easily evolve into the general intelligence suggested by Andrew Ng's 2016 comment that AI would either "now or in the near future" be able to do "any mental task" a person could do "with less than one second of thought".[22] In making sense of today's VUCA world, humans draw on a wealth of tacit knowledge about emotion, human behaviour and culture, to say nothing of the ambiguities of business and society, in ways that are virtually impossible to encode – at least in the foreseeable future.

5.2 The nature of the professional relationships between the people

Besides evolving relationships between humans and technology, an organisation's structure is also heavily influenced by the ways in which people interact during the course of their work. Much has already changed through remote work becoming a mainstream reality, through levels of skill and competence becoming detached (at least to a degree) from seniority, through disaggregation of value chains both by clients and by law firms seeking greater efficiencies, and through more porous professional relationships between lawyers and other disciplines.

---

22 Ng, A, "What Artificial Intelligence Can and Can't Do Right Now", *Harvard Business Review*, 9 November 2016. Available at https://hbr.org/2016/11/what-artificial-intelligence-can-and-cant-do-right-now.

(a) ***Hierarchical structures***

Figures 1 and 2 illustrated the strict hierarchy and also a flatter, more collaborative variant on this. The latter is probably the closest parallel to where law firms have evolved, as they migrate away from the 'Tournament of Lawyers' pyramid. Areas that need to be hierarchical in nature in order to deliver optimum performance still exist, but other areas exist where such a structure can be stifling. An example of such a practice might be where employees need to follow carefully defined protocols and deviation from these can damage performance.

(b) ***Open organisational structures***

At the opposite extreme from a hierarchical structure is an open or 'flat' structure (see Figure 13) where everybody is of the same level of seniority. Such structures allow decisions to be taken very quickly and require little or no investment in bureaucratic and management resources. Senior fee earners can focus far more on serving clients, without having to multitask with management roles and supervising subordinates.

On the other hand, such a structure can become a problem, especially in larger organisations where the lack of control and accountability can create risk. Difficult decisions, especially those that require other people to modify the behaviour in ways that they would prefer not to, are difficult to take and even more so to implement.

Figure 13. An open organisational structure

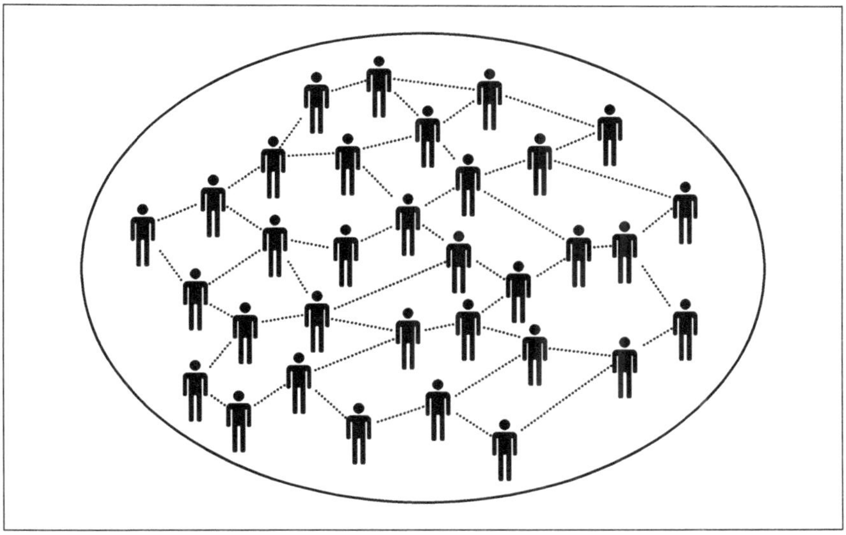

Source: Author.

Nonetheless, elements of such a structure may be usefully incorporated into business units and teams where the level of seniority is similar across the members and the highly agile, egalitarian relationships that result make it more likely that the group will meet its strategic objectives.

(c) Holacracies

Another form of structure that would seem to have application in some areas is a holacracy (see Figure 14). With its roots in complexity theory, the term is derived from the Greek *holon* which is something that is simultaneously a whole and a part. Holacracies are a form of decentralised, highly participative organisational structure in which authority and decision making is delegated to self-organising teams. The intent of a holacracy is that accountability and leadership are equally distributed among the workforce. Leaders change according to which person is best placed to lead a particular activity. People are organised according to roles, which are more fluid than positions or job titles. Each circle defines its roles through a collective governance process. These are updated periodically to adapt to changing needs. Holacracies work best where:

Figure 14. A holacratic organisational structure[23]

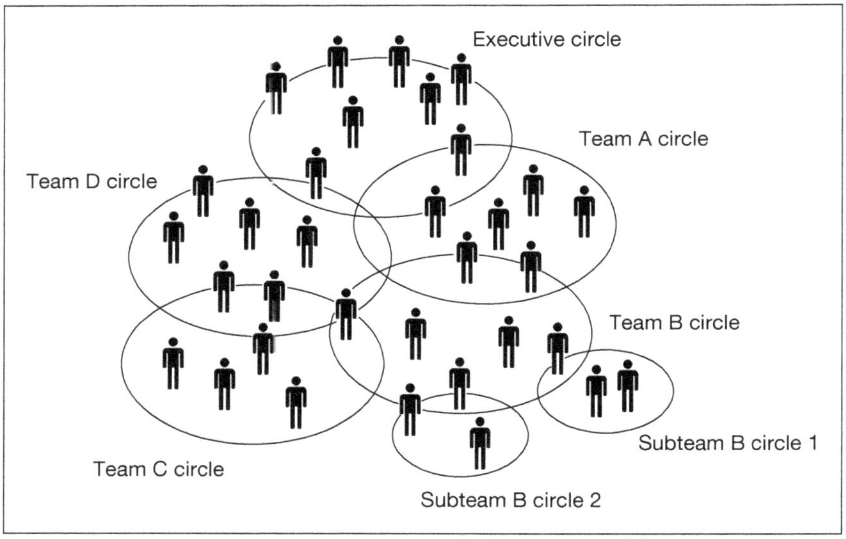

Source: Adapted from Robertson, 2015.

23 Robertson, BJ, *Holocracy: The Revolutionary Management System that Abolishes Hierarchy*, 2015, Henry Holt & Company.

- the teams delivering the work are highly skilled and able to deliver their best work with minimal supervision;
- the work itself is complex and ambiguous and each engagement needs to be creatively/innovatively approached; and
- the composition of the teams changes significantly from engagement to engagement.

Whether entire firms will organise themselves into holacracies in the future is debatable, but teams that adhere to very similar principles already exist in many law firms and other organisations. As with all the other structures, holacracies have pros and cons. It is also entirely possible that a structure that meets the needs of a group at one time might not be the best at another time.

(d) The need for professionals to determine their own structures and business models

No firm should slavishly adopt any of these generic structures, whether at the firm-wide level or for a particular business unit or

Figure 15. A hybrid organisational structure, with different models at business unit level that are aligned with the performance drivers of that business unit, and varying combinations of human versus algorithm value creation

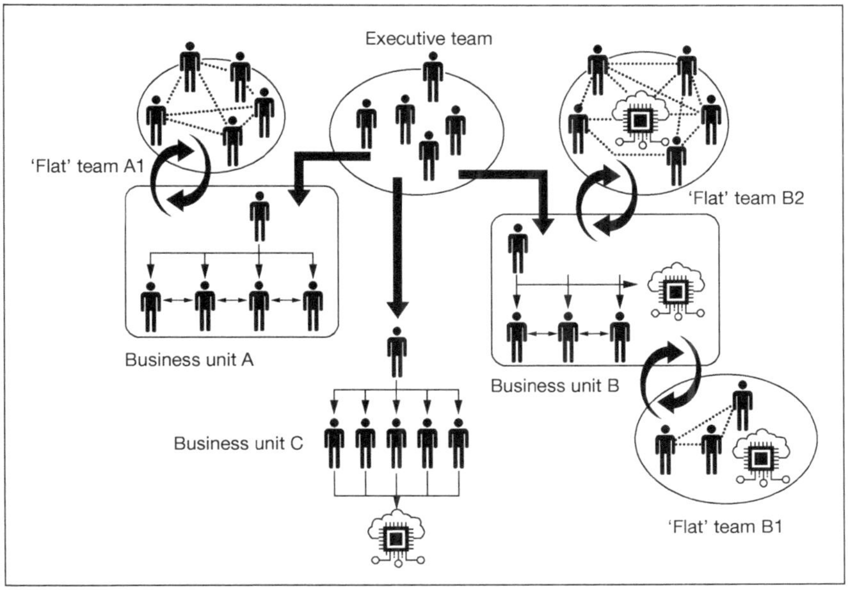

Source: Author.

other group. It is the characteristics of each model, and its 'fit' with the needs of the group, that must determine the degree to which it should be built into the design of the business model for a particular group.

A firm that is open to developing business models and structure at this lower level is likely to find that each group will have its own ideas about what it would take to deliver the best results. In groups of professionals especially, allowing the group to have a significant hand in the way in which it organises itself is a key driver of performance. Setting the criteria based on the "fully loaded revenue generation potential" (see earlier section 3.4 on Profit model) sets a good foundation for discussing the kind of business model that is required to deliver that, in that group in particular.

Figure 15 shows an entirely hypothetical schematic of a firm with multiple business units, each with a different business model with structures and with human + technology combinations that best align with their respective CVPs. Performance would be measured primarily on the basis of profit contributed/value added, not simply revenues and less still on input metrics such as hours worked.

6. Conclusion

It seems clear that over the coming three to five years the pressure on law firms will increase to combine human and digital inputs in the firm's service delivery and business processes. The existing core businesses that currently deliver the mainstream of a firm's work will become even more heavily contested and adjacencies will become more difficult to exploit. Under this scenario, it is crucial to be able to effectively shift focus to Johnson's 'white space' and win work that is currently uncontested. Doing so is a matter of business model transformation, not strategy, and needs to be approached as such. Areas of 'white space' exploited will in due course be emulated by competitors, so the capability that a firm develops to be able to do this might ultimately prove more valuable to the firm than the value won in the short term, each time.

At the core of all this lies a very different approach to clients. In a world where clients themselves do not have a clear view of how their legal needs are evolving, and have a jaundiced view of the ability of outside counsel to be able to help with this, any firm that can prove them wrong can entrench relationships and differentiate themselves in ways that are extremely difficult to achieve by other means.

Matter management in law firms – the emergence and impact of legal project management

Ignaz Fuesgen
smartvokat

1. Introduction

'Legal project management' has become one of the buzzwords of contemporary management practices in the legal profession. This chapter introduces the concept of legal project management and highlights aspects related to its application and implementation in comparison to a traditional matter management approach. The chapter's objective is to familiarise the reader with a basic understanding of the framework and embedded elements.

The transformation of legal service delivery from a viewpoint of technical excellence as the only differentiator towards a process-driven management framework becomes apparent in the discussion of significant elements of legal project management. Each element indicates and prompts numerous opportunities for technology enablement and new organisational structures. Within its limitations, reference is made to the differences arising from transitioning a law firm's approach from traditional matter management to legal project management and its corresponding Waterfall and Agile principles and practices.

2. Efficiency and value creation in the context of contemporary law firms' strategies

For many years, law firm leaders have been recognising the permanent trends in practice management aiming at fundamentally reshaping the legal landscape. The strategy agenda of all large and medium-sized corporate law firms is influenced by the need to find the balance between the following:

- Sustained top-line growth – that is, increasing revenues from fees and other services and products;

- Overall competitiveness based on a relevant portfolio of services and digital products; and
- Reduced costs of delivery.

While striving for widening the gap between revenue and corresponding delivery costs, the previously quite successful assortment of offerings is facing serious headwinds. A significantly higher number of new legal service offerings, driven by the emergence of alternative legal service providers and smaller law firms leveraging technology and process management, have attracted the interest of a more sophisticated community of legal services buyers.

Ultimately, many incumbent traditional law firms have found themselves caught in a peculiar situation, needing to redesign their matter delivery model and, at the same time, fundamentally rethink their service portfolio. The former clearly points to the input side of law firm operations and opportunities for efficiency gains, whereas the latter relates to the type and format of services offered – that is, the output. As a reminder, 'efficiency' defined in the law firm context is about "the time it takes to complete a given task … it pertains to the time and effort needed to carry a matter from intake to paid invoice".[1]

Value is by definition a combination of perceived service benefits coupled with expectations derived from the advising law firm's brand equity.

However, identifying and realising efficiencies in matter management alone would fall short of meeting client expectations, as Aileen Leventon argues. She resorts to an article by Michael E Porter called "What is Value in Health Care?" published in *The New England Journal of Medicine*.[2] Leventon substitutes the phrases "legal services" and "hours or billing value/hourly-based fees" in Porter's article with "health care" and "volume" respectively. Porter noted:

> *since value depends on results, not inputs, value in health care [legal services] is measured by the outcomes achieved, not the volume [billing value] of services delivered, and shifting focus from volume*

1 "Understand the Importance of Law Firm Efficiency", *Thomson Reuters*, available at https://legal.thomsonreuters.com/en/insights/articles/the-importance-of-law-firm-efficiency (accessed on 7 April 2020).

2 Porter, Michael E, "What is Value in Health Care?", *The New England Journal of Medicine*, 23 December 2010, quoted in: Leventon, Aileen, "What Is Legal Value?", *Edge International*, 24 April 2018, available at www.edge.ai/2018/04/what-is-legal-value/ (accessed on 6 April 2020).

[hourly-based fees] to value is a central challenge ... Since value is defined as outcomes relative to costs, it encompasses efficiency. Cost reduction without regard to the outcomes achieved is dangerous and self-defeating, leading to false "savings" and potentially limiting effective care.[3]

Research on law firm leaders' views, such as the annual survey amongst US law firms conducted by Thomas S Clay and Eric A Seeger on behalf of consultancy Altman Weil,[4] confirms that a focus on improved practice efficiency is a permanent trend in the profession.

While measuring and monitoring of time allocated to client matters has been alleviated by more sophisticated practice management frameworks and systems, the same cannot be said for value creation. From a client's perspective, "value" or "added value" is by definition a combination of perceived service benefits coupled with expectations derived from the advising law firm's brand equity. In simple terms, "value" comprises the following dimensions in line with the CIRS model used by Avuka Training and Coaching (see Figure 1):

- *Situational context:* Has the lawyer developed a comprehensive understanding of the client's assumptions, experiences, preferences, objectives and resources which define the need for legal advice?
- *Relevance:* Has the lawyer[5] offered the client solutions, rather than legal advice, that address the client's objectives? For illustration, a client does not instruct lawyers to conduct a due diligence or draft a share purchase agreement for the sake of it, but the legal advice serves to find the most economically viable way to acquire a company.
- *Interest:* Have probing questions been asked by the lawyer to further explore the matter? Has he or she demonstrated a sufficient degree of empathy and interest towards the client?
- *Comfort:* How responsive was the advice given to the client? Has a collaborative working style been established between client and lawyer? Have client suggestions in terms of document formats, writing style and so forth been taken into consideration and implemented?

---

3 *Ibid.*

4 95.9% of respondents state that focus on efficiency is a permanent trend according to Clay, Thomas S and Seeger, Eric A, "2019 Law Firms in Transition – An Altman Weil Flash Survey", *Altman Weil Inc*, May 2019, available at www.altmanweil.com/LFiT2019/ (accessed on 3 April 2020).

5 The term 'lawyer' is synonymously used throughout the chapter for all regulated legal advisory roles, such as attorneys, solicitors, barristers and advocates.

Figure 1. The CIRS model

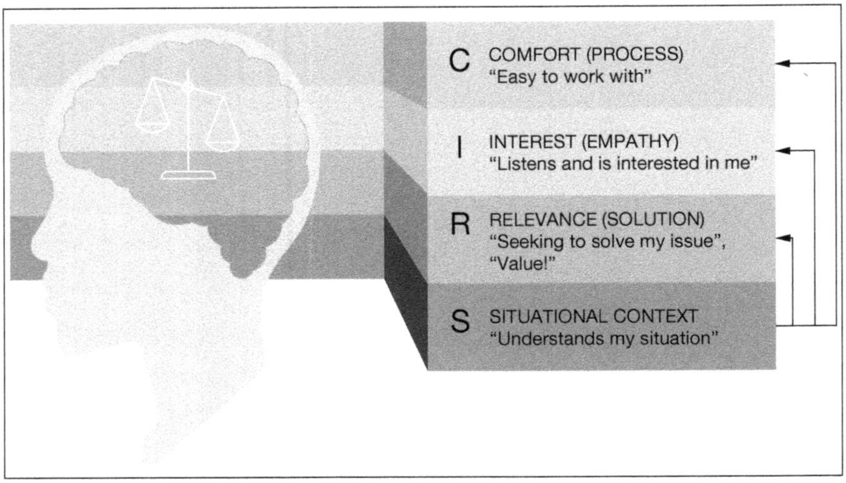

Source: Avuka Training and Coaching.

Leo Staub summarises the importance of value creation in the context of holistic solutions as follows: "The provision of the minimum legal service (correct legal advice) only results in a situation whereby the client is not dissatisfied. Clients are only satisfied or even enthusiastic when a service meets their other requirements or even exceeds their expectations."[6]

Notably, those value dimensions are entirely based on the client's perception derived from his or her working style, personality and professional background, not necessarily any factual foundation. Furthermore, many aspects are admittedly difficult to monitor and measure by mere observation only. Therefore, structured feedback interviews, a key element in the close phase of the matter management lifecycle, are the only way to capture and validate the degree of fulfilment.

Efficiency and value creation are central themes to the emergence and application of legal project management. The selection and validation of legal project management elements and techniques in client situations is inevitably tied to the question of whether it improves efficiency and value creation.

---

6 Staub, Leo, "The Client, the Unknown Entity – Understanding Client Requirements", *Vista blog of ES-HSG*, 30 August 2019, available at www.vista.blog/en/der-mandant-das-unbekannte-wesen-kundenbeduerfnisse-verstehen (accessed on 29 March 2020).

3. Managing matters by legal project management principles and practices

3.1 Definition of legal project management

Without knowing it, many lawyers have been project managers or played a minor or major role in managing a project. However, this was often done unknowingly and not in a structured and targeted manner. Legal project management transforms this set of unconscious actions into a coherent framework of project management principles and practices, fully adapted to the requirements of the legal profession.

The Project Management Institute, one of the foremost standards associations in the field of project management, defines a project as "a temporary endeavour undertaken to create a unique product, service or result".[7] Consequently, the notion of a temporary activity implies a defined beginning and end in time, and therefore defined scope and corresponding resources. The uniqueness distinguishes the project from a routine operation (ie, repetitive actions governed by process management). However, this does not rule out the likelihood of having standardised processes embedded in a project, such as invoicing clients. In essence, a specific set of tasks and activities is identified and implemented to accomplish a singular goal.

Legal project management is the application of project management principles and practices to enhance the delivery of legal services.

All legal matters, irrespective of their transactional or ongoing nature, being litigious and non-litigious or based on their duration, fulfil the criteria of a "temporary endeavour" with a defined starting and end point. Even *ad hoc* enquiries, potentially requiring not more than a few hours of legal research and drafting, may most likely resemble the characteristics of the traditional project management practices, albeit not fully reflecting all elements in each phase (refer to section 3.2). The uniqueness is to be judged from a client's perspective where each matter offers a bespoke client experience – that is, a combination of technical expertise, personal interaction and communication between client and lawyer, and

---

7 The Project Management Institute, *What is Project Management?*, available at www.pmi.org/about/learn-about-pmi/what-is-project-management (accessed on 11 April 2020).

the underlying process flow. Legal project management (frequently abbreviated nowadays to LPM) made its first official appearance as a discipline and methodology during the period between 2009 and 2016 with the publication of a series of groundbreaking books.[8] Its emergence was preceded by the rise of numerous other process-focused methodologies in the final decades of the last century, which focused on efficiency and effectiveness, measured by quality management, process control and continuous improvement.[9]

Back then in the said period between 2009 and 2016 and in this context of process improvement, legal project management achieved a certain degree of popularity amongst in-house legal operations specialists and law firm advisers who had experimented with various other methodologies, including TQM and Six Sigma. Its final breakthrough, however, happened only over the past four years, illustrated by the launch of the International Institute of Legal Project Management (IILPM), the introduction of legal project management modules or sessions in law school curricula,[10] the creation of dedicated legal project manager roles at global law firms and other indicators. The steady increase of cloud-based technologies in the form of workflow automation, document review and virtual collaboration enables process orientation irrespective of type of legal content.[11] The relevance of technology is reflected in the legal project management framework depicted in Figure 2.

---

8 A representative sample of publications includes:
Levy, Steven B, *Legal Project Management: Control Costs, Meet Schedules, Manage Risks and Maintain Sanity*, 2009; Hassett, Jim, *Legal Project Management, Pricing and Alternative Fee Arrangements – What Firms Are Doing*, 2013; Waldow, Pam and Richardson, Doug, *Legal Project Management in One Hour for Lawyers*, 2013; Lambreth, Susan Raridon, Leventon, Aileen R and Rueff Jr, David A, *The Power of Legal Project Management: A Practical Handbook*, 2014; and Lambreth, Susan Raridon, Leventon, Aileen R and Rueff Jr, David A, *Implementing Legal Project Management: The Legal Professional's Guide to Success*, 2016.

9 Renowned Yale Professor William Edward Deming's Plan-Do-Check-Act (PDCA) cycle is a pivotal concept to the understanding of any project management methodology, including legal project management.

10 For example, the following leading law schools have introduced LPM modules in their programmes: Vanderbilt Law School (https://law.vanderbilt.edu/academics/academic-programs/law-and-innovation/index.php); IE Law School Madrid (www.ie.edu/law-school/executive-education/degrees/legal-project-management-gateway-program-in-english/); and Seattle School of Law (https://law.seattleu.edu/continuing-legal-education/cle-on-demand/on-demand-webinar-library/practice-management-programs/2015-legal-project-management) (accessed on 6 April 2020).

11 William Edward Deming's famous quote "If you can't describe what you are doing as a process, you don't know what you're doing" highlights the necessity to dissect every single legal matter by process steps to benefit from proactive matter management.

Numerous definitions exist for legal project management and most, if not all of them, focus on the application of project management principles and practices in the legal context. The IILPM defines legal project management as "application of project management principles and practices to enhance the delivery of legal services".[12]

Is the prefix 'legal' justified even though legal project management operates at the core on the same basic principles and practices used by engineers, management consultants, IT developers and other professional service providers? Antony Smith emphasises the strong signal sent to lawyers: "Arguably, the 'legal' prefix acted, and still acts, as a signifier. It says to lawyers: project management is for you too."[13]

Other aspects include:

- terminology (eg, referring to clients instead of customers);
- regulatory obligations (eg, related to client confidentiality, formal requirements etc);
- costing and billing models (eg, prescribed rates, alternative fee arrangements etc);
- the relevance of certain project management functions (eg, procurement plays a rather minor role in legal service delivery); and, last but not least,
- legal technology with specific focus on legal delivery processes.

The definition as such does not prejudice whether the application of legal project management is based on a Waterfall or Agile methodology. Both families of methodologies are explained in more detail in section 4.5.

3.2 A legal project management framework

A number of legal project management frameworks have been devised and promoted by law firms, consultants and other industry experts. They may differ in detail but share all the core guiding principles.

- *Solution orientation:* Any legal advice given by the lawyer serves the purpose of achieving a client's business objective. The difference between a solution and pure technical advice lies in

12 Available at www.iilpm.com/about/explaining-lpm/ (accessed on 4 April 2020).

13 Smith, Antony, "Why it's Called Legal Project Management", blog post, 16 October 2018, available at https://legalprojectmanagement.co.uk/why-legal-project-management/ (accessed on 16 April 2020).

the contextualisation of legal content – that is, interpreting a paragraph cannot happen in a vacuum. The client's objective directs and informs the decision-making process.

- *Transparency:* The way a client matter is handled forms an important part of the client–attorney relationship. Clients should know about the progress of their matters (as do all team members of the law firm), understand the impact of external forces and be involved in the decision-making process. When and as required, both client and attorney should be capacitated to deliberately plan and monitor each activity and task with the context or related to the matter in a timely, coordinated and meaningful manner (no surprise). Ultimately, some authors also argue that transparency and a higher degree of predictability contribute towards lowering stress levels and promote the wellbeing of those involved in the matter management.[14]
- *Communication:* The establishment of transparency will fall short if not linked to a comprehensive and proactively managed communication approach, which acknowledges the importance of direct and indirect stakeholders to the matter management process and outcome. Therefore, different contents – targeting different stakeholders with potentially distinct interests, preferences and requirements – demand a diversification of communication channels, formats and frequencies.
- *Cost control and resource allocation:* The application of contemporary management and leadership techniques and insights warrants a proportional investment of resources (eg, attorney time) to the benefits and risks inherent in the matter. The creation of a realistic, detailed and reliable budget, which is consistently monitored in terms of performance against budget during the engagement's full course, constitutes the core of legal project management. Effective usage of templates, guidelines and checklists, and technology complements this approach.

---

14 Compare Esteve De Miguel, Sergio, "Legal Project Management: the Ultimate Guide to Boosting Efficiency (step by step)", *Bigle Legal* blog, 15 May 2019, available at https://blog.biglelegal.com/en/boosting-efficiency-with-legal-project-management-ultimate-guide (accessed on 3 May 2020); Smith, Antony, "5 Examples of How Legal Project Management Can Reduce Stress", blog post, 14 September 2018, available at https://legalprojectmanagement.co.uk/5-examples-legal-project-management-reduce-stress/ (accessed on 20 April 2020) and others.

Utilising the core principles of legal project management as guideposts for the overall matter management design and planning will greatly benefit the completeness of the approach.

- *Risk management:* Often confused with the legal risk addressed by matter itself, risk management is crucial in addressing stakeholders and processes effectively during the course of the matter lifecycle. Risk management in legal project management serves the purpose to identify risks, such as sponsorship of the matter, scoping risks etc, and continuously monitor them to enable a proactive matter management.

The introduction of a dedicated legal project management framework in law firms establishes a common language, as well as a guide for governance and orientation purposes. Lawyers will greatly benefit from such a framework as many of them have at some stage of their legal career been exposed or involved in some project management activities, but:

- have not been trained in project management methods;
- are usually not aware of the bigger context, the full sequence and nature of activities; and
- appreciate a legal project management framework for guidance.

A legal project management framework should recognise the following elements:

- The lifecycle stages, usually comprising four phases (define, plan, deliver and close) in case of a Waterfall project management approach;
- Key functions and elements under each phase;
- Productivity tools and enabling approaches; and
- People and organisational capability elements.

Framing the four phases, productivity tools and enabling approaches, as depicted in Figure 2, include but are not limited to legal design, workflow management, templates and any type of technologies, such as document management and review systems, collaborative platforms and so forth.

Finally, people and organisational capabilities play a major role in the framework. The legal profession (or the regulation thereof) in general and law firms in particular have developed specific leadership models and legal service delivery cultures, distinct from other private sector operators. The interpersonal communication element, essential to legal project management, deserves a special mention in this regard.

To those readers who are concerned about the vast number of tasks and activities involved, legal project management is a toolkit and philosophy of proactively contributing to a trusted client–lawyer relationship.

Legal project management is a toolkit and philosophy. The nature of the matter and client preferences decide on the elements to be implemented.

The nature, size and scope of each matter, client preferences and situational circumstances are only some aspects to be considered when deciding on which elements of legal project management to be applied. For instance, matters with a duration of only a few hours do not require a detailed and very granular work. However, a quick reflection on which direct and indirect stakeholders may be affected by the matter using the appropriate stakeholder mapping tools may benefit the relevance and impact of the document drafts and subsequent communication.

It is worth mentioning, Figure 2 depicts a legal project management approach based on a Waterfall project management

Figure 2. Legal project management lifecycle

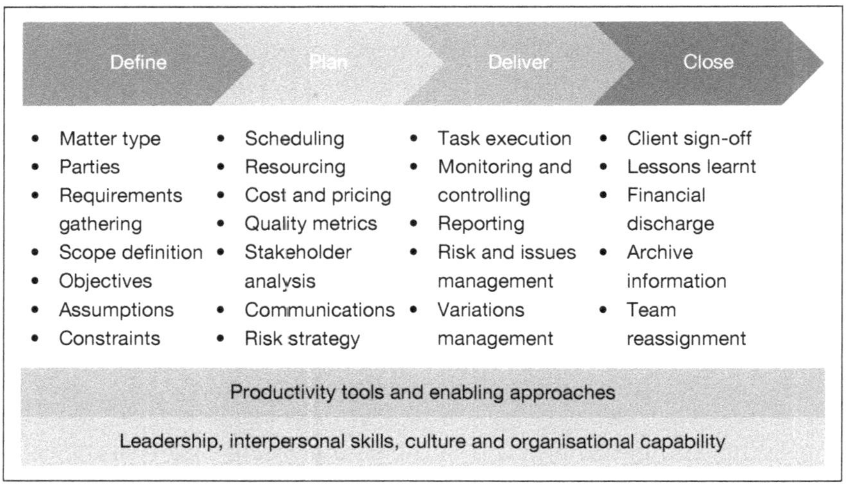

Source: Simplified version of IILPM LPM Framework.

methodology. The differences between Waterfall and Agile methodologies are further explored in section 4.5.

3.3 Legal project management – a new approach or an extension of today's practices

Neither application of project management nor the provision of legal advice have been new developments. By using project tools and techniques in the context of legal project management, a law firm can better plan, budget, schedule and allocate resources to progress client work. Profits and profit margins can be better tracked during the execution of matters, not just at month end when invoices are raised. Identifying and managing risks attached to the matter management process, managing issues effectively as they arise and dealing with scope changes that often lead to either write-offs or at least potentially unpleasant fee-related conversations are at the core of what legal project management achieves.

In principle, each matter follows the lifecycle illustrated by Figure 3 with varying nuances on each phase in terms of phase-specific activities applied.

Following legal project management practices, the overall process of assessing a client's situation (define), planning the matter with respect to deadlines (plan), conducting the matter (execute) and eventually concluding it (close), is not new. However, legal project management puts a greater emphasis on the first phases (define and plan) and, subsequently, the control phase, which may create a false and misleading impression that legal project management adds another administrative layer to matter management. While the

Figure 3. Comparison of the traditional legal advisory process with an LPM-orientated approach

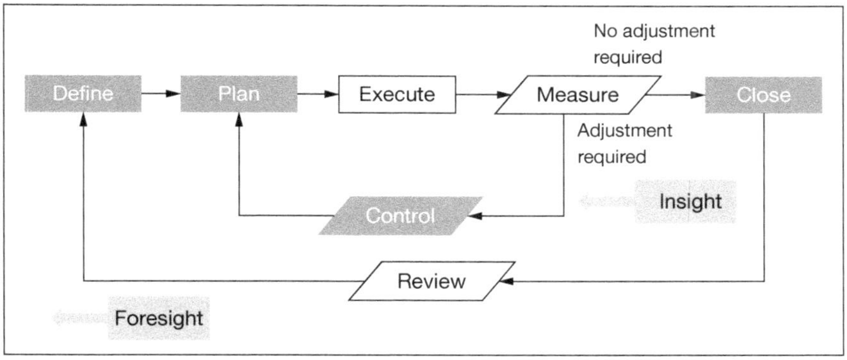

Source: Original source unknown, modified by author.

absolute effort, such as time invested, may be bigger than compared to today's traditional approach, the total effort over the course of the matter lifecycle should be smaller due to efficiency gains.

What is new is the rigorous application of review and feedback loops with the matter management team, clients and stakeholders, aiming to secure the full alignment of matter resources with client expectations. Insights assist with the effective adjustments during the delivery of the matter. Foresights, in addition, consider the overall management of the matter and target improvements of process steps, such as application of templates, effort estimation and so on.[15]

Three main activity streams are fundamental during the define and plan phases:[16]

- Scoping the matter;
- Scheduling and costing the matter; and
- Devising a risk strategy (in combination with stakeholder and communications management).

The quality of upfront planning and considerate matter management design will significantly assist the matter later on and overall reduce the total matter management effort.

Those three activity streams introduce a data-driven plan that must be monitored against predetermined key performance indicators (measure). If those indicators deviate from the plan, root cause analysis has to be conducted and approach and plan re-calibrated as required (control).

Defining the legal matter's scope is the starting point for effective legal project management. The scope identifies what the legal matter is to encompass and what it is to accomplish – that is, a definition of success, which is not to be confused with promising success! Without a clear and mutually understood and agreed definition of success, lawyers and clients will struggle towards the end of the matter lifecycle, trying to determine the quality of the outcome. It is necessary to remind oneself that success is about

15 A key element of the close phase is the structured and consistent capturing of client feedback by means of interviews succeeding the completion of the matter. The details of this element are not covered by this chapter. Readers are strongly advised to consider client feedback during their implementation efforts of legal project management.

16 For the sake of clarity, the outlined sequential steps follow the terminology of a Waterfall project management approach.

the value perceived by the client, which goes way beyond the technical expertise. For instance, it is the expected merger control notification leading to a completed merger, not a set of specific provisions in the share purchase agreement.

The scope should be specific and realistic, and divisible into discrete tasks as a prerequisite for further scheduling and costing activities in the plan phase. The scope should clearly address exclusions to manage client expectations (eg, determining the format of data to be submitted for the data room in a vendor due diligence). As a general directive and best practice, the scope of the legal matter should reflect alignment with the client's objectives. Checklists with probing questions are a proven means to guide lawyers through this exercise, support conversations with clients to frame the matter accordingly and enforce a quality standard across the firm.

Once the scope has been determined, a matter (or work) plan is devised aligning scope with milestones, a matter schedule, responsibilities, estimated costs and budget. Building on insights from the scoping exercise, the pool of tasks and activities is revised and extended as required to achieve the specified outcome.

Subsequently, scheduling comes into play to identify major divisions – legal matter phases and milestones (specific events demonstrating progress or completion of a phase) – before itemising and "resourcing" the tasks in the work breakdown structure.

In simple terms, the work breakdown structure deals with five salient aspects:

- What must be done?
- When should it be done?
- Who is doing it?
- At what cost is the task or activity completed?
- Which impact could cause delays and changes?

How does one estimate the activities in the matter schedule and overall work breakdown structure?

The level of detail and structure of a work breakdown structure should reflect the needs and nature of a matter.

First, one identifies the activities and arranges them in sequences (dependencies). In a second step, the matter team drills down to itemise specific tasks and activities within each phase, and the sequence in which those tasks ought to be completed. For instance, tasks in the document review phase of a legal case might include defining and developing a protocol for reviewers, training reviewers, and the reviewers conducting the actual review of the documents. The number and expertise level of people required for each activity and the amount of time it will take them to complete each task must be factored in. For completion of each task and activity, the responsible and accountable person is assigned. Finally, concrete start and end dates for each task and activity are established considering annual leaves, national holidays, weekends etc. Past experiences of those professionals devising the work breakdown structure, estimates of similar matters and, last but not least, contingency are all key to estimate times.

The level of detail applied to a work breakdown structure should resemble the following:

- Knowledge and experience of the legal team;
- Level of accuracy needed;
- Level of clarity to responsibilities; and
- Alignment to reporting requirements.

Finally, a budget based on estimates for all individual tasks is developed, taking into consideration schedule, staffing requirements and funding for other expenses. It is understood that the level of granularity depends on the matter size and scope.

The third main activity during the define and plan phases focuses on devising a risk strategy. Every legal matter has risks linked to the way the matter is delivered. It is important at the outset of the matter and continuously thereafter to project the potential risks as follows:

- Identify each risk;
- Evaluate its probability of occurring;
- Evaluate its impact on the matter progress if the risk were to occur, such as scheduling, costs or people;
- Identify significant dependencies between inputs;
- Develop mitigation plans; and
- Monitor risks and, if required, amend mitigation plans.

Identifying a risk means considering its impact on the progress of the matter. Can a possible cause and its consequences be identified? The degree of risk tolerance demonstrated by stakeholders is another important aspect of risk planning. The impact and probability of a risk can be captured in a risk matrix in order to prioritise those with the highest probability and biggest impact first. Thus, a risk mitigation plan simply mirrors the risk matrix in priorities and resource allocation.

Figure 4. Overview of risks occurring in legal matter management

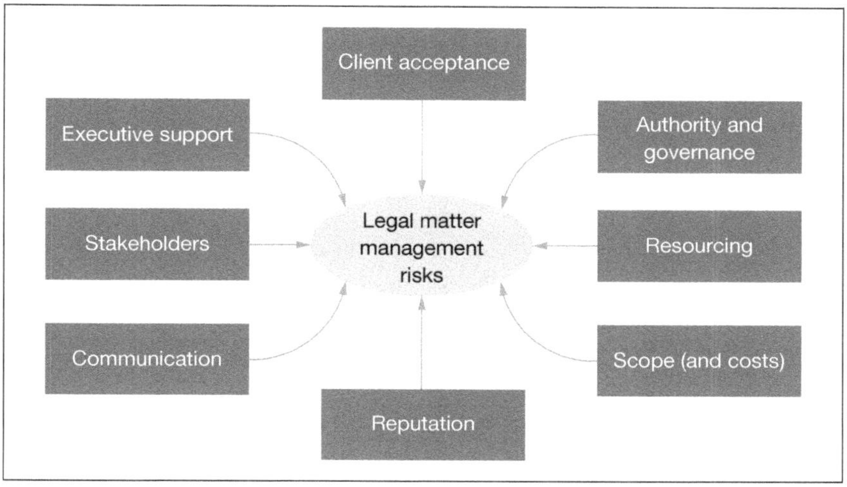

Risk can materialise in many different forms (see Figure 4) and at any given point in time. Therefore, it is of utmost importance to monitor identified risks consistently during the matter lifecycle and frequently interrogate the situation to spot new risks potentially emerging from issues. Assigning an owner to a certain area or type of risk shall definitely support the monitoring process.

As a matter of fact, risk planning cannot be viewed in isolation as it is deeply correlated with stakeholder management and communications.

The trio of managing risks, stakeholders and communications substantially influences the matter process (efficiency) and outcome (value). The interdependencies between the three elements are best illustrated in the context of key considerations for a matter communication plan:

- The communication plan should acknowledge the identities and interests of stakeholders at all levels. This information is usually sourced from the stakeholder analysis.
- Importantly, the plan contemplates what each party really needs or wants to know, input sourced from risk analysis.
- The scope and reach, the best method of information sharing and the corresponding timing of each communication 'event', is a combination of insights from the risk and stakeholder analysis.

Figure 5. Interdependencies between risk, stakeholders and communications

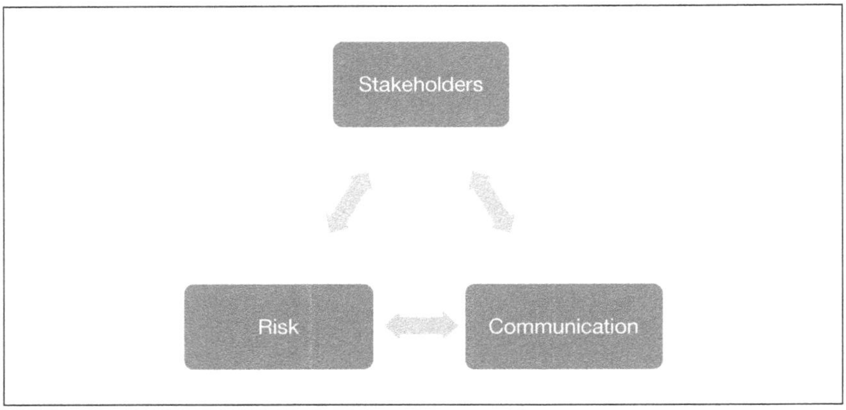

- The responsiveness – that is, how promptly changes, urgencies or emergencies have to be flagged – is, again, derived from the risk and stakeholder analysis.

In summary, matter scoping, scheduling and costing and risk management are essential to any legal project management approach. Hence, legal project management is not revolutionising the traditional matter management lifecycle but accentuating the initial planning activities to build a foundation for extending the traditional approach towards continuous monitoring and reviews. Intensified communication, transparency and continuous improvement are the main outcomes of the approach.

4. The application of legal project management

4.1 Change management – more than timesheets and project plans

Change management activities (ie, internal communication featuring success stories, digital billboards providing e-learning and templates etc) should be tailored towards "institutional inertia" first and foremost. Introducing legal project management is about addressing existing traditions and belief systems, which may hamper the collective and individual willingness to embark on a change of mindset. Insufficient awareness and training as well as a lack of a known methodology contribute to the individual's unease to interrogate current workflows and procedures. Finally yet importantly, gaps in interpersonal skills and ineffective systems and tools let individual lawyers think of an unsurmountable paradigm change.

In the author's experience, lawyers frequently express three major myths and prejudices:

- The fear of an additional administrative layer in matter management;
- Applicability of legal project management only in relation to large matters; and
- Legal project management means new technology licences.

One of the biggest concerns of lawyers is the creation of another administrative layer in the matter management process, simply reducing legal project management to keeping timesheets and updating matter plans. In reality, legal project managers and their teams build trust through transparency and predictability in the course of a matter. Proactive management of the matter, stakeholder identification and tailored communication, efficient meeting facilitation and comprehensible status updates are just a few examples.

The application of legal project management differs in relation to the nature of the client and matter.

The size of the matter is irrelevant insofar as legal project management is a toolkit and philosophy. Its application differs in extent and number of tools applied based on what is appropriate in relation to the nature of the client and matter ("fit for purpose") as explained in section 3.2. Likewise, smaller law firms and solo practitioners are not disqualified from applying elements of legal project management.

Finally, legal project management is not dependent on the introduction or existence of a certain kind of technology. It is methodology, framework and toolkit, while technology may support its application with structured data and reporting.

The actual change management process commences with soliciting buy-in from senior management and other internal stakeholders. For the latter group, assessing the needs and potential contributions by legal project management in daily routines is mandatory. Any rollout of legal project management should start small with a manageable matter and limited complexities. In conclusion, the most important recommendation is to document processes, templates, checklists and so forth. By doing it, legal project management becomes 'real' in the eyes of affected lawyers as most will struggle envisioning its actual application in daily routines. Visualisation techniques (ie, pre-designed charts and tables) support the adoption rate.

4.2 The role of the legal project manager

Lawyers have effectively been project managers since the profession's inception, but only a few have deliberately nurtured and leveraged the underlying skills. In that context, the International Institute of Legal Project Management (IILPM) has come up with three different functional contributors related to legal project management:

- The supporting function carried out by those supporting legal matters;
- The delivery function carried out by those in the legal matter project team; and
- The leadership function carried out by those individuals leading the legal matter.

According to the IILPM: "educational requirements for personnel at both the support and delivery function level was deemed to be largely the same ([collectively] defined as a *project associate* role), with the leadership function requiring a high level of project manager expertise (defined as the *project practitioner* role)".[17]

More and more legal project manager vacancies are now being advertised. Albeit similar in job descriptions, the positioning and implementation of those roles significantly differ from law firm to law firm. Defining the role of the legal project manager in accordance with IILPM's project practitioner aspiration, one must explore two fundamental questions:

1. What does the law firm expect from a legal project manager?
2. Who is best suited from a technical and personality perspective to meet those expectations?

The first question references the role and impact the collective of all lawyers in a firm assigns to legal project management in their

17 IILPM, *Legal Project Management Competency Framework*, available at www.iilpm.com/wp-content/uploads/2020/01/IILPM_LPM-Competency-Framework_Exec-Summary_1.00.pdf (accessed on 27 April 2020).

daily routines. In a short survey conducted by Antony Smith and the IILPM,[18] one of the respondents describes the challenge as follows: "A lot of partners are still apprehensive about 'letting you in', so quite often the first few times you work with them it is only on financials or billing, their understanding of what legal project managers can/should do takes time to build."

Involving legal project managers predominantly in monitoring the financial aspects of matter management indicates an administrative expectation towards the nature of the role, thus a 'project associate' in IILPM terminology. If that is the case, legal project management tasks can be regarded as a mere extension of a practice manager's portfolio.

However, in the author's view, legal project managers should be regarded as change agents rather than matter administrators. Strong communication skills, resembled in excellent moderation and facilitation skills, are necessary to promote a cultural change. Introducing principles and practices of legal project management is not a "quick fix" and demands a clear demonstration of the value the change will bring to the firm's operations and, ultimately, financials.

Legal project managers should be change agents, rather than matter administrators.

Who should fill in the project practitioner role and which skills beyond the above-mentioned proficiency in context-driven communications should be catered for? In principle, the role of legal project manager as a project practitioner may be occupied by the lead lawyer in the context of each matter. However, we have lately noticed, at least for medium-sized to larger law firms, the recruitment of professionals who possess a background in project management, legal tech or innovation management and are not legal practitioners themselves, albeit they may have a legal degree and have gained experience in the legal profession before. It is fair to say that no statistics exist at this stage confirming the percentages of former practising lawyers turned dedicated legal project managers and those with no legal qualification or background working in those dedicated roles.

18 Results are discussed in Smith, Antony, "Here Are the Key Challenges Facing Legal Project Managers", 7 February 2019. Available at https://legalprojectmanagement.co.uk/key-challenges-facing-legal-project-managers/ (accessed on 28 April 2020).

Dedicated experts in legal project management positions are meant to act as catalysts and subject matter experts helping law firms to better manage the legal matter process, aimed to free up the time of expensive senior associates and partners. The latter shall benefit from additional time capacity to focus on actual legal tasks, while the legal project manager looks after the key stakeholder engagement, process management, technology infrastructure and communication processes.

Exemplary project practitioner tasks include:

- upfront planning to define and gain consensus on the scope and required effort;[19]
- coordinating resources – people, financial and other;
- establishing communication mechanisms and rules in the context of direct and indirect stakeholders;
- identifying and respectively moderating a process identifying interdependencies between tasks and resources;
- managing the work plan and updates;
- connecting people to resolve questions, risks and issues, and being the central point of contact; and
- balancing project scope, time, people and cost to manage quality delivery while hedging risks.

Notably, the carving out of a dedicated legal project manager capacity creates often the perception of an "outsourced function", relieving the pressure on partners and associates to embrace project management practices. Furthermore, in more conservative law firm cultures it bears the risk of falling into the "administration trap", morphing the role into a glorified and sophisticated assistant or project associate.

4.3 Alignment of legal project management in the law firm organisation

Once a decision has been taken in favour of introducing legal project management as a cross-functional service philosophy in the firm, a place for bundling the expertise and subject matter experts ('centre of excellence') needs to be identified in the organogram.

The most common approach is footed in the entrepreneurial freedom of individual partners and their teams. A "progressive"

19 In Agile, the product owner, a defined role in Agile methodologies, together with the team would ensure the compilation of all client requirements in the backlog.

Figure 6. Potential alignment with legal project management centre of excellence in law firm structure

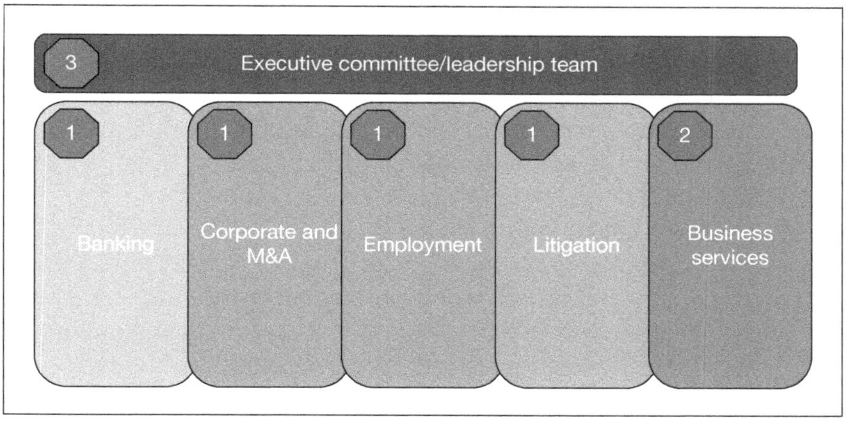

Source: Avuka Training and Coaching.

lawyer team would be in favour of option 1 – that is, retraining a fellow team member, dedicated professional support lawyer or practice manager to introduce legal project management just to this specific practice area. Advantages include the high proximity to client matters and any aspects particular to the area of expertise. In return, sharing of know-how beyond departmental practice area boundaries may be limited.

Option 2 reflects a truly cross-functional and specialist approach similar to business development, marketing and HR functions. However, a legal project manager may not be regarded as deeply interwoven in the fabric of the practice and its matters. Allocating costs (time spent on matters) to the respective practice area may be another issue.

Finally, legal project management is occasionally implemented as a service in the office of the managing partner or a similar advisory function to the leadership team. This approach assists with positioning legal project management as a strategic service while adding a layer of authority to it. On the downside, there is a risk of creating overhead costs that cannot be fully traced and charged back to the individual matter.

These are just a few brief aspects and law firms need to consider carefully the way they intend to position legal project management in relation to their leadership and corporate culture.

4.4 From costing and pricing to value creation

Many analysts and commentators of the legal profession point to the introduction of "alternative fee arrangements" ("AFAs"),[20] that is, fee models other than those based on the billable hour, as one of the key drivers for the introduction of legal project management.

Planning matters by breaking them up into phases, activities and tasks empowers law firms to estimate efforts much more precisely and monitor awarded budgets in relation to progress ("estimate to complete").

Two costing approaches exist:

- *Bottom-up costing* takes all possible costs into account (assisted by the visual work breakdown structure). It is a popular approach in particular for well-defined legal processes such as conveyancing, potentially including tariff components.
- *Top-down costing* assumes working with a set budget, starting on a very high level (main deliverables) and breaking task bundles further down. Assumptions assist with curbing costs to meet budgets. It is, for example, often used for budget-based pricing models (fixed or capped fees), where the law firm assumes a certain market-relevant fee range. It may also prove useful for outcome-based and value pricing models to determine a baseline.

Figure 7. Comparison of the lawyer perspective vs perceived client value

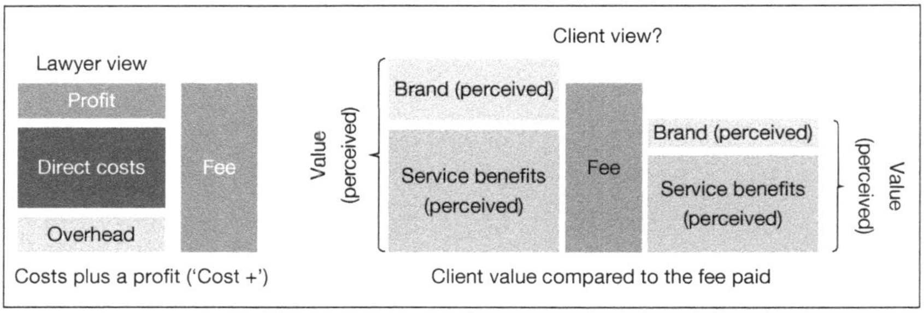

Source: Avuka Training and Coaching, adapted from Isaiah Adams, 2014.[21]

20 For instance, refer to Marra, Anna and Hutchison, Todd, "The Rise and Future of Legal Project Management", available at https://lawahead.ie.edu/the-rise-and-future-of-legal-project-management/ (accessed on 30 April 2020).

21 Adams, Isaiah, "How to Shift From a Cost-Plus to a Value-Based Pricing Strategy", *Optimization Group*, 5 May 2014, available at www.optimizationgroup.com/how-to-shift-from-a-cost-plus-to-a-value-based-pricing-strategy/ (accessed on 30 April 2020).

Combining the internal perspective of a more rigorous cost planning and monitoring approach versus fee offered with the external (ie, the client's) perspective of received value versus fee paid offers a significant competitive advantage.

If the client perceives a value that is greater than the fee paid, one can assume value creation. Figure 7 demonstrates once more – just on a financial level – the direct relationship between efficiency (lowering input costs) and value creation as a central element of legal project management.

4.5 Waterfall, Agile or hybrid?

The traditional approach to project management, also called "Waterfall", is based on clear end goals and schedules. It is characterised by a sequential series of steps, one after the other. Progress of the matter is seen as flowing steadily from the top to the bottom (as in a waterfall). A key aspect of the Waterfall approach is the strict adherence to the phased approach of define–plan–execute–close, linking a defined scope to a project plan and corresponding deliverables. What about situations where rapidly changing business needs, complex cross-functional work streams and potentially adversarial counterparts with no interest in collaboration exist?

Figure 8. Agile legal project management based on Scrum[22]

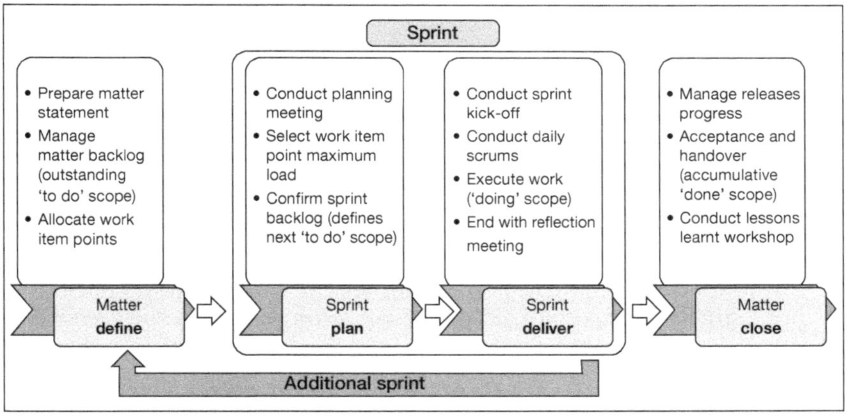

Source: Todd Hutchison, International Institute of Legal Project Management.

22 NB: Scrum does not recognise the concept of 'scope', a fixed set of requirements. Its counterpart in Scrum is called Backlog and is continuously revised and never set.

These may be opportunities to consider Agile project management methodologies. Agile is an umbrella term for several different frameworks or methodologies.[23]

Originally developed and applied in software development, many legal leaders are attracted by Agile's promise to foster flexibility and quicker turnaround cycles for draft versions of documents, concepts and legal tech applications. Immediate feedback loops are meant to drive alignment between client expectations and those who are supposed to provide advisory services and thus prevent developments in the wrong direction. Workload allocated to "sprints" is based on "work item points", a value attributed to each task by the matter team.

Agile project methodologies go beyond a working method and emphasise a mindset that prioritises the "what" over the "how" of a process. Collaboration matters more than hierarchical structures.

The Agile Manifesto[24] summarises those aspects in four simple directives:[25]

- Individuals and interactions over processes and tools;
- Working software over comprehensive documentation;
- Customer collaboration over contract negotiation; and
- Responding to change over following a plan.

From a legal perspective, "working software over comprehensive documentation" translates into a "reader-friendly, concise and pragmatic advice, comprehendible also for non-legally trained readers", as opposed to lengthy, academic papers.

The iterative approach is a core element of Agile. In Scrum, a popular Agile methodology, "decisions are made based on observation and experimentation rather than on detailed upfront planning. Empirical process control relies on the three main ideas of transparency, inspection, and adaptation."[26] Continuous improvement is driven by regular client and stakeholder feedback.

Applying Scrum, a matter is divided into short and incremental phases of work (so-called "sprints"), which usually last for a week. During each sprint, the team independently organises its work and

23 Key terms of Agile are summarised in Milnes, Michael, "Agile Project Management for Lawyers: Beyond the Hype", *Thomson Reuters*, 20 March 2019, available at https://insight.thomsonreuters.com.au/posts/agile-project-management-for-lawyers (accessed on 29 April 2020).

24 The four directives are complemented by 12 principles, available at http://agilemanifesto.org/ (accessed on 27 April 2020).

25 *Ibid.*

26 SCRUMStudy, "Empirical Process Control", available at www.scrumstudy.com/whyscrum/scrum-empirical-process-control (accessed on 27 April 2020).

reallocates capacities where needed by way of conducting daily scrums – short meetings focusing on the achievements on the previous day, plans for the actual day and potential impediments regarding planned activities. Once a sprint is completed, it is followed by two reviews:

- One review (sprint review) inspects the actual content against the definition of "done" and acceptance criteria and gathers client and stakeholder feedback.
- Another review (sprint retrospective) looks at the sprint delivery process.

The approach allows the matter team to re-prioritise tasks and adapt their planning to reflect what the client may expect next. Client requirements can continuously evolve following the emergence of new information, new actions set by opponents in court and so on, resulting in a great degree of flexibility and adaptability.

Each sprint must deliver a result that is immediately workable, or in other words provide an outcome of value to the client. While in software development, this outcome is referred to as a "potentially shippable increment", which is an upgrade or feature that the client could feasibly release to its software users, what could that be in legal?

In legal, a 'potentially shippable product' refers to a version of a document or a phase in a transaction.

Let us consider a practical example.[27] Traditionally, law firms follow a linear approach with respect to drafting and reviews of legal documents. Junior lawyers review all the documents, followed by scrutiny of senior lawyers. Client interaction is limited to a review subsequent to this internal process and typically only solicited towards the end of the review process.

In contrast, structuring the matter management in workflows based on iterative and incremental process steps (ie, sprints), the sequence of activities would start with planning the task in terms of responsible team members (delivery and review) and the way to complete the task. A sample of documents is considered for the first

27 Example taken from LegalVision, "How Agile Project Management Can Revolutionise the Legal Industry", 14 August 2019 (updated on 11 November 2019), available at https://legalvision.com.au/legal-agile-project-management/ (accessed on 26 April 2020).

sprint. The process is reviewed afterwards in terms of the approach and efforts involved drafting the documents. This review would involve the client and stakeholders. Subsequently, the process itself would be vetted and required changes adapted before taking on the next batch of documents.

The most obvious difference between Agile and Waterfall is the upfront planning effort incurred by Waterfall methodologies, which causes four challenges for most law firms:

- A significant part of the planning effort is centred on scoping and scheduling. Often, larger matters require lawyers to address those two aspects during the pitching phase (eg, in the context of a request for proposal). Who will be willing to take on these costs without any potentially guaranteed return? This argument often serves a purpose to avoid applying project management practices at all, albeit it ignores the so-called "legal project management debt", which is the accumulation of additional and unnecessary work and rework that is caused by a lack of application of project management principles at each stage of the matter lifecycle.[28]

  Although, Waterfall methodologies are subject to the general understanding of legal project management as a comprehensive toolkit and framework to choose from, the upfront planning elements enjoy some prominence in the context of a rigorous Waterfall approach.
- Project plans, in particular those aligning interests of many stakeholders (eg, in corporate reorganisation projects). Once put in motion, they may become a very rigorous framework to avoid continuous debates towards the entire approach.[29]
- A number of practice areas are based on a high number of short-term, *ad hoc* assignments, such as regulatory practices. Drafting a project plan may not be feasible and cost effective in the context of the overall matter duration.
- In case of longer transactional matters, the learning cycle for team members may just be too slow.[30]

---

28 Law360, *Getting Out Of Legal Project Management Debt*, available at www.law360.com/articles/1158534/getting-out-of-legal-project-management-debt (accessed on 28 April 2020).

29 For an extended discussion of the topic refer to Grant, John E, "Legal Project Management: You're Doing it Wrong", *The Agile Attorney*, 7 July 2014, available at https://agileattorney.com/legal-project-management-youre-doing-it-wrong/ (accessed on 27 April 2020). Grant quoted Jason Fried and David Hansson (Rework, 2010), who state that "planning" is just another word for "guessing".

30 *Ibid.*

Table 1. Relative comparison of Waterfall approach vs Agile

	Waterfall approaches	**Agile approaches**
Degree of matter complexity[31] and/or number of stakeholders	Low	High
Initial planning (eg, scoping, scheduling, costing)	High	Low
Volume of solely text-based documentation as opposed to visualisation or other formats with respect to team minutes, memos, etc	High	Low
Communication complexity (diverse audiences, channels) and frequency amongst team members, with project sponsor and stakeholders	Low to medium	High
Degree of expected changes in requirements in the course of the matter/project	Low	High
Responsiveness to changes in requirements (tempo of the matter/project)[32]	Low	High
Reassessment of activities and tasks as during the matter/ project lifecycle	Low to medium	High
Client and stakeholder involvement in progress monitoring and evaluation	Low	High

continued on next page

31 Refer to Craig, Kim and Lee, Jenny, "Agile – A Non-Traditional Approach to Legal Project Management", p2, published in ILTA's December 2013 white paper entitled *Business and Financial Management: Wrangling the Wild Ride*, available at www.seyfarth.com/images/content/6/9/v1/6965/ILTA122013.pdf (accessed on 24 April 2020).

32 *Ibid.*

	Waterfall approaches	**Agile approaches**
Control/supervision of matter delivery team	High	Low
Autonomy of individual team members	Low	High

Source: Adapted from Jim Hassett and Ed Burke, 2017.[33]

Agile addresses those four challenges. In spite of the many advantages of Agile methodologies, we need to concede the high degree of communication intensity. Agile encompasses the need for daily interactions in the matter team, as well as frequently between matter team and clients and stakeholders due to the relatively high complexity of matters. Furthermore, the idea of completely aligning oneself with client requirements may quickly collide with tight budgets and cost-effective 'quick fixes', where compromises may be needed.

Matters with low numbers of interfaces with other departments and experts, stable delivery processes and matter scope with a clearly defined end goal may be better suited to Waterfall methodologies, such as identified in the framework in section 3.2.

A limited number of indicative aspects is listed in Table 1. In essence, the author recommends carefully considering the full range of principles, practices and techniques from both Waterfall and Agile methodologies. Only subsequent to this thorough assessment should the team embark on a hybrid "cherry-picking approach", which talks to the objectives and the nature of the matter. Sufficient experience in the various methodologies is key to this selection.

In conclusion, Jim Hassett and Ed Burke made the important observation that "to date, Agile has had its greatest impact on LPM as a general mindset rather than as a specific collection of well-defined techniques".[34]

33 Hassett, Jim and Burke, Ed, "Why the Agile Approach Is So Important to Law Firms", *Of Counsel*, Vol 36, No 10, October 2017, p7. Available at www.legalbizdev.com/files/Agile-LPM-from-Of-Counsel.pdf (accessed on 25 April 2020).

34 *Ibid.*

5. Conclusion and outlook

Legal project management is not a radical new approach to legal matter management. Instead, it elevates fragmented inherent working patterns to a framework of proactive and deliberate management interventions. Its ultimate goal is derived from the process improvement methodologies at the end of the last century, aiming for better service and better results (ie, efficiency, effectiveness and client satisfaction). In our terminology, effectiveness and client satisfaction are merged to 'value creation'. Rolling out legal project management principles and practices is essential to providing a first-rate experience to clients and strengthening a firm's competitiveness.

Proactively entering into the matter management lifecycle based on a holistic understanding of the matter and planning of next steps offers a distinguished and repeatable service experience to clients. Costs play a huge role. Taking the time to listen and capture your client's requirements and systematically fulfilling them demonstrates the firm's interest in a meaningful client relationship but also controls costs of wastage (ie, hours that did not result in valuable outputs).

As the nature of each practice area and single matter requires a distinct combination of legal project management elements, it is crucial to educate the entire firm on the scope and availability of these tools and techniques, and own legal project management as a collective discipline.

Looking ahead, the introduction of legal project management is a non-negotiable item on each law firm leader's agenda. In a saturated legal market, deploying a firm-wide legal project management strategy ensures that a law firm can compete with other law firms and, as importantly, alternative legal service providers, and deliver a cost-effective legal advisory service that keeps clients coming back for more.

COVID-19 has proven that contemporary online collaboration platforms offer an unprecedented degree of virtualisation of team structures and processes hand in hand with comprehensive planning and communication – a key boost for effective project management. While many law firms are still experimenting with Waterfall methodologies, we will experience more introductions of Agile approaches. With Agile, many legacies in the context of hierarchical organisational structures must be reviewed (eg, considering the

Agile notion of self-organising teams) and new forms of cooperative leadership roles introduced.

Ultimately, legal project management is a mindset shift from a reactive, technically outstanding piece of legal advice towards a human-centred, client-focused and meaningful service process experience.

Legal tech as a factor in strategic law firm development

Felix Dette
METIS Rechtsanwälte PartGmbB

1. Introduction

1.1 Legal tech as a megatrend

'Legal tech' – or the digitalisation and automation of the legal market – has been one of the legal megatrends of the last decade. Few other legal topics have occupied a comparable number of publications, blogs and conferences in recent years.

As in other areas of digitalisation, there is a variety of views and opinions on the effects the future development and spread of technology will have on the legal market, the legal profession and, in particular, the way lawyers will provide legal services in the future. Some rather bullish forecasts from the past – according to which even complex tasks and large areas of legal services could soon be performed by legal tech solutions, thereby significantly replacing the lawyers in these areas – have not yet come true. It is therefore not surprising that the question has been raised as to whether legal tech is still more of a hype or fashionable buzzword. However, even doubters must concede that a number of changes and tendencies can be observed in the legal market that are associated with what is known as legal tech.

1.2 Current changes in the legal market associated with legal tech

In recent years, numerous new players with technology and web-based business models have entered the legal market which, for example, attempt to compete with traditional law firms in certain areas (eg, enforcement of consumer rights) or, as another example, operate internet-based platforms that bring together lawyers and clients seeking legal advice.

In addition, there is a large and constantly growing number of legal tech companies that develop technology-based solutions especially for law firms and other legal professionals. Their promise is to prepare the ground for better, faster and more efficient legal services – for example, by speeding up internal and mandate-related processes, improving the collection, review and flow of information, and facilitating the processing of documents and the communication within the firm as well as with its clients.

Moreover, many law firms have themselves built up legal tech know-how as well as accordant personnel capacities, and have even started to develop their own legal tech tools. Certain legal tech providers offer special programming software for law firms to facilitate the development of their own legal tech tools. Some law firms have entered into cooperations with legal tech start-ups or other legal tech providers, or have organised "legal hackathons" to draw attention to the topic. Others have joined forces in networks to work together on the development of future legal tech solutions.

1.3 Impact on own business?

Irrespective of whether these developments should be regarded as an opportunity or a threat, the key question for law firms in the current environment is less whether legal tech will change the way legal advice is provided in the future and more to what extent and at what speed.

Beyond the changes in the legal market and measures already taken by other law firms, increased time and competitive pressure, as well as higher efficiency expectations of clients, could be good reasons and motivation for law firms of all sizes to take a closer look at the available technology-based solutions, examine the potential for their own practice and include legal tech on the agenda when considering strategic law firm development.

This chapter aims to provide food for thought for such further considerations and is based on personal practical experiences, observations and discussions with colleagues.

2. What is legal tech?

What is behind the term 'legal tech'? Almost every law firm already uses technology-based solutions, especially in data processing, communication and legal databases. But does that make this technology 'legal tech'?

There are different approaches to the definition of 'legal tech'. They all describe in different facets the development and use of digital technology to support or automate legal activities,[1] both by

1 https://en.wikipedia.org/wiki/Legal_technology.

and for traditional and new players in the market. In addition to software solutions for the core tasks of legal work (eg, research tools, document analysis tools, document automation and processing tools), tools for administrative processes within law firms (eg, process management, time recording), legal departments (eg, legal spend management) or for connecting law firms with their clients (market places) are commonly summarised as legal tech.

Some definition approaches differentiate according to the degree of technological progress, in particular the degree of automation achieved. The frequently quoted definition by Vermont Law Professor Oliver R Goodenough[2] divides legal tech into three levels based on the systematics known from other contexts of digitalisation.

"Legal Tech 1.0" refers to those applications that support the work of the lawyer within the existing system, whereby the actual legal work is still performed by the lawyer. Research tools, document tools and law firm management tools that are already widespread on the market serve as examples.

"Legal Tech 2.0" describes such (also already existing) applications through which – in particular by means of artificial intelligence and machine-learning tools – sections of legal work are carried out to a higher extent automatically by technology. To a certain extent, the lawyer is replaced. Examples given are the automated execution of document reviews and the (partially) automated creation of contracts and other legal documents.

The third stage, "Legal Tech 3.0", describes a future scenario in which technology has changed the legal working environment and legal processes more comprehensively. Legal norms are then written in the form of computer code and operate more or less autonomously – for example, on the basis of self-executing "smart contracts". Large parts of the previous processes of finding and enforcing law have then, according to this classification, been replaced by alternative technology-based processes and solutions.

Other categorisation approaches focus on the current legal tech landscape and divide it into categories such as "managing the business" (eg, tools for HR, management and finance purposes), "performing the work" (eg, tools for document creation and contract analysis), with the overlapping area of "managing the business and/or performing the work" (eg, knowledge management), each

2 www.huffpost.com/entry/legal-technology-30_b_6603658?guccounter=1.

with certain subcategories, and "consumer services" for solutions providing direct legal advice.[3]

3. Step 1: Needs analysis and market overview

The strategic considerations of whether and, if so, which technologies are likely to offer added value for the firm's practice should start with an analysis of the firm's own processes and demands. Even the most elaborate legal tech tool will be useless if it does not meet the demands of the firm's practice or if there are no matters suitable for the use of the tool. As in other areas of digitalisation, technology-based automation can create added value, especially in connection with frequently recurring, similar work processes. However, there is no one-size-fits-all solution for law firms. Rather, the specific circumstances – such as the jurisdiction the law firm is working in, its range of services and practice groups, size, existing infrastructure and client/matter-structure – place different demands on the functionality of any technology-based solution.

The firm's own needs analysis should be accompanied by an intensive assessment of the legal tech solutions available on the market. In view of the variety of different legal tech tools and their dynamic development this can be a challenging task. Business consultants for legal professionals specialised in this field offer their assistance in connection with the selection and implementation of legal tech solutions. Legal tech handbooks, market guides and blogs may also be helpful sources to achieve an overview of the legal tech market and a better understanding of the offered solutions.

4. Step 2: Make it or buy it, alone or in cooperation with others?

While many legal tech solutions can be purchased 'off the shelf' or used with only little further adjustments, others – in particular, document review tools using artificial intelligence – often only deliver their full potential after further individual training. To enable these tools to recognise specific clauses or patterns in documents, sample documents must be uploaded and the corresponding sample clauses must be earmarked manually by the lawyer. The more extensive and better such training is, the better the work results of the tool will be. Even if certain functionalities are already available or training has already previously taken place, the program capabilities may

3 https://legalsolutions.thomsonreuters.co.uk/content/dam/openweb/documents/pdf/uki-legal-solutions/report/tr-legaltech-startup-report-2019.pdf.

have to be further trained for individual matters and the purposes specifically required in it.

In light of the time- and cost-intensive implementation and training of these tools, it could be worthwhile considering joining forces with other law firms to achieve a higher training level more quickly at lower personnel costs. The disadvantage of this option is, however, that the real value of the trained artificial intelligence would then also be available to other market participants. Furthermore, potential confidentiality and quality assurance issues would have to be taken care of.

5. Potential benefits

Used sensibly, legal tech solutions can significantly improve a law firm's own practice, both with regard to administrative processes and the core legal work. The following three practical examples highlight how legal tech solutions enable lawyers to benefit from technology in connection with document processing, document review and process management.

5.1 Example: Document automation and document processing

A broad field for legal tech solutions is the automation of documents and the improved document processing. Legal tech solutions not only facilitate and accelerate the process from the (automated) template or sample document to the finished document draft, but also facilitate, for example, the joint processing of a document by several lawyers at the same time, which can be particularly helpful in matters where larger teams have to contribute to the same document.

5.2 Example: Document review and contract analysis

Document review and contract analysis tools with artificial intelligence can provide particular added value and leverage the human resources of the law firm. The volume of data generated is increasing worldwide. In many circumstances, lawyers have to review ever-larger volumes of data and documents in a limited time (eg, due diligence reviews in mergers and acquisitions or real estate transactions, eDiscovery, internal investigations or mass procedures). Document review and contract analysis tools are able to automatically review machine-readable data records such as emails, contracts, pleadings or other documents for specific types of clauses or contents. Data volumes that would take lawyers days or even weeks to review can be analysed and categorised swiftly with the help of legal tech applications for previously defined or specifically trained patterns, terms and filters, and are then available for further legal review by the lawyer. For the lawyers involved, this can significantly reduce time-consuming preparatory work with the effect that they can concentrate at an earlier point in time on the actual legal assessment.

Artificial intelligence tools with high accuracy can also increase the quality of the work results where more comprehensive data (pre-)analyses can be carried out. In particular, this holds true for cases where, due to time constraints, otherwise only random samples could have been taken.

The time and efficiency gains can also lead to the indirect advantage of allowing law firms to expand their range of activities and apply for new types of mandates. On the one hand, efficiency-increasing legal tech solutions can enable the firm to leverage its own personnel resources and handle mandates that would otherwise exceed pure personnel capacities. On the other hand, the use of legal tech solutions can lead to an improvement in the cost structure, which, due to economies of scale, may make mandates that could otherwise not be handled profitably more commercially attractive.

5.3 Example: Process management tools

Especially for complex matters or matters that involve larger teams, there are legal tech tools available that facilitate process management for law firms. Certain solutions aim at improving the workflow management and work allocation, while others allow the client to track the progress of the matter or improve the internal communication within the law firm as well as the communication with the client and its other advisers. Improvements in this area are also attractive for marketing reasons. Not only does every client appreciate a well-managed and smoothly run process, but legal tech solutions in this field are also particularly visible to clients who can directly experience their benefits when working together with the law firm.

The above-mentioned advantages are only exemplary. In summary, however, it can be stated that a broader replacement of core legal advisory activities by legal tech tools (ie, "Legal Tech 3.0" in the above nomenclature) cannot be observed at present. Rather, the advantages of using legal tech currently lie in a complement to the work of lawyers by supporting and enhancing the human working skills.

6. Cost, risks and challenges

The potential benefits from the use of legal tech solutions have to be set against the costs as well as certain risks and challenges associated with their implementation and use.

6.1 Acquisition and running costs

The investment in legal tech solutions is initially associated with not inconsiderable one-off and often-ongoing expenses for the acquisition of the software and/or licensing fees. Despite the above-mentioned advantages, the costs are not always offset by an immediately measurable financial benefit that is likely to amortise the costs.

6.2 Time expenditure

Also the considerable time and personnel expenditure for the implementation and, depending on the solution, the further "training" of legal tech applications should be taken into account and not underestimated. Personnel capacities can be tied up to a considerable extent outside the actual mandate work. The more the law firm aims at further developing its own legal tech solutions, the more the necessity of also building up special personnel capacities comes to the fore.

6.3 Acceptance within the firm

In addition, there may be internal challenges for the implementation of legal tech solutions in terms of lacking acceptance and willingness to rely on new technological concepts instead of the "tried and tested" and well-established methods in law firm management and client work. The best legal tech application is useless if not used in practice. It is therefore key to carefully prepare and accompany the change process at all levels, and to evaluate the actual use from time to time.

6.4 Dependence on provider

The most difficult decision is the selection of the right product from the right provider. The large variety of legal tech providers and solutions has already been pointed out. Due to the dynamically developing market, it is often hardly possible to predict which technology, provider and product will succeed in the long term. Obviously the decision in favour of a particular provider can, depending on the product or service, come with a certain degree of dependence. A change in provider at a later stage may then entail the risk that own developments or product adaptations (eg, specific templates and samples) that have been created by means of the application in the meantime cannot simply be used in a new application from another provider.

6.5 Pitfalls and challenges for the use of artificial intelligence tools

Not every transaction or other matter involving the review of larger databases is suitable for the use of artificial intelligence tools such as document analysis and contract review tools. Even where this is the case, the use of such legal tech tools may be confronted with specific practical challenges.

(a) *Training errors and unusual formulations*

As mentioned above, artificial intelligence tools often require previous training. Training errors may adversely affect the analysis result. Moreover, new clauses or unusual formulations in documents bear the risk of being overlooked or misinterpreted by the tool. Against the background of possible professional liability risks, special attention must therefore be paid to quality assurance during the training phase as well as in the subsequent use.

(b) *Access to data and data quality*

Access to the database is a prerequisite of the use of any such artificial intelligence tools, which in practice can be challenging depending on the data room and/or legal tech provider.

In addition to availability, the quality of the existing database plays a significant role, especially with regard to its readability for the application. The readability can, for example, be impaired by poor scan quality or handwritten notes in documents. Depending on the application used, additional problems in document analysis can arise due to the language of the documents, even though many applications can operate with documents in different languages.

7. Conclusion

Recent developments and the solutions already available on the market demonstrate that there are very good reasons to see legal tech primarily as an opportunity for lawyers; an opportunity, however, that requires a substantial investment of time and money.

If used sensibly, legal tech applications can considerably support lawyers in the management of the law firm and the performance of client work and, in combination of "man and machine", significantly speed up and improve the quality of the legal services. This finding alone should be reason enough to put the topic of legal tech on the agenda for strategic law firm development.

Beyond that, the costs for the implementation of legal tech solutions and the internal development of corresponding experience and know-how should not only be measured by the currently realisable advantages, but should also be seen as an investment in the future and competitiveness of the firm. Development in the area of legal tech in general and in the area of applications for law firms in particular continues to be very dynamic. With regard to other, already more advanced fields of digitalisation, it is not expected that the development will slow down.

Even if the firm's own clients are currently not proactively requesting the use of legal tech or making it a selection criterion in the awarding of mandates, it is likely that this could change if legal tech applications develop further and become established as the market standard in certain areas. The stronger the impact of legal tech solutions on factors that are relevant to the awarding of a mandate such as quality, time and cost becomes, the more important the law firm's ability to innovate in this respect will be. The greater then will be the competitive disadvantage for and the *de facto* pressure on those law firms that cannot take advantage of legal tech.

Winning and keeping clients

E Leigh Dance
ELD International LLC
Global Counsel Leaders

1. Introduction

This chapter aims to get to the heart of key issues in the age-old challenge of client development. Many of the fundamentals are the same, but to provide valuable and actionable guidance, we must also focus on the circumstances that affect how legal services are used by companies today.

The greatest impact today is caused by the breadth and pace of digital transformation in business, which is only just beginning for the legal sector.

As you read this chapter, repeatedly ask yourself three questions:

- What can you do to help make your clients perform better and make their stakeholders happy?
- Do you have solutions that are aligned with digitalisation of legal services delivery?
- How agile is your approach to winning and keeping clients?

The answers will be found, and your strategy perfected, through your understanding of the client, your awareness of the legal services marketplace (discussed in other chapters of this book), your actions and how consistently you practise them, and continual improvement. This is how you will succeed at winning and keeping clients.

If you have not yet begun to think differently about these issues to how you did a few years ago, now is the time to start. Expect it to be both confusing, often non-linear, and fun – especially when you start to see clients respond to you differently and see that your hard work is paying off.

We will look at the theme from three angles: (i) re-examine how you win and keep clients; (ii) adapt your actions and your offers to the client's current problems; and (iii) renovate your client development practices and determine priorities.

2. Re-examine how you win and keep clients

Trusting relationships are more important than ever, especially in a client relationship where the client is in many locations or in many countries. In those client relationships, trust and loyalty is built and maintained in a very different way. Its glue is threefold: clear and transparent advice that is provided in concise communication; consistent service delivery; and top-notch reporting.

There are more and more of what we initially called 'alternative service providers' (ASPs) on the market. Every day clients demonstrate their readiness to drop the 'A' in ASPs and adjust their spend to many different types of service provider, not just law firms. We are all seeing the plethora of small and larger businesses that aim to profit by helping legal services buyers leverage digital and take new approaches to cover demand and deliver value.

Unfortunately, all too often the sellers of legal tech solutions are pushing a product and are not attuned to or clear about their understanding of the client's situation and problem. In-house counsel notice this and have become more vocal about their frustrations with it.

When general counsel speak about their allies in improving their own productivity, efficiency and performance, it is interesting that law firms are often named rather than legal tech. This is not only because these firms have made great strides in adopting and using new technologies, but also because they are willing to dig deep into the client's issue and work with them to solve their root problem.

It is not complicated. For the lion's share of work that clients give their law firms, it is the approach and delivery that counts as much as your legal advice. You need to get into the client's shoes and find out really what their pain points are, where they need help. Then you can begin to re-evaluate your priority client service or offering around the pain points and adapt as those pain points change. Making work easier for your clients is essential to winning and keeping them.

2.1 Think differently

Get ready to think differently. In the legal services arena, "thinking differently" means taking off your lawyer hat and mindset and pushing yourself to re-examine everything about what you currently do, in light of what you find out about your client's problems. Only then can you consider what you want to keep and what you want to change in order to deliver results – and how to prioritise.

Take a select group of your clients and look at their situation with new eyes, as if your old preconceptions might all be wrong. If you do not know enough, ask them. Turn your classical practices upside down, drop everything, and reconsider. See what you can toss out, and what you must keep or improve. Dump what you do not need, see what new practices you will need. And again, fight the desire to diagnose and immediately plan.

Before you reconstruct your client development programme, focus 90% on the problems you are trying to solve for each of those clients. Write down those problems and work in groups to refine them to the very core issues that you and your firm can solve – this is where agility pays off.

2.2 Consider these data points

These data points underscore why you must rethink how you win and keep clients. Look for insights and data in a number of places to supplement these points – and focus primarily on clients' real risks and threats and day-to-day situations, not on the like/do not like studies on their outside counsel experiences. Think more broadly. These points are drawn from my hundreds of in-depth conversations with general counsel and their teams, and from the research of AdvanceLaw.[1]

- Clarity and brevity of your advice wins you big points. Less translation to business eases ability for executive leaders to make decisions. Plus, many general counsel will not stand for long and laborious law firm opinions that lack succinct recommendations. It is a sign that the provider has no understanding of their day-to-day demands, and many in-house counsel find it not just inconvenient, but a sign the outside counsel does not understand their situation or needs.
- New and unknown products/delivery channels are being introduced all the time in some companies, creating more demand on your clients.
- Many firms seek to add value through key client programmes. Another way to add value is to give your clients some of the professional skills and experience you possess in your firm. Help your clients win awards, get media coverage, speaking opportunities, soft-skills training, and improve their presentation skills.

---

1 See www.advancelaw.com.

- In-house counsel look at risk and financial forecast effect. They no longer approach issues or define support by legal practice (with few exceptions).
- Your clients' bosses expect continual efficiency gains. Move lawyers up the value chain with more "legal professionals" and automated ways to do your work.
- A top driver of value from external counsel is regular feedback, including reverse feedback, from the law firm to the client.
- Tighter budgets mean corporate counsel need to show their internal stakeholders the proof of value delivered for the expense. In-house counsel are generally poor on key performance indicators. How can you provide practical help that your client needs to demonstrate value and defend against budget cuts that may happen a few times this year?
- Many clients have learned about value through practice. They are finding that flat fees are a consistently effective way of reducing costs without hurting quality.
- There are concerns among clients about endless demand for legal services and finite supply. The demand is caused by uncertainty as well as regulation, creating legal and reputational risk.
- Competition for the middle market company work is growing dramatically, as law firm profit margins from large, operationally sophisticated legal departments begin to shrink or be dispersed among old and new providers.
- As important as legal advice is to many clients, so is reputation. Today, the company's ethics stance can damage brand value, popular issues mushroom, perception can bring regulator inquiries and disputes, plus unfavourable media attention. How can you help your clients with this?
- Lawyers need to learn and upskill to serve their clients. This is one of the drivers of increased industry sector focus to spotlight and solve client needs in specific fields.

3. Adapt your actions and your offers to the client's current problems

Remember my earlier comment about clarifying your client's problems. This evolves – your client's primary problems today could be different from the last time you spoke, so always ask again. In every conversation, you must repeat your understanding of the key client's problems and which aspect of them you are trying to solve. It is not just responding to an instruction. It is how you deliver, in a way that is tailored to your understanding of the client's problem. A key element of winning and retaining clients is to understand and help with the external and internal situations that cause concern for your client, as well as the fundamental shift towards digital business that many of your clients experience. Let us look at some of those situations and explore what the digital shifts are about.

3.1 Are you "there" yet?

Every corporate legal department is trying to make big changes, "find a better way", improve and prepare. Many in-house legal functions have made enormous advancements and are prepared to speed their pace of change in the future, but nearly all will admit "we're not there yet".

Clients are pressed to simplify and reduce process to survive, not to mention disrupt their own products and services before a wily competitor does so. As the general counsel of CVS's Aetna division explains, "We're asking how to dramatically shorten cycle times on some tasks. Our legal department wants to move from 6 years to 6 months – and why not 6 days? But before we start that process, our first question must be: 'Why are we doing this?' or 'Do we really need to do this?'"

3.2 Integrate a digital mindset

It is essential to work a digital mindset into how you win and keep clients and solve their specific problems.

The pressures come from the top: given that 76% of CEOs of 400 large US companies believe that their growth relies on their ability to challenge and disrupt any business norm.[2] Digital transformation is a core business strategy of just about every company in every sector.

For the last five years that we have gathered data on the demands of global clients, we find that the lion's share of in-house counsel see an increase in their workload year after year. It is an unsustainable predicament. As a result, they rightly conclude that process and technology can do more to save the legal department than really good answers to legal questions.

2 KPMG 2019 US CEO Outlook.

3.3 Take to heart what others are saying

But what does digital mean for the legal world, and corporate legal and compliance departments? Here are a few comments I have received from current general counsel. As you read them, note what sorts of ways you or your firm can assist them to do what they are determined to do.

Chris Fowler, general counsel technology with BT in London, characterised digital transformation in legal as "the replacement of customised, manually intensive tasks (such as custom-built contracts) with automated, data-driven repeatable outputs (such as a negotiated contract/early case assessment)". Chris believes that "data-rich legal areas like higher-volume enterprise contracts and claims are obvious early adopters of digital. But as legal data structures mature, there is no reason why other areas – such as anti-trust assessments – can't be automatically produced."

Chris noted, "To truly benefit from digitalisation, we have found at BT that it's essential to devote significant time to plan the strategy and clarify the goals for our end-state operating model. Transformation of in-house Legal requires department-wide plans for technology implementation, tool and process adoption and management of strategic partners. It's not a finite destination – we continue to revise the plans as we learn and as our business changes. If you have these plans and execute well, you can demonstrate that your team proactively supports the strategic priorities of the business."

According to Lucy Fato, executive vice president and general counsel for AIG in New York, "A digital law department is one where decision-making is driven by data. Access to real-time, insightful metrics and key performance indicators (based on clean data) is critical. At AIG, our global legal operations group is modernizing our technology application infrastructure. We're also focusing on consistent data element capture to ensure that our data is good. The primary goal of a digital law department is much the same as it was 15 years ago: a race to absorb and process critical data points quickly enough to proactively manage your legal matter portfolio, while reducing enterprise risk and efficiently managing your organization."

Bill Deckelman, executive vice president and general counsel with Fortune 250 company DXC Technology, explained, "Our clients have been implementing digital transformation in their businesses for a few years. Now many general counsel are expected to transform the legal function too. Digital transformation of Legal should use the same approaches employed to transform business functions. The specific goals may vary by company but the focus of digital in Legal is to increase meaningful collaboration with our business clients and deliver measurable business value."

Deckelman continues, "Technology can enable much of this collaboration, but transformation equally involves people and processes. To be a digital legal department our people must be proactive, agile, collaborative, creative, resilient, and have a global perspective and cultural awareness. Each of us must constantly learn and improve our ability to connect law with technology and business. At the end of the day, it's all about serving our business client and our end customers.

"To evolve Legal into a client-centric organization we must continually move the needle on value. With technology advances, we can now manage our legal function and identify risks much more effectively through data analytics. That added value, and the close business connections that digital transformation brings to Legal, is what it's all about."

3.4 Consider a law firm leader's approach

It is valuable to have a law firm leader's perspective on the digital shift as well. Law firms often share best practices and lessons with each other on how they are approaching their own transformations to respond better to client demands. Participate in those valuable discussions when you can.

Eversheds Sutherland's global co-chair and US managing partner Mark Wasserman describes some of the changes in outside counsel behaviour that he finds necessary to be a true and trusted ally to the client.

According to Mark, "For us, digital in the context of law means thinking strategically about the best ways to use technology and data in new or innovative ways to provide better (and usually more efficient) solutions to client needs and problems. Most importantly, it is not about the technology itself, but rather about changing mindsets, processes and possibly business models to attack problems in a different way."

Mark explains, "Speaking from our firm's experience, delivering on digital requires experimentation with different tools and detailed conversations with clients about their needs," he continues. "We have worked with several AI and machine learning developers on various projects with clients and within the firm. Recently, we saved a client nearly $45,000 on a project by using a software that analyses text in contracts and other legal documents.

"We have created apps that provide information enabling our lawyers and our clients to access what they need when they need it. And we now have a captive alternative provider that will use technology and alternative staffing to assist clients with appropriate projects. Technology is involved in all of this, but at the end of the day it is all about lawyers thinking about the delivery of services in a different way."

4. Renovate your client development practices and set priorities

Here is where we take the old tried and true client development practices and update them to the present before we begin implementing the same old stuff. Today, with geopolitical and economic uncertainty, tensions are felt by business.

As you circle back to the ground rules of good client development techniques, try some of the following approaches tailored to our volatile, uncertain, complex and ambiguous times that should reap benefits for you in the short and longer term.

You can achieve an impact when you apply the following steps.

4.1 Provide advice using a helpful approach

Your partners and colleagues cannot always give sure answers or absolute advice on the right step forward in today's unpredictable environment. Yet, your advice can be valuable to give your client the way to educate and tell their board of directors intelligently that they have some scenarios, but they "just don't have an answer".

Your best approach is to be helpful. Give a concise review of what we know now, key points where there is no clarity, and timelines on when clarity may come. Give your service providers with a few options and examples of what your other clients are doing, specifically within their sector. A decision will need to be made no matter the weather, and the valuable outside counsel will be the one that helps the company make important decisions in areas that are very grey.

4.2 Provide a unique perspective and special expertise

Clients are eager to get a diversity of perspectives from professionals in different industries and roles that are not just your accountants or lawyers. Change up your events to include insights from clients and other relevant experts, and offer your professionals to do the moderating and introductions.

4.3 Have fun

Build relationships and win the goodwill of many influential clients by providing more social interaction among the rising professionals on your own client teams that are one or two steps below leadership level. Allow the millennials to choose a simple theme for the event, with the goal being to host a simple and original activity that brings professionals together to talk and have fun.

4.4 Prevent surprises with transparency

When there is uncertainty, work environments are stressful and fuses may be short. Surprises are more aggravating than ever in this climate, so it is best to be transparent about the scope, fees and deliverables.

'No surprises' also means providing guidance to your clients on avoiding the unknown. Keep them abreast of what is on the horizon that could impact their business by sending them relevant alerts that are focused and specific to the services you offer, accompanied by a calendar whenever possible.

4.5 Give tips in conjunction with diagnostics

Most businesses have their focus trained to the near-term these days and a sales pitch that raises fears of an imminent risk (unless it is real, of course) will not be appreciated. Instead, always include your informational communications with clear steps on what to do next (eg, "here's what we're seeing, here's what you may want to do"). Tactical tips are more useful to your clients than strategic advice.

4.6 Bring clients and peers together

Our current global climate has created a need for views from our peers in other respected companies. Simple events, such as for breakfast, lunch, dinner or a drink with five to six people, where your clients can benefit from the reassurance that they are not alone, and they will get cred for sharing 'prevailing views' when back at the office.

As the host, you can moderate the conversation and keep them away from any legal 'landmines' such as pricing or inside info.

5. Winning and keeping clients

You have all the puzzle pieces, now it is time to put them together, see the big picture and make it yours.

Trust and loyalty are paramount in your client relationships – know how to build and maintain them. Have a clear and full understanding of your client's pain points. Think outside of the box to adapt for these pain points, and make your client's work easier by providing transparent advice, consistent service and quality reporting.

Stay cognisant of how digital trends in all arenas impact your clients, and take steps to leverage digital to your advantage. Be informed of how your in-house peers and your competitors approach digital innovation. Regularly critique your own practices, keeping an eye on how to improve decision making within a world of geopolitical and economic uncertainty.

With some thinking outside of the box, a different perspective to client development, and a little hard work (with a bit of fun mixed in), you will reap the benefits of long-lasting client relationships.

Reputation management in professional service firms

William S Harvey
University of Exeter Business School
Timothy Morris
Michael Smets
Saïd Business School, University of Oxford

1. Introduction

Research in the field of management on the concept of reputation has drawn on several disciplines, including economics, sociology and psychology. Each discipline has contributed to the definitions of the concept that exist in management. For example, economics focuses on the relationship of reputation and firm performance, and sociology focuses on status and legitimacy of organisations in particular fields. The management literature has built upon these core disciplines to develop the concept of reputation in terms of quality, prominence (or familiarity) and in terms of esteem (or favourability) among a set of organisational stakeholders. The literature has also focused on the importance of both character reputation (focused around issues such as integrity or ethical conduct of an organisation) and capability reputation (the perceived quality and performance of an organisation).[1] There have also been important distinctions made between organisations that 'look good' and those that are 'being good'.[2]

2. Theoretical perspectives of reputation

There have been many attempts at defining reputation that suggest the concept has different perspectives. Rosa Chun has argued that there are three different schools of thought on reputation.[3] First, the

1 Mishina, Y, Block, ES and Mannor, MJ, "The Path Dependence of Organisational Reputation: How Social Judgment Influences Assessments of Capability and Character", *Strategic Management Journal*, Vol 33, No 5, 2012, pp459–477.

2 Chun, R, Argandoña, A, Choirat, C and Siegel, DS, "Corporate Reputation: Being Good and Looking Good", *Business & Society*, 58(6), 2019, pp1132–1142.

3 Chun, R, "Corporate Reputation: Meaning and Measurement", *International Journal of Management Reviews*, Vol 7, No 2, 2005, pp91–109.

Evaluative School where there is an emphasis on an organisation's financial performance. Secondly, the Impressional School that focuses on the overall impressions of an organisation. Thirdly, the Relational School explores the gaps between perceptions of internal and external stakeholders. Davide Ravasi *et al* refer to six perspectives.[4] First, Game-Theoretic, which reflects expectations about future behaviour. Secondly, Strategic, which argues reputation is an intangible asset that reflects the multidimensional and comparative evaluations of stakeholders. Thirdly, Macro-Cognitive, which refers to the socially constructed evaluation and prominence of organisations. Fourthly, Micro-Cognitive explains the individual comparative and evaluative judgements of organisations. Fifthly, Cultural-Sociological are the broad evaluations of organisations in relation to moral, technical or artistic criteria. Sixthly, Communicative is the broad evaluation of the actions of organisations.

3. Definitions and dimensions of reputation

It is generally agreed that there are three important attributes of reputation. First, it is based on the perception of organisations; secondly, it is based on the perceptions of internal and external stakeholders; and thirdly, it is a comparative measurement made in relation to competitors or the relevant peer group.[5] In the absence of a comparator group, stakeholders typically look to an organisation's past when reflecting on its current and future prospects. Reputations can be positive or negative, but are generally stable and enduring rather than changing with each event or new piece of information; although there have been some challenges to the notion that reputation is sticky, arguing that it can be more dynamic, especially in response to stakeholder expectations of change.[6] Others have argued that it is not feasible to talk of an aggregate reputation among a diverse set of stakeholders, because each stakeholder may have different concerns and ways of interpreting the focal firm's behaviour.[7] For instance, the firm could be highly profitable and viewed favourably

---

4 Ravasi, D, Rindova, V, Etter, M and Cornelissen, J, "The Formation of Organisational Reputation", *Academy of Management Annals*, 12(2), 2018, pp574–599.

5 Fombrun, CJ, *Reputation: Realizing Value from the Corporate Image*, 1996, Cambridge, MA: Harvard Business School Press.

6 Tetrault Sirsly, CA and Lvina, E, "From Doing Good to Looking Better: The Dynamics of CSR and Reputation", *Business & Society*, 58(6), 2019, pp1234–1266.

7 Harvey, WS, Tourky, M, Knight, E and Kitchen, P, "Lens or Prism? How Organisations Sustain Multiple and Competing Reputations", *European Journal of Marketing*, 51(4), 2017, pp821–844.

by investors but have a reputation as a tough employer and be viewed less favourably in the labour market. Therefore, reputation must be stakeholder-specific.[8] Charles Fombrun has proposed a definition of reputation which aims to address these points:

> *A corporate reputation is a collective assessment of a company's attractiveness to a specific group of stakeholders relative to a reference group of companies with which the company competes for resources.*[9]

Thus, reputation focuses on the distinctiveness of a focal organisation from others in its peer group and its attractiveness to external stakeholders.[10] Further, by focusing on attractiveness to stakeholders, this definition proposes that reputation is something which organisations project from within, but which is judged from the outside. It is a socio-cognitive concept based on peer group perceptions, or what is called a social fact[11] and the signals that an organisation sends are important for building reputation among external stakeholders.[12] Reputation reflects past behaviours or outcomes that are salient to stakeholders.[13] In other words, stakeholders are selective in the information they use and the inferences they make about that information based on what is salient for them (rather than what the firm deems as salient). Underlying this process of judgement, stakeholders assume that the present and future behaviour of a firm can be revealed by looking at its past performance (however defined). The notion that under conditions of imperfect information the past is a guide to the future explains why reputation is important.

Other work has noted that the concept of reputation incorporates different dimensions (see Table 1) and unfortunately there has

---

8 Jensen, M, Kim, H and Kim, BK, "Meeting Expectations: A Role-theoretic Perspective on Reputation" in Barnett, ML and Pollock, TG (eds), *The Oxford Handbook of Corporate Reputation*, 2012, Oxford: Oxford University Press, pp140–159.

9 Fombrun, CJ, "The Building Blocks of Corporate Reputation: Definitions, Antecedents, Consequences" in Barnett, ML and Pollock, TG (eds), *The Oxford Handbook of Corporate Reputation*, 2012, Oxford: Oxford University Press, pp94–113.

10 Bitektine, A, "Toward a Theory of Social Judgments of Organisations: The Case of Legitimacy, Reputation, and Status", *Academy of Management Review*, Vol 36, No 1, 2011, pp151–179.

11 Rindova, VP, Williamson, IO and Petkova, AP, "Reputation as an Intangible Asset: Reflections on Theory and Methods in Two Empirical Studies of Business School Reputations", *Journal of Management*, Vol 36, No 3, 2010, pp610–619.

12 Bergh, DD, Ketchen, DJ, Boyd, BK and Bergh, J, "New Frontiers of the Reputation – Performance Relationship: Insights from Multiple Theories", *Journal of Management*, Vol 36, No 3, 2010, pp620–632.

13 Velamuri, R, Venkataraman, S and Harvey, WS, "Seizing the Ethical High Ground: Ethical Reputation Building in Corrupt Environments", *Journal of Management Studies*, Vol 54, No 5, 2017, pp647–675.

been something of a proliferation of terms in defining these dimensions. Michael Barnett *et al* summarise the different ways in which reputation is defined by suggesting that stakeholders have three levels of engagement with reputation: reputation as a state of awareness, reputation as an assessment and reputation as an asset.[14] Awareness occurs when actors know of a focal organisation's name or logo, but make no judgement about its activities. Assessment implies more than awareness, as stakeholders judge the attributes or quality of the focal organisation. Asset refers to the proposition that a corporate reputation holds a particular value for the focal firm. Donald Lange *et al* summarise the definitional landscape in a way that substantially overlaps with the above typology, suggesting that being 'known', being 'known for something' and 'generalised favourability' are three significant dimensions for building reputation.[15] Being known refers to different stakeholders having familiarity with the activities, products and services of an organisation, and the reputation of the organisation tends to be stronger when different stakeholders have a broad awareness as well as a distinct understanding of its activities. This form of reputation is also referred to as prominence. Being known for something is when a particular aspect of the organisation is of interest or holds value for a stakeholder, and an organisation holds a reputation for something such as producing high-quality products. This form of reputation is referred to as quality. Generalised favourability is a broad assessment of the organisation based on multiple as opposed to specific attributes. These multiple attributes are aggregated into a single judgement, which varies depending on the stakeholder.

Violina Rindova *et al* compress the definition of reputation somewhat, proposing that there are essentially two dimensions that they call quality and prominence.[16] Perceived quality is defined as how stakeholders evaluate the particular attributes of organisations (similar to Lange *et al*'s concept of being known for something) and prominence is defined as a collective awareness and recognition

---

14 Barnett, M, Jermier, J and Lafferty, B, "Corporate Reputation: The Definitional Landscape", *Corporate Reputation Review*, Vol 9, No 1, 2006, pp26–38.

15 Lange, D, Lee, PM and Dai, Y, "Organisational Reputation: A Review", *Journal of Management*, Vol 37, No 1, 2011, pp153–184.

16 Rindova, VP, Williamson, IO, Petkova, AP and Sever, JM, "Being Good or Being Known: An Empirical Examination of the Dimensions, Antecedents, and Consequences of Organisational Reputation", *Academy of Management Journal*, Vol 48, No 6, 2005, pp1033–1049.

that an organisation has accumulated in its field (similar to Lange *et al*'s concept of being known).[17]

One issue which is pertinent to professional service firms (PSFs) is the level at which reputation is judged. It is clear that much of the work on reputation discusses corporate reputation, or the reputation of the overall organisation such as McKinsey & Company, Goldman Sachs or PwC. However, given the breadth and diversity of many large organisations and the multiple brands and different environments in which they operate, it is logical to disaggregate reputation under certain circumstances, notably where the core operating organisation is not closely associated with its parent, or where its brands are run autonomously from other parts of the organisation. GE or Coca Cola's multiple businesses might be a case in point. Furthermore, it is worth noting that brand represents the internal efforts to project a statement about the value or benefits of a product or service, which is sometimes referred to as intended image (what it wants others to think about it), but this is not the same as reputation, which is based on what stakeholder actually thinks about the organisation.[18]

For PSFs, which are often a relatively loose confederation of different practices and driven by the expertise, efforts and connections of individual partners, the notion of a unitary corporate reputation may therefore make little sense to their clients. Indeed, it can be argued that PSFs are essentially built by the interaction of individual and corporate reputations. Partners win business with their professional teams based on their own market reputations but are aided by the reputation of their firm; in turn, the firm's reputation is sustained by the actions of its individual partners and their teams. The dynamics of this interaction will depend on how far the firm is internally integrated, shares work and projects a unified image.

Finally, it is worth noting that reputation is closely linked to other social evaluation concepts.[19] For example, status is based on

---

17 See also Rindova, VP, Williamson, IO and Petkova, AP, "Reputation as an Intangible Asset: Reflections on Theory and Methods in Two Empirical Studies of Business School Reputations", *Journal of Management*, Vol 36, No 3, 2010, pp610–619.

18 Brown, TJ, Dacin, PA, Pratt, MG and Whetten, DA, "Identity, intended image, construed image, and reputation: An interdisciplinary framework and suggested terminology", *Journal of the Academy of Marketing Science*, Vol 34, No 2, 2006, pp99–106.

19 Pollock, TG, Lashley, K, Rindova, VP and Han, JH, "Which of These Things Are Not Like the Others? Comparing the Rational, Emotional, and Moral Aspects of Reputation, Status, Celebrity, and Stigma", *Academy of Management Annals*, Vol 13, No 2, 2019, pp444–478.

possession of desirable or socially approved attributes and the status of an organisation is defined by how closely it can demonstrate those appropriate attributes. Such attributes might include where a corporation's stock is listed or with whom it is associated. Indeed, status is frequently generated by association with others who already have some form of status, such as by doing business with high-status partners, by having high-status advisers or bankers and by hiring high-status directors. Status is somewhat different from the concept of reputation insofar as it is based on similarity or convergence around a set of attributes rather than positive difference, which is at the heart of a strong reputation. However, the concept of status is extremely useful because it emphasises how reputation is not simply built on the actions of the focal organisation, but is influenced by the way in which intermediaries, recommenders or connectors provide information about it to external parties. Again, incomplete information is key here: in such circumstances, these third parties are filling in the gaps by summarising relevant information and offering judgements to others about the reputation of the organisation. Another important social evaluation construct is celebrity, which describes the strong emotional responses an organisation evokes from the public,[20] often because they wish to identify with that organisation; but like with reputation, celebrity can be positive and negative,[21] and can be strongly influenced by social and mass media.

In light of different definitions and dimensions of reputation (and related constructs), our working definition of reputation is:

Comparative evaluations by different stakeholders based on the prominence, favourability, perceived qualities, character and potential future contribution of organisations.

3. Reputation in professional service firms

'Reputation' and 'quality' are often assumed to be one and the same in relation to PSFs. We set out to test this assumption by exploring how far reputation of the firm was matched by the quality of projects in a leading international management consultancy and found that the reputation of the firm by no means necessarily aligns

20 Rindova, VP, Pollock, TG and Hayward, ML, "Celebrity firms: The social construction of market popularity", *Academy of Management Review*, Vol 31, No 1, 2006, pp50–71.

21 Zavyalova, A, Pfarrer, MD and Reger, RK, "Celebrity and infamy? The consequences of media narratives about organisational identity", *Academy of Management Review*, Vol 42, No 3, 2017, pp461–480.

Table 1. Summarising the reputation terminology and our definition

Chun (2005)	*Evaluative School.* The evaluation of an organisation's financial performance. *Impressional School.* The overall impression of an organisation. *Relational School.* The gaps between perceptions of internal and external stakeholders.
Rindova *et al* (2005)	*Perceived quality.* How stakeholders evaluate a particular organisational attribute. *Prominence.* Collective awareness and recognition that an organisation has accumulated in its organisational field. *Favourability.* Not defined.
Barnett *et al* (2006)	*Awareness.* Individuals know about organisations, but make no judgement about their activities. *Assessment.* Stakeholders' judgement of the attributes or qualities of organisations. *Asset.* The proposition that reputation holds a particular value for organisations.
Rindova *et al* (2007)[22]	*Quality.* Not defined. *Prominence.* Not defined. *Favourability.* More difficult to build than visibility and therefore potentially more valuable.[23]

continued on next page

22 Rindova, VP, Petkova, AP and Kotha, S, "Standing Out: How New Firms in Emerging Markets Build Reputation", *Strategic Organisation*, Vol 5, No 1, 2007, pp31–70.

23 See also Greenwood, R, Li, SX, Prakash, R and Deephouse, DL, "Reputation, Diversification, and Organizational Explanations of Performance in Professional Service Firms", *Organization Science*, Vol 16, No 6, 2005, pp661–673.

Lange *et al* (2011)	*Being known for something.* When different stakeholders are familiar with the activities, products and services of an organisation. *Being known.* When a certain organisational attribute holds particular interest or value for different stakeholders. *Generalised favourability.* A broad comparative assessment of an organisation based on multiple attributes which are aggregated into one single judgement.
Ravasi *et al* (2018)	*Game-Theoretic.* Expectations about future behaviour. *Strategic.* Intangible asset that reflects the multidimensional and comparative evaluations of stakeholders. *Macro-Cognitive.* The socially constructed evaluation and prominence of organisations. *Micro-Cognitive.* Individual comparative and evaluative judgements of organisations. *Cultural-Sociological.* Broad evaluations in relation to moral, technical or artistic criteria. *Communicative.* Broad evaluation of the actions of organisations.
Pollock *et al* (2019)	*Rational.* Reputation's sociocognitive content is mainly rational. *Emotional.* Good and bad reputations can create positive or negative emotions. *Moral.* Some stakeholders are focused on morals when considering reputation.
Our definition	Comparative evaluations by different stakeholders based on the prominence, favourability, perceived qualities, character and potential future contribution of organisations.

with quality. Not only is the relationship between reputation and quality uncertain in management consultancies, the process of building and sustaining reputation is complex and various. It is a process of overriding importance to both consultancies and clients, and demands to be better understood and carefully managed.

4. The relationship between reputation and quality in PSFs

4.1 Reputation matters to firm and client alike

To date, most of the evidence used to analyse issues of reputation and quality has focused on consumer products where reputation is strongly aligned with the actual physical quality of the product. However, the role of reputation in the professional service sector, where judgements of quality are far harder to make at all stages (ie, before, during and after a service has been delivered), is much more complicated. The 'products' in PSFs consist of complex, customised solutions devised for clients who themselves are often required to play a key collaborative role in helping create them. This coupling of the service provider and the client makes judgements of quality difficult.

Beyond this there are other uncertainties. One is the lack of institutional standards in the profession, such as legal regulation, fee rates and necessary qualifications. Another is 'transactional uncertainty'. This refers to the way in which 'experience goods' cannot be inspected, compared or controlled for quality by the client in advance. In choosing between competing professional service organisations, therefore, the client often has to fall back on other signals, notably reputation.

Reputation is important in other ways for PSFs, in that it helps guarantee a continuing flow of business. Professional service clients experience a high degree of risk at the point of purchase and they often have to defend their choices to others. Choosing reputable providers and turning to them for repeat work helps to reduce some of that risk for clients. Hence, clients will be tempted to repeat purchases with a highly regarded PSF because this reduces the uncertainty of switching to an untried and untested firm.

In addition, reputation plays an important role in PSFs' own labour market. The work of PSFs involves delivering knowledge-intensive services, whose knowledge is embedded in professional staff and delivered through individuals and teams of employees interacting with clients. Hiring and retaining professional staff of the appropriate quality is therefore critical to the competitiveness of

PSFs, especially as such members of staff are relatively mobile. Elite professional service firms typically seek to hire employees from elite universities because the universities' reputation is a marker of high quality.

In short, reputation matters a great deal for both PSFs and their clients. This is broadly accepted, but how reputation is formed and what specific aspects of reputation are particularly critical in choosing PSFs are little understood. The received view rests on two untested assumptions, both of which merit challenge: first, that reputation and service quality are identical; and secondly, that a PSF's reputation is the same for all its stakeholders.

4.2 Quality is an uncertain quantity

As noted above, the general assumption seems to be that reputation is built through consistently delivering high-quality services. Once a firm's reputation is established, so the thinking goes, there are spillover effects that it can exploit in new practice areas that, if successfully developed, can further generate or consolidate its reputation. The process can be summarised in Figure 1.

However, before accepting this model at face value, a number of qualifications need to be made. Reputation is most strictly applicable in situations when transactions of the same kind are repeated. Even then, reputation is only relevant if processes are the

Figure 1. The interaction of reputation and project quality

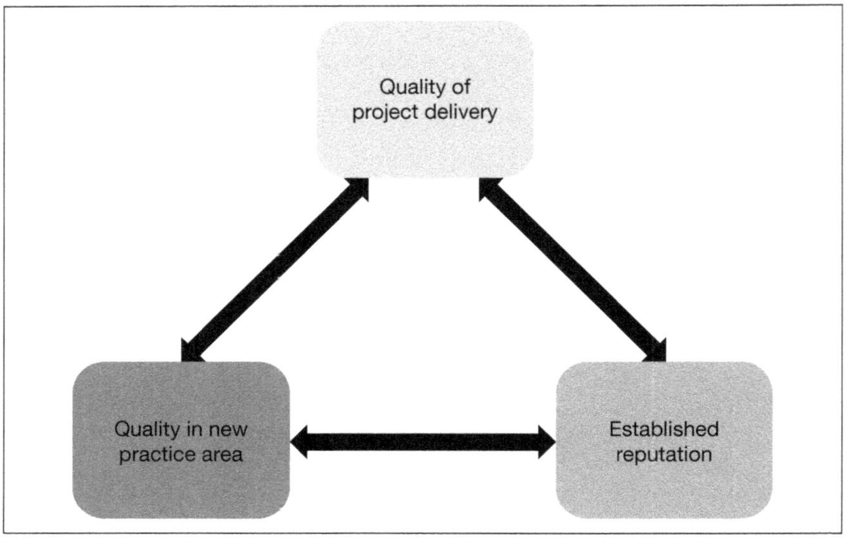

same across all transactions, and, unlike in many product-based organisations, in the case of PSFs, no project is ever exactly the same as another in aims, content, delivery or personnel. This raises the question of whether perceived quality in one project is similar to perceived quality in another, particularly if different clients are judging quality.

Overall, there are two main dimensions to service quality. The first is 'technical quality', which refers to the core service of what is being delivered. The second is 'functional quality', which refers to how the service is delivered. The quality of what is delivered may be very different from how it is delivered, but the two dimensions are not mutually exclusive and each affects how clients perceive the quality of the other.

The distinction between the two dimensions matters, however, because they demand different skills. Technical competency depends on firms applying their core knowledge and skills to deliver tangible results to clients. Functional competency depends far more on interpersonal skills, style of delivery and expectation management. In both cases, managing relationships is essential, and regular communication between the service provider and the client is important for instilling trust and reducing the risk of failure in the relationship. This is particularly important because the expectations of clients regarding their service providers will change over the life of the project.

In transactions with PSFs, clients are exposed to considerable risks in terms of the confidentiality, integrity and commitment of a consultant. Keeping promises has therefore been singled out as the most important aspect of engagement success. Relationships between PSFs and clients demand empathy, responsiveness and reliability – with reliability often cited as the most important dimension.

5. Choosing a professional service provider: the interplay of networks, trust and knowledge

Three factors are of overriding importance in helping build reputation among PSF stakeholders: networks, trust and knowledge.

5.1 Networks are key

Client and employee alumni networks can result in significant financial returns. According to one survey of management consultancy firms across three different countries, some 80% to 85% of their fees resulted from such networks. Networks not only generate positive word-of-mouth, or peer recommendations, but are even more important when one takes into account clients' tendency to repeat purchases and their resistance to competitive offers. However, while the importance of networks is generally accepted, the interaction between reputation and trust is less well understood.

5.2 Two types of trust

As noted, projects within the professional service sector are particularly difficult for clients to evaluate. How do consumers not trained in law, for instance, know whether they actually received the best legal advice? As a result, clients have to rely heavily on their trust in the service provider. This is what Glückler and Armbrüster refer to as experience-based trust and a mechanism that they label as networked reputation.[24] There are two important types of trust that management consultancies need to nurture: 'competence trust', which rests on the service provider possessing the necessary qualifications, skills and capabilities to fulfil a particular task; and 'goodwill trust', which turns on the moral and ethical commitment of service providers not to behave opportunistically and is therefore similar to the character dimension of reputation.

Competence trust is more one-sided and easier to signal and recognise, whereas goodwill trust is more reciprocal and therefore involves the motives and actions of both parties. Clients may trust a firm to deliver a high-quality project, but not necessarily that it will treat its information confidentially. Moreover, different projects demand different types of trust. Clients may be more interested in competence trust in short-term strategy projects than long-term cost-cutting projects, where they may be more interested in goodwill trust.

The relationship between trust and reputation is problematic in other ways. A client may be well satisfied with how a management consultancy has used its confidential information on a particular strategy project, and this will help to instil trust; however, this is only the first step. The firm needs to exhibit consistent behaviour over time in different projects with key individuals to build this form of reputation on a solid basis.

24 Glückler, J and Armbrüster, T, "Bridging Uncertainty in Management Consulting: The Mechanisms of Trust and Networked Reputation", *Organisation Studies*, Vol 24, No 2, 2003, pp269–297.

5.3 Knowledge trade-offs

Clients' choices of management consultancies and other providers are influenced not only by networks and the types of trust they inspire, but also by the type of knowledge involved in the project. This is particularly important as the knowledge requirements of clients is rapidly evolving. Projects which demand a greater degree of client-specific and client-intensive knowledge tend to be placed with existing consultants. This is not to say that clients are not open to working with new management consultants, but there is a strong preference towards using consultants with whom they have established business relationships when the project involves sensitive information. In contrast, in projects that are more functional and industry-specific, clients often prefer to use external consultants with whom they hold looser business relationships. In short, the type of knowledge that a particular project entails and the politics of the project have important implications.

When clients are reaching decisions about which management consultants to use, they often have to make trade-off choices between the type of knowledge and the level of confidentiality. If they are less concerned about innovative knowledge, but confidentiality is a key factor, they will err on the side of using established consultants and prefer 'goodwill trust'. In contrast, when clients are more concerned about innovative knowledge and confidentiality is not so important, they will err on the side of using new consultants and prefer 'competency trust'. The process can be summarised in Table 2.

Table 2. Client criteria for choosing a consulting firm

Choice of management consultants	Established management consultants	New management consultants
Type of knowledge	Less innovative/ routine knowledge	More innovative knowledge
Level of confidentiality	High	Low
Political nature	Sensitive	Uncontroversial
Form of trust	Goodwill trust	Competency trust

To an extent, therefore, clients could be said to act rationally in their choices of management consultancies. But in other ways they appear to be driven by other criteria such as internal political pressures or risk aversion. This is one of the reasons why clients typically rely on other criteria, in particular reputation, as a signal of quality and appropriateness.

In order to study the significance of reputation and the process of reputation formation across different competencies and stakeholder groups, we looked at a global management consultancy, examining offices in various countries and markets, and interviewing clients, key intermediaries, employees and alumni.

6. Findings

Below and in Figure 2 we summarise nine key considerations that PSFs must keep in mind when it comes to how reputation is developed, leveraged and transmitted.

Figure 2. Reputation management in professional service firms

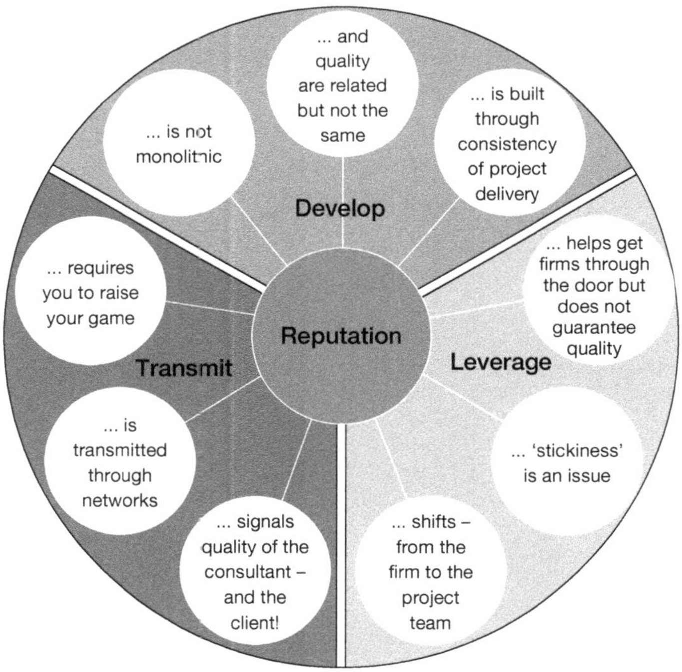

6.1 Reputation is not monolithic

Consultancies have multiple reputations. Firms' reputations not only vary widely among clients and potential clients, but even, we found, within the consultancy itself. Even its own employees' assessments of functional expertise, quality and reputation varied significantly, and they identified a wide variety of different reputations based on factors such as office location, the respondents' area of expertise or their positions in the company.

6.2 Reputation and quality are related but not the same

While reputation and quality share similar characteristics, they are not the same. Reputation is the judgement of a firm's ability to deliver future value among a wider group of stakeholders. Quality is the impression among clients of the service that has been provided to them by the firm in the past.

6.3 Reputation is built through consistency of project delivery

The consistency of project delivery is an important bridge between quality and reputation. Consistency encompasses both predictability for the client on a particular transaction and similarity of standards across different projects. The view of the quality of project delivery by the firm, particularly in its core markets, was not always consistent in all its international offices. Although the firm's reputation for particular projects was very strong across a range of clients, this was not the case among all clients and for all competencies. Consequently, clients often received mixed signals across different jurisdictions about what to expect from the firm. Resolving these differences in perceived quality to ensure consistent delivery is essential.

6.4 Reputation helps get firms through the door but does not guarantee quality

A strong reputation undoubtedly helps consultancies get to the starting line in the race to win a project. Both internal and external stakeholders frequently referred to the tendering process as a 'beauty contest', implying that invited participants need a minimum reputation simply to be considered. However, once a certain level of reputation is reached, the quality of particular projects is not considered because it is assumed that if a firm has an excellent reputation then it must be delivering high-quality projects. Consequently, firms with strong reputations do not need to exceed the expectations of clients and may be evaluated more generously by buyers.

6.5 Reputation 'stickiness' is an issue

One problem with transferring reputation from the firm to a specific project team is 'reputation stickiness', whereby clients are unable or unwilling to transfer reputation from one type of work to another until they are clear that the firm holds an established position in that service line. In cases of uncertainty, clients will tend to opt for firms who have established reputations in those areas to minimise risk. Or they look for other forms of evidence of quality in those areas, for instance high-profile and relevant thought leadership in reputable outlets.

6.6 Reputation shifts – from the firm to the project team

Reputation is important, but during the tendering process potential clients become more interested in the potential quality of the project. At this stage the focus of the firm's reputation shifts significantly from the firm to the project team. Clients not only focus on how their project needs tally with what the consultancy is proposing in terms of the process of addressing the project goals, but also whether the experience and skills of the firm's proposed project team fit with the needs of the project.

The seniority of the consulting team is an important proxy for skill and experience. Consulting firms with weaker reputations often have to allocate more senior and expensive consultants than those consulting firms with stronger reputations. In turn, this affects the relative profitability of the consultancies, with the more reputable firms able to generate greater profits per assignment on average. Higher profitability in turn also attracts higher-quality staff who see the opportunity for greater earnings from higher profits, thus setting in motion a virtuous circle arising from reputation in both labour and client markets. Service providers need to manage their teams carefully because discerning clients are keen that they have the right level of experience ('grey hairs') on their projects.

6.7 Reputation signals quality of the consultant – and the client!

Some clients select a management consultancy on the basis of their reputation for expertise in a particular type of work rather than what they deliver, because they want to signal to a range of stakeholders such as board members, asset managers and the media that they are taking a particular issue seriously by hiring a market leader. Often clients also need to validate their own policies or proposals or obtain an insurance stamp in case problems crop up later. This tactic has been termed reputation borrowing.[25]

6.8 Reputation is transmitted through networks

The relationship between consultant and client may transcend the purely commercial relationships and become a strong personal relationship. This is important not only in generating repeat work from the client, but also in referrals. Consultants and clients both agreed that strong referral networks are important for securing projects, and some even felt that reputation built through these networks is a more decisive factor than quality when clients are deciding which firm to choose for a project. Networks can help overcome a lack of information and experience in selecting a competent supplier. In this regard, the reputation of the network connecting the client and the consulting firm acts as a critical factor in selection.

6.9 Reputation requires you to raise your game

Both clients and the consultancy employees agreed on the rising expectations of clients. Many clients had previously worked in the management consultancy sector and therefore had an intimate understanding of the industry and what they can realistically expect in terms of price, consultancy team and quality. However, firms who had extensive alumni networks had an advantage because they had established strong ties with clients and potential clients. This has important implications for reputation as it implies the assumed uncertainty problem, whereby clients find it difficult to judge the quality or performance of PSFs with whom they interact, is diminishing. Yet, given that clients are more knowledgeable, firms need to raise their game and live up to the higher expectations of their clients in order to maintain their reputation.

7. The lessons

In practice, quality and reputation are by no means aligned. One consequence is that firms with strong reputations, for instance, can get away with poorer-quality service, and a strong reputation can buffer firms against mistakes. In contrast, firms with weaker

---

25 Petkova, AP, "From the Ground Up: Building Young Firms' Reputations" in Barnett, ML and Pollock, TG (eds), *The Oxford Handbook of Corporate Reputation*, 2012, Oxford University Press, Oxford, pp383–401.

reputations not only have to work harder but often over-deliver on the quality of projects. This can have the unintended consequence for firms of coming across as needy. That said, quality and reputation can also diverge due to the conflicting interests of clients (who are looking for both high quality and low costs from consultancy firms) and consultancies (who are looking for high returns from their clients who are sufficiently satisfied with the quality of work).

There can be damaging repercussions for consultancies whose reputation does not keep pace with their quality of service. Our subject firm experienced great difficulties winning bids against competitors, even though the client considered them in certain contexts as delivering the best quality, because other competitors had a stronger reputation for a wider range of expertise. Firms with strong reputations are theoretically able to expand into practice areas in which they are not necessarily strong, while firms with less-strong reputations cannot diversify either so widely or successfully. One consequence is that firms with less-strong reputations may lose the opportunity to bid for larger projects in which several practices are involved.

Building and sustaining reputation is a many-sided, open-ended activity and demands continuous, sophisticated management. Consultancies need to decide exactly what reputation and, more specifically, what aspects of reputation they wish to communicate, and then clearly project these to both their internal and external stakeholders through the three interrelated channels of signalling, networks and client relationships. Consultancies also need to focus on the functional as well as the technical aspects of their projects – the 'how' as well as the 'why' and the 'what'. Trust and knowledge are key. So, in parallel with this they need to develop trust of two different kinds: 'competence trust' and 'goodwill trust'. And, on an individual basis, project by project, partners and their teams must ensure they apply the types and levels of knowledge demanded by clients.

How to merge: lessons from 20 years of law firm mergers

Lisa R Smith
Fairfax Associates

1. Introduction

The legal industry continues to consolidate. *The American Lawyer*'s 2019 Global 100 (October 2019) included 23 firms with more than 2,000 lawyers and 57 firms with over 1,000 lawyers. One firm is approaching 10,000 lawyers. Many of these firms have completed at least one merger as part of their growth strategy and in several cases the firms themselves have been created as a result of a substantial merger. In fact five of the 10 largest firms in the Global 100 have completed significant cross-border mergers.

Of course, many firms smaller than these global powerhouses have also completed mergers, further contributing to the consolidation of the legal market.

Despite the multitude of mergers over the last two decades, the legal market remains much less consolidated than other professional service sectors. The top 10 investment banks, accounting firms and advertising agencies hold a much greater share of their overall markets than the top 10 law firms do of the legal market. While there are some natural barriers to consolidation in the legal industry – conflicts being chief among them – it is likely that the market will continue to consolidate for the foreseeable future.

While law firm mergers have become increasingly common, the outcomes of mergers are decidedly more varied. Many have been successful, while some have been spectacularly unsuccessful (to the point of firm dissolution). Some have exceeded expectations, while others have had little impact on the overall competitiveness of the combined firm. Our experience, having consulted on many mergers over the last two decades, indicates that there are two key variables to predict success in mergers. The first is the strength of the business case for the merger. The second is the effectiveness of execution and integration (see Figure 1). A weak business case for merger is unlikely to succeed even with flawless execution.

Figure 1. The key variables for successful mergers

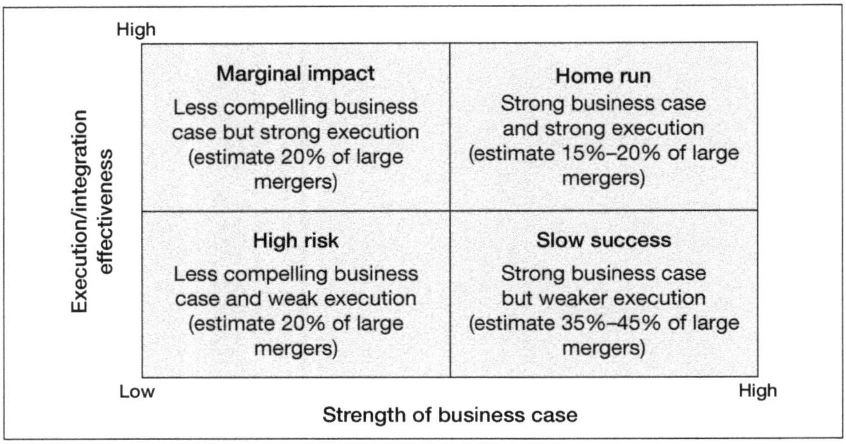

Likewise, we have seen some combinations with very strong business cases take much longer to reach their full potential because execution was weak or an afterthought.

This chapter will address both of these dimensions, as well as the key strategic drivers of mergers and the effective management of the merger process. While the focus is on mergers, many of the principles can be applied to large lateral groups as well.

2. Why merge?

The answer to the question 'Why merge?' is actually quite simple. A merger between two firms must improve competitiveness in pursuit of specific strategic objectives. A merger is a way to execute a firm's strategy. Of course, there are nuances to the simple answer and a range of reasons why firms pursue mergers.

2.1 Build geographic capability

Building geographic capability is one driver of mergers and is particularly relevant for cross-border mergers. In fact our analysis of large mergers indicates that geography is the primary or at least secondary driver of the majority of mergers. Leading companies are continuing to build their business around the world. The global economic balance of countries is shifting and will continue to shift, with emerging market economies overtaking many Western market economies over the next several decades. This dynamic creates a need for global law firms, and perhaps ones that look different to the current set of global firms.

The first question a firm needs to answer is how or if a new jurisdiction will help build competitive strength. That competitive strength could come from a number of sources – does it help you provide services that are or could be demanded by your current clients? Would it build on a particular industry or practice strength that would allow you significantly to raise your profile and attract new clients? Is it a critical jurisdiction in your network?

It is also useful to think about the question from the defensive perspective. What are the competitive disadvantages of not pursuing a global strategy or not being in a particular jurisdiction? Will having only a domestic presence limit the work the firm will be considered for? Is this work that the firm could realistically expect to compete for with a presence in a new jurisdiction?

It is important to remember that not all firms have a client base or practice mix that requires a multi-jurisdictional presence. Some mergers have failed to meet expectations because opportunities for the two legacy firms to work together, whether across state lines or across oceans, simply did not exist. For those firms that do require a broader domestic or a global platform, a merger can be an effective way to build that capability.

2.2 Build practice and industry depth

Building practice and industry depth is another key driver of mergers. Most companies with significant legal needs are sophisticated buyers of legal services. They are increasingly buying legal services on the basis of specialist expertise and deep knowledge of the business that can be applied to their specific legal problem. The ability to access public information on firm expertise and success has accelerated this trend. Quality of legal services is not a differentiator, but a given. Merger can be a way to build practice depth and to solidify both firms' presence in one or more industry sectors, allowing the combined firm to be a 'known for' firm in the area.

Similar to the geographic dimension, the first question that needs to be asked in the context of a merger is how combining practices will build competitive strength. Do the two firms have practices which, when combined, will create or have the potential to create a market-leading practice? Or will the combined practices simply be larger, but still lack the critical mass to be competitive in the market? Do the firms bring complementary practices that can realistically be offered to clients? Would the combined firm increase its profile in key industry sectors? Would this industry profile add value to clients in that sector and attract new clients?

2.3 Grow with clients

Ultimately, a merger must be driven by the needs of the firm's current and future clients. If a client's business has grown rapidly, a firm may find that it no longer has either the depth of experience or the breadth of practice to adequately serve the needs of that client. A merger that brings breadth and depth can help better serve (and retain) the client. It also gives the combined firm the opportunity to displace other firms on the client's approved list.

When two firms have clients in common it can help both the client and the firm. Many clients are looking to reduce the number of outside counsel with whom they work. Combining work in one firm can help them achieve this. It also helps the firm increase its ties to the client and solidifies the relationship.

2.4 Build scale

While bigger is not necessarily better, there can be benefits to scale in a law firm. Larger firms tend to have better-known brands. They are more likely to have one or more leading practices, and these practices can create a halo effect for lesser-known practices. Further, larger and better-known firms may be seen as a 'safe choice' for matters that rise to the board level.

Increased scale also brings internal advantages, including the ability to make investments, be it in technology, process innovation, marketing initiatives or talent additions. In addition, there can be economies of scale when it comes to costs. While there may be short-term costs associated with a merger, over the longer term the cost base of the firm can be reduced.

2.5 Address internal issues

Finally, there are some internal factors that can contribute to a firm looking at merger. While internal factors should not be a primary driver of mergers, they can be factors that cause firms to consider merger more seriously. Some firms find that a merger is a viable way to address leadership and succession issues in the firm. A firm may find that there is no one interested in or capable of taking over the leadership role in the firm. This is not uncommon in closely held founder firms. In considering a merger of this type it is important to ensure there will be an adequate transition and that the clients are likely to survive the retirement of the founding partner or partners.

Mergers can also be a catalyst for change. Some firms find that while they know they need to make certain structural changes in the firm – for example, change the partner structure, eliminate an unfunded retirement plan, close an office – they do not have the fortitude or stability to make those changes as a stand-alone firm. A merger can present the opportunity to move the firm forward and make long-needed changes.

3. Building a business case for merger

Once the question "Why merge?" has been answered, it is critical to build the business case for a specific merger. First and foremost, the discipline of building the business case helps to ensure that a strong case actually exists. Sometimes it is easier to talk about the mechanics of merger than the strategy, so it is not unheard of for discussions to progress to a term sheet without having taken more than a superficial look at the business case.

Secondly, it is critical to be able to articulate the business case for the merger to various audiences during the course of discussions and after the announcement of the merger. Leaders need to build support and enthusiasm from the firm's partners by explaining the business case. Partners need to be able to explain to their clients why the merger makes sense. The chairman needs to be able to explain the rationale for the combined firm to the press and to the marketplace. Associates and staff need to understand what opportunities the combined firm will create for them.

Finally, merger discussions can fall apart when inadequate time is spent on developing the business case, because the negotiating team can lose enthusiasm when the discussions hit the first hurdle if the ultimate objective is not clearly understood and articulated.

The business case for merger starts with a clear strategy for the firm. The strategy should focus primarily on the firm's desired market position, the basis for the firm's competitiveness and differentiation in the marketplace and the firm's target client base. The strategy should also address internal factors, including talent management priorities and cultural underpinnings. A merger is a way to execute the strategy, not a strategy in and of itself. The strategic underpinnings of a business case become more complex in the context of merger because the merger needs to align with the strategy of two different firms.

The business case must address not only the current position of the combined firm, but the likely position in the evolving market. The market is moving too quickly to create a firm that is only competitive today. The firm must be competitive on a going-forward basis as well.

Key components of the business case generally include:

- Strategic aims for the combined firm:
  - basis of competitiveness;
  - market position, including future position;
  - core practices and industry sectors.
- Key practice opportunities:
  - creation of market-leading practices;
  - additional depth in core practices;
  - addition of complementary practices.
- Key client opportunities:
  - opportunities to expand the relationship with existing clients through additional services, deeper services, or new geography;
  - opportunities to gain new work (including capturing recent lost opportunities);
  - potential business conflicts which will impact growth of certain practices.
- Key geographic compatibilities:
  - market position in key markets;
  - impact of expanded geography;
  - potential markets for the combined firm.
- Financial profile and opportunities:
  - key performance indicators and projected performance of the combined firm;
  - merger-related synergies and costs.
- Risks and obstacles:
  - key risk factors;
  - potential barriers to success.

The development of the business case will typically be an iterative process. The initial case will be developed in early meetings. Detail will be added as practice groups meet, as pro formas are developed, and as client opportunities are identified. It is important to step back periodically to ensure that the case is still as strong as initially thought, and to communicate that strength to the partners.

4. Effective management of the merger process

Managing the merger process is critical. Unlike a corporate merger, where the discussions and negotiations take place at the top levels and are announced to the employees and the market when it is a done deal, mergers of law firms must build support among the partners from the early stages. Not only is it important that the partners are onboard with the merger in order to achieve an effective integration, but from a more practical standpoint a majority of partners, and in some firms as many as 80% of partners, must approve the combination.

While this chapter will not address the full scope of the merger process, there are four key aspects to focus on that can help to ensure a smooth process.

4.1 Plan the process

Not surprisingly, planning the process and the timetable is the critical first step. This includes identifying the key steps required in the different workstreams, setting the merger teams and sub-teams, and establishing a desired target effective date.

The value of the planning process is that it helps to ensure that all involved recognise at the outset the scope and scale of the issues that need to be agreed, and to manage expectations among those directly involved in the discussions and the partnership at large. While discussions rarely go entirely according to plan, the merger plan can establish the framework for moving forward. Planning also helps to ensure that both firms have similar expectations of timing. If one has a greater sense of urgency than the other, both will likely be frustrated.

4.2 Be realistic about effort and resources

In our experience there is an almost universal underestimation of the effort and resources required to complete a merger. This can be in part related to the time required to resolve unanticipated issues, but in the main tends to be related to the underlying complexity of merging law firms and the breadth of issues that need to be addressed. The time and commitment required to complete a merger are considerable. Those involved must be able to give sufficient priority to the role or there is a high risk that the talks will drag on too long, enthusiasm and momentum will be lost and eventually the process will stall entirely.

The time commitment will vary with the role a person is playing in the process, and the size and complexity of the merger. The managing partner and/or chairman typically needs to be prepared to devote half or more of his or her time to the process at key stages.

Because of the time commitment required, merger discussions are not something to be entered into lightly. Protracted discussions can distract the management team from other strategic initiatives and can result in the firm treading water for a period of time.

4.3 Anticipate and address hurdles

Hurdles and challenges are likely to arise during merger discussions. The stronger the business case and the relationship between the two firms, the more likely it is that solutions will be found. As with all aspects of negotiations, the primary consideration in addressing such challenges should be maximising the competitiveness of the new firm rather than adopting the approach of one or the other firm. This is particularly true if the merged firm will be competing in a market position and be of a scale that is very different from that of either legacy firm.

There is sometimes a temptation to defer addressing some issues until after the merger has taken place. While that can be appropriate for some issues, it is important that not too many substantive issues are deferred. The drawback of deferring is that the merged firm starts life with an overly introverted focus – addressing internal issues of organisation and structure, or profit sharing or management roles – rather than being focused on the far more important issues of serving existing clients, winning new work for the combined firm and creating opportunities for lawyers to work together.

4.4 Keep the partnership informed

Considerations such as the scale of a firm, its culture and the impact of the potential merger will influence the level and detail of communication between the firm's management and the partnership during merger discussions. Experience has shown that in most circumstances it is more effective to keep a partnership informed of progress as discussions proceed and to seek partners' input, endorsement and commitment on a step-by-step basis rather than attempting to 'sell' what may be regarded by partners as a done deal. Keeping the partnership informed and consulting as appropriate requires significant time from firm leadership, but results in the case for merger being tested throughout the process and builds partner commitment.

While each firm is different, some firm leaders have found it important to have key influencers involved in the merger discussions from an early stage. This includes those who are potentially sceptical of the combination, as their early involvement in and support for the business case can be crucial for gaining overall partner support. At a minimum the sceptics and key influencers may require additional attention and communication during the merger discussions.

5. Merger structure and impact on business case and process

Historically, law firm mergers were expected to be fully integrated and to replicate the model that would have been obtained had the firm grown organically. More recently, and particularly in the context of cross-border mergers, an increasing number of firms have adopted firm structures that facilitate cross-jurisdiction combinations. These are typically a 'Swiss verein' structure, although other forms exist as well. A verein firm effectively operates like a holding company with member firms. While the verein is governed by a board under an 'advise and consent' type arrangement, the member firms are separate financial entities and can have their own management structure and compensation arrangements. In fact, sharing of profits is prohibited, although sharing of expenses and joint ventures is permitted. Some vereins are highly integrated while others are quite loosely integrated and allow significant autonomy to the member firms. Some have two member firms, while others have many.

A verein can certainly ease some of the challenges that impact cross-border combinations. It facilitates combinations of firms that may have different fiscal years, different tax and accounting methodologies or that operate in jurisdictions with very different financial models. It is also easier to defer the resolution of some issues (eg, a common approach to compensation), as they are not required for the firms to begin operating on a side-by-side basis.

Regardless of the structure a firm might take, it is important to approach the development of the business case with rigour. While there may be less immediate financial interdependence in a verein structure, there will certainly be brand interdependence. The strategy of the combined firm and the relative market positions of the member firms must be largely aligned in order to facilitate cross-servicing and cross-selling of clients. The approach to client service and the underlying culture of the firms must be compatible to facilitate strong working relationships. The financial strength is important, even with separate profit centres, because instability in one segment of the firm could be problematic for the whole firm. And comparable financial strength will be critical should the firm move to closer financial alignment at some point.

While there is a set of issues that are verein-specific, such as the financial structure, the governing approach and structure at the global level, and even branding, we recommend that firms which are considering merger under a verein structure discuss and address the same issues that firms contemplating a fully integrated structure would be addressing.

6. Keys to effective merger execution

The key to effective merger integration is to ensure a balance between client, practice and people integration and administrative and structural integration. Too often the administrative integration becomes the primary focus, and the client, practice and people side is left to its own devices. While the firm may ultimately achieve its expected objectives, it is likely to take five years instead of two. The true success of the merger will not be measured by the immediate compatibility of the billing system, but instead by the ability to deliver on the potential identified in the business case. This can include, for example, delivering on a competitive strength, delivering integrated services to clients across jurisdictions and winning new work.

Throughout the integration it is important to keep the majority of the lawyers focused on continuing to serve clients. The merger should enhance client service, not distract from it, and client perceptions can be formed in those early days.

This chapter will not address the full scope of the merger execution and integration but will focus on the three aspects we find to be the most critical to success.

6.1 Plan the process

As with the merger process, effective planning of merger integration is critical. It helps to establish the roadmap and expectations, as well as allow the leadership of the firm to delegate where appropriate and focus on the most value-added initiatives. Too often leadership gets caught up in the minutiae and then does not have adequate time to address the important issues. This is not meant to diminish the importance of getting the small things right, but the big things will be the ones that make the long-term difference.

The starting point for developing the merger integration plan is to establish the gap between where the combined firm will be on day one, and where it would like to be at key future points – six months, one year, two years and three years. Taking this approach, as opposed to focusing on the immediate steps that need to be achieved in the first 90 days, ensures a longer-range outlook and plan. Of course, there are aspects of the plan, particularly the administrative integration plan, which will have to be planned out week-by-week in the early stages; but the strategic plan needs a longer-term focus.

While the specifics of the execution plan will depend on the size, scale and objectives of the merger, as well as whether it is a Swiss verein or similar structure, we recommend that the following be specifically addressed in the plan.

- Cultural integration:
  - definition of core values;
  - approach to client service.
- Practice group integration:
  - leadership assignments and responsibilities;
  - partner assignments and roles;
  - planning process and goal setting.
- Client integration and development:
  - integration of key client programme and client teams;
  - communication and business development plans for key clients;
  - integrated business development programme.
- Human resources:
  - partner performance expectations and metrics (typically detailed before the effective date but often requiring refinement post-merger);
  - alignment of talent management initiatives and policies;
  - alignment of recruiting initiatives.
- Communications plan:
  - clients;
  - internal;
  - market.
- Financial plan:
  - alignment of financial and billing policies;
  - alignment of metrics and reports.
- Risk management:
  - alignment of risk management policies;
  - establishment of an integrated conflicts and client acceptance process.
- Technology and administrative integration.

6.2 Be clear about expectations and success metrics

People typically have expectations, often unrealistic ones, about what the merger will deliver and when. It is critical to be clear about what the expectations are around a number of dimensions, and what metrics will be used to define success.

Financial expectations are subject to the most scrutiny, in part because they also often factor in the public perception of the success of the merger. Setting realistic financial performance metrics and budgets for the first two years of the merger should be done in advance of the combination. The partners need to understand the underlying financial drivers and what performance levels are required to achieve the objectives.

The leadership should also set at least broad expectations and metrics around practices and clients. While it can be dangerous to be too specific (eg, expanding work for Client C by 30%), it can be useful to identify overall expectations for expansion of existing clients, winning of new matters and new clients, growth in key markets, and the like.

6.3 Pay attention to communications

Not surprisingly, effective communications are critical in a post-merger environment. There are at least four dimensions to consider in communications – the frequency, the content, the tone and the medium.

(a) Frequency

Typically, firms under-communicate rather than over-communicate. Managing partners are often surprised to find that a message that they feel has been delivered has not in fact been heard by the majority of the partners (or others). It is important to keep messages simple and direct, and to communicate them more than once, sometimes in more ways than one. In the early days a weekly leadership update may be appropriate. After the first 90 days or so it may be that monthly or bi-monthly updates are enough. This should be augmented by communications from practice leaders, key client leaders and C-level staff.

(b) Content

In keeping with the simple and direct idea above, it can be useful to build messages around a few key themes. These might be client successes, practice successes and a people update. If you provide too many details, the key message can get lost.

(c) Tone

The tone of messages can make a difference. This is not just about highlighting positive messages, but also making sure that there is no 'us' versus 'them' language that slips into the messages.

Emphasise the new firm that has been created. Some firms, for example, have specifically banned the use of terms like 'legacy firm', as that perpetuates a two-firm mentality longer than need be. At some point it is useful to move on from merger integration to simply firm management and planning to emphasise the future rather than the past. This point is typically after 12 to 24 months but could be shorter in smaller combinations. When doing cross-border combinations, it is also important to be culturally aware in your tone.

(d) Medium

The appropriate vehicles for communication will depend to a degree on the culture of the two firms. Typically, there is no substitute for face-to-face contact, and moving management meetings around the offices, having in-person practice group meetings, having partner retreats, and visiting other offices whenever possible provides the best forum for communication and interaction. Regular video conferences, telephone conferences, emails or video messages can be effective supplements to the in-person meetings. If you are adding several time zones as part of a combination, be sensitive to that in scheduling.

7. Conclusion

We expect merger to continue to play a significant role as the legal industry consolidates globally. In order to increase the percentage of 'Home Run' mergers (see Figure 1), leadership must increase the focus on ensuring that there is a strong business case for the merger and that the post-merger integration is well planned and effectively executed. Too few mergers historically have succeeded on both of these dimensions and the market is less forgiving today than it was a decade or two ago.

How to screw up your international expansion: a 15-step guide

Robert C Bata
WarwickPlace Legal LLC

Preface to the second edition

It is now eight years since my "15-step guide" was first published, and its lessons have remained relevant to this day. Indeed, one might even modestly assert that the admonitions of the original chapter have been heeded rather well, given the spate of international expansion we have seen during this period. That is not to say that all recent cross-border ventures have been unqualified successes – we need only recall the recent flirtation (but no engagement, much less wedding bells) between a Magic Circle firm and a Californian stalwart. But never mind; now that Brexit is done, there is a renewed impetus for UK firms to get it right in the United States.

It has certainly been a busy number of years for international expansion. One would think the current climate of trade wars, social and political upheaval, anti-globalist and nationalist sentiment (and, as of this writing, the novel coronavirus outbreak) would suggest caution; however, there is every indication that there will be no slowing down of law firms' quest for market share and the need to be responsive to global client demand.

Over the past eight years there have been 89 cross-border combinations where at least one of the firms was from the United States, and that does not even include domestic mergers that also involved combinations of the firms' existing international offices (eg, Squire Sanders/Patton Boggs and Arnold & Porter/Kaye Scholer). Granted, the numbers are skewed by serial acquirers, such as Dentons and DLA, and some of the narrow specialist firms, such as employment shop Littler Mendelson, but there is little doubt that the trend has been in favour of global expansion.

It is not just the Americans who have been active entrants into foreign markets. British firms have not been idle, with expansion into Australia (Ashurst), Africa (Clifford Chance) and a variety of Western European locations. In Eastern Europe, German firms such as Noerr have stepped up their presence, while regional firms such as Kinstellar and Arcliffe have taken over territory left behind during the exodus of many of the major Western law firms. The Italians liked the Middle East (BonelliErede into Dubai and Gianni Origoni into Abu Dhabi), while Spanish firms, such as Uría Menéndez, have been aggressive in their push into Latin America, and local regional firms, such as Ferrere, have also made cross-border moves there. Japanese firms, following the lead of Mori Hamada & Matsumoto, have opened in Singapore, and Chinese firms, such as Zhong Lun, have made their global ambitions known, including along the old Silk Road as part of the Belt and Road initiative.

The Chinese–Australian merger resulting in King & Wood Mallesons took a hit with its ill-fated merger in Europe with SJ Berwin (hint: you really need to understand the financials of your target). And finally, several firms have realigned their international strategy, meaning that they just gave up in some locations (eg, Vinson & Elkins in Asia, Troutman Sanders everywhere outside the United States, and Weil Gotshal & Manges and K&L Gates in Eastern Europe).

But for those who have tried and failed, and for those who are yet to dip their toe in international waters, let us remember that there are always second chances. Not many years ago, a small Chicago firm named Sonnenschein, Nath & Rosenthal opened a London office and managed to commit many of the screwups we counsel about in this chapter. The firm left London with its tail between its legs, derided by the legal press and widely believed to have been finished with its international experiment for good. Today, that firm is named Dentons.

So you want to be an international firm? You want to open offices in exotic locales? Good for you. We live in a thoroughly interconnected global economy. Increased access to information, greater ease of communication, expanded global markets and proliferating cross-border transactions and disputes have transformed your clients' expectations. The action is … everywhere! If you can't look after your most valued clients wherever in the world they may need you, well then it's *adiós, amigos*!

The trouble is that, as it turns out, going international is not easy. The global legal landscape is dotted with flags planted by law firms dashing to establish themselves in the hottest new markets – and littered with the wrecks of efforts gone wrong. There are a myriad of ways to fail at it. In the end, if you foul up, you will have spent an awful lot of time and end up losing money, losing clients, losing colleagues, losing your reputation and quite possibly losing your very existence. So it actually may be viewed as a public service of sorts for us to lay out a set of concrete steps to ensure you will make a shambles of it without investing too much time. And for those inspired souls who prefer to learn from the mistakes of others rather than their own, there may even be a road map here for getting it right.

Not all of the 15 measures described below are necessarily fatal in and of themselves, but they each contain the seeds of fiasco. By the same token, one need not slavishly take each of the actions highlighted by this guide in order to achieve a complete mess. But taken together, these 15 suggestions, or guidelines if you will, are as good as a guarantee that your international expansion will fade, fizzle and flop in pretty short order.

Finally, it may seem to the sceptical reader that some of the scenarios described below are too silly, too outlandish and too implausible to have happened in our learned profession. Please be assured that, while we have named no names, in order to protect the innocent (or just the plain foolish), each example has an antecedent in the real world.

1. The vision thing

The accumulated wisdom of the firm's *éminence grise* is one of the treasured assets of many partnerships. These elder statespersons, although still firmly in charge, can look beyond the mundane affairs of firm management and devise strategies for the future. Although well-intentioned, their visionary strategies can sometimes soar beyond the practical and the necessary, and occasionally they are just a means to enshrine the leader's personal legacy. Whatever the motivation, however, the bigger the vision, the bigger the need to achieve 'buy-in' from the partnership. And yet, when it comes to one of the most transformative of strategies – international expansion – senior partners often ignore the fact that it is the firm's most productive partners, the ones in the prime of their careers, with active practices, for whom the strategy must work. If those partners' practices will not be enhanced by an international strategy, if their practices are distinctly domestic, if in fact they see the cost of cross-border expansion as a hit on their profit share and no more, the project is doomed. This is especially so when the leader is held in such high esteem that the partnership goes along with the plan out of deference to their wishes. Once the senior partner exits the stage, it will be curtains for the foreign office too.

A corollary to this phenomenon is that of the passport-happy partner, who insists that a foreign office is essential to their practice, or else all of their clients (who until now had mysteriously been content to work with them without such offices) will disappear into the clutches of more nimble competitors. Is this just someone who wants a lot of air miles, or perhaps live the glamorous expat life? Or is it someone who would like to find a nice hiding place from the rest of the partnership? Or maybe it is someone who has been freshly recruited from an international firm and now claims that their practice will only follow if the new firm opens up foreign offices in the same locations as the old one. (Now *there's* a case of the unasked question coming back to bite the recruiting committee.) Let these characters have their way, and you can be pretty sure the new office will end up as nothing more than a frolic and a detour.

2. Geography is overrated

The world is a confusing place. Regimes change, place names change, countries get carved up, people insist on speaking incomprehensible languages. Who can keep up with all that? Even so, a few years ago some partners with a burgeoning practice in Central and Eastern Europe thought they had made a persuasive argument to their colleagues for opening an office in Budapest. The business case was strong, barriers to entry were low, the field was still wide open. It was therefore all the more disheartening for them to be solicitously asked by the firm's management committee whether it wasn't too dangerous to set up shop in such a volatile region of the Middle East ... The atlas-challenged firm never did get past its confusion. It ended up losing the lead partner to a competitor, missing out on several waves of groundbreaking privatisations and having to play catch-up when it was too late. This was an efficient failure, streamlined and elegant: if you can't tell your Azores from your Elba, your foreign venture is doomed from the get-go.

3. *J'aime Paris!*

Lest we become overly smug in our assessment of those who did not pay attention in geography class, there is plenty of potential for a belly-up when the impetus for international expansion comes from a misguided focus on a particular location. This happens when you think you know something about a market when actually you don't. Take for example the China Syndrome, which goes something like this:

China's population is more than one billion people, so the demand for legal services must also be astronomical. And everyone else seems to be opening offices there. Therefore we should be there too. We'll need to figure out what we can offer, but that's a minor issue: once we build it they will come.

But the truth is that the big numbers in China – huge population, giant country, enormous resources, warp-speed development – don't necessarily translate into big numbers on your bottom line, as many firms have learned. For every firm that has the talent and resources to handle a big-ticket arbitration, or a Red Chip IPO or a behemoth infrastructure financing, there are plenty who have merely bounced along the bottom, handling routine company formations, low-end real estate and rubber-stamp labour and employment matters. If you barge into a market on a wing and a prayer, you're likely to end up crawling and cursing.

Even worse is the wanderlust approach to expansion. Say for example that one of the partners has handled a matter in Laos or Mozambique or Tahiti and has simply fallen in love with the place. She persuades her partners that this could be a fantastic opportunity to get involved in more of the same type work if only they had an office there. Local businesses, ministry officials and a member of one of the leading families have all told her they would send work. Before you know it, a presence is established, and the wait begins … and continues … and continues, because no one in this enchanting locale is willing to pay your home country billing rates. But even if rates are not the issue – and when aren't they? – allowing a partner to commit the firm to an expansion that serves little benefit other than to indulge his or her enthusiasm for a place, be it Paris, Milan or Rio, all on the hopeful supposition that a practice 'could turn into something', is sheer folly.

4. Seeing is believing

You are well-informed about the difficulty of entering a foreign market. You've heard some horror stories, and you're not too sure you believe the tales of success. What you do know is that your firm needs to be seen to be in a particular location, so your competitors across town don't steal a march on you. It also happens to be a nice recruitment tool to be able to say that you've got an office in an important and possibly fascinating city. But you're not going to risk your partners' money, because that would be imprudent.

So you do the next best thing, which is to rent some space and trumpet an office opening to the world. Your website is updated to show the lawyers 'in' that office, even though when you look closely, those lawyers are actually sitting at their desks in their original locations. You might even give these lawyers a separate identity, like the 'Gulf States Team', or the 'Iceland Desk'. These are superbly evocative designations: 'Team' suggests a well-oiled machine ready to spring into action, while 'Desk' conjures up a busy newsroom, with typewriters furiously clacking, or possibly a kind of foreign ministry warren where diplomats work the night away gathering intelligence and negotiating secret protocols.

Yes. Well, the problem is that the 'teams' and the 'desks' are illusory, and clients catch on to these things. You assure them you can fly hordes of lawyers to your new foreign location at the drop of a hat, but the client won't pay for that, and you can't eat the cost. Local businesses will not take you seriously if you can't make yourself available on short notice. And you can't very well schedule meetings in the back room of the bodega you were able to get on the cheap. Bottom line: if you're renting space without anyone to put in it, you're better off staying home.

This is a good place to mention another smoke-and-mirrors approach favoured by some: the 'International Practice Group'. This can be wholly innocuous in intent – it's a way of advertising that your firm has dealt with matters outside its home jurisdiction and is, perhaps, comfortable with doing so again. Unfortunately it can also turn into an admission that, in fact, you have nothing like an international practice, but that you have cobbled together a hotchpotch of incidental projects you've handled in order to make it appear that you do. An international practice is, after all, not a practice area, like corporate or real estate or tax, unless your firm has a Law of the Sea speciality. A genuine international practice is one where you can routinely find cross-border elements in your substantive practice areas – simply saying you have one won't make it so.

5. Reinvent yourself

You've arrived at the decision to enter a foreign market. Your reasoning is pretty sound. You know where you want to go, and you want a real presence, not a Potemkin village. You understand that merely being in some unusual location is not enough to qualify your firm as having an international practice. You've done research, and you know the strengths of particular locations. You've concluded, correctly, that London is a major financial centre, or that Hong Kong is huge in capital markets, or that Ulaanbaatar is the next big thing in natural resources.

In fact, you've gone an extra step. You've looked at your firm's performance in its home market and realised that things are not looking so good there. Your partners are complacent and not working hard enough; your marketing and practice development are non-existent; your brightest associates are being poached by your competitors; and worst of all, your profits have been on a downward curve for some time. So you've found the perfect solution: enter some of the world's most competitive jurisdictions, where no one has heard of your firm, and act as though you belong there. Go ahead, start an energy practice in Houston, even though you wouldn't know a pipeline from a chorus line; start a telecoms practice in Düsseldorf, even if you think a megahertz is a limousine rental company. Hire some locals to provide you with cover, and hope their practice will be good enough to let you survive. And then, your theory holds, you can set to work fixing what's wrong back home and possibly transforming the firm into something completely different.

Wake-up call: never in a hundred years will this work. Firms with a well-thought-through strategy have done plenty of reinventing of themselves, and quite successfully too, whether they were once a standard practice in the Midlands of England now grown into a global megafirm; or a small bankruptcy shop in New York's Midtown that is today one of the world's most successful and sophisticated international capital markets firms. But you cannot magically metamorphose into a different firm – much less solve your domestic problems – by bolting on a novelty practice in a foreign country.

In the first place, you will most likely not find anyone interested in joining your firm in the foreign location. After all, where for the foreign practice group is the synergy, the cross-sell, the prospect of fruitful integration into a firm whose practice has nothing to do with theirs? Even worse if you do find some interested recruits: chances are their business is in the 'rebuilding phase' (ie, they don't have any); or they have no interest in integration, because after they've spent a few years with you they will move on to the next highest bidder.

Secondly, your domestic issues must always take precedence over foreign experiments. An unproductive partner will remain unproductive no matter what a colleague in another country in another practice area may be doing. Your core clients will not suddenly send you new work at home, on the strength of what you may be doing overseas. You want to tell your real estate clients in St Louis that your London office is tops in AIM listings of mining company shares in London? Knock yourself out, but they won't care. What those clients really want to know is how you can serve them better at home. International expansion is not a cure for what ails you at home.

6. Goals versus own goals

You have avoided all of the major pitfalls. You know where you want to be; you know why this location is important; you're satisfied that being there is not simply a whim or a masquerade. You are not merely ducking intractable problems at home, and you know you'd better not pretend to be something you are not. All set to go? All set to fail if you don't have a clear strategy for what you want to accomplish once you've arrived.

A particularly big way to fail in this regard is through a merger that is really nothing more than a work in progress. For example, a prestigious City firm learned the hard way that marrying up with a US firm which, although most distinguished in its heyday was suffering declining fortunes, gave it little more than an expensive beachhead in a competitive location. The thought behind this kind of merger is that getting into the market is more important than figuring out how to succeed in that market. Yes, the thinking went, at some stage steps will have to be taken to rationalise the merger, but for starters it was perfectly OK to gobble up an amorphous, undifferentiated mass and put off into the future shaping it into something that made sense. Of course the opposite turned out to be true, a costly and painful lesson for all concerned.

Another but no less effective way to fail in a foreign jurisdiction is to hire everyone who comes through the door and is willing to accept a paycheck from you. You can report staggering advances in your headcount: a bankruptcy team here, a credit card expert there, a litigator or two, some real estate and insurance specialists, online gambling, structured finance, venture capital … it makes one's head spin just to contemplate the variety. It doesn't matter that the office has no recognisable identity, you say, because you are determined to reach 'critical mass', whatever that may be. Once you get there will be time enough to decide which way to jump, right? Dead wrong. How could you know what size you need to be when you don't know what you want to be? Depending on the practice you are building, a small headcount can be sufficient and still profitable. Yes, size matters – except when it doesn't.

7. I've got a secret

However sound your strategy for international expansion may be, you can still drop the ball if you mishandle the way you communicate it to your partners and the outside world.

In the world of law firms, surprises are generally unwelcome and almost always unpleasant. It is therefore remarkable how often a very small group of firm leaders decides it is a good idea to keep from their partners any notion of a potential international expansion, only to spring it on the unsuspecting populace as a *fait accompli*. This is a poor idea for many reasons, particularly because, no matter what the firm leaders say, the rest of the partners will assume they have been cut out of some sweet deal the seniors have arranged for themselves.

Treating sensitive and proprietary information as confidential is of course crucial in any phase of planning an international expansion, especially when it involves a merger. But there is no message more toxic than one that implies that the firm's leaders do not trust the partnership to maintain confidences or to discuss the issues in a constructive way. The result: demoralised and sceptical partners withhold their support, or walk out the door, or take it upon themselves to initiate discussions with third parties, thereby derailing the original plan.

8. Alert the media!

Fearing precisely the dire results described in the previous section, the firm's leaders embark on a strategy of letting the sun shine on every fresh idea they come up with. A memorandum is circulated to all staff describing the decision of the management committee to seek to expand internationally. Although the committee has reached no decision on how, where or when the expansion will occur, they are now committed to this goal. The memorandum is circulated to the media, and within a day or two the world is aware that this firm is on the march.

A flurry of press attention, accompanied by a tsunami of approaches from recruiters and law firm management consultants, takes place over the next few months. But nothing happens and the story becomes yesterday's news. Then an announcement is made that discussions are taking place with a particular firm. Rumours fly, partners are preoccupied with how the combination will affect them. Meetings are arranged for practice groups to meet their counterparts. Heads of terms are drawn up and leaked to the press. Speculation abounds regarding name changes, leadership roles, expected lay-offs. Partnership votes are scheduled and postponed. Interest blocs spring up within the partnership – some love the idea of the merger, others see the seeds of their practice's very destruction.

And then the whole thing goes nowhere, the two firms announcing that they part as friends. But a few months later the process starts again with another firm and goes nowhere again. And the same a year later. And again. The continued, repeated and much-discussed failure of the expansion project puts the world on notice that it will never happen. Finally the prophecy becomes self-fulfilling, or, perhaps worse, the firm, now desperate to have its strategy validated, is forced into the embrace of the wrong suitor. It is a long and painful road to failure.

9. Democracy is wonderful

Managing a law firm, particularly one with international ambitions, is far too complex to be done successfully by just one person. (There are some notable exceptions, but they are truly exceptional.) Sometimes though the task seems so daunting that major decisions get delegated to a task force or a committee, and the deliberations of these bodies are then supplemented by partnership-wide discussion groups, focus groups, head-scratching groups and of course votes. Lots of votes.

Well and good in the interest of openness, but not so good when it comes to following a straight line toward the goal of international expansion. Take the case of the 'International Committee', which some firms set up to investigate possible approaches to expansion. These committees are usually made up of a handful of partners who meet the following qualifications: they like to travel; they have time on their hands; and they have fixed ideas as to what would benefit their practice the most.

Having spent a good bit of time and money on exploratory travel and meetings, the committee will make a recommendation to the firm's leadership, which is usually too busy to second-guess them. The recommendations therefore either get shelved until some later date, or passed on to another group of partners, or to the full partnership for some kind of discussion or vote. Inevitably someone will have a better relationship with another firm in the target country and will want in on the decision-making process, or will want to form her own committee. In the meantime, one of the members of the original committee retires or gets de-equitised, or worse. Ultimately, another person with a different idea for a strategy emerges and recommends abandoning the entire project.

There is no substitute for well-informed and open discussion among partners; but failure is certain if there is no overarching guidance from the firm's leadership. Without that, any semblance of an international strategy becomes the domain of competing interest groups.

10. Strangers in a strange land

Once you've decided on your approach to expansion and are ready to set up your office – whether starting from scratch, recruiting locals or joining an existing firm – the most important decision you can make is who, if anyone, from your firm should be assigned to the new office. This person or group will be ambassadors for your firm, crucial cultural translators between the new office and the rest of the firm and of course inspirational characters with a strong work ethic and an interest in ensuring smooth integration. Too often, however, these people are not to be found. It turns out that the partners whose practice is most relevant to the new foreign office are too busy to move; or they want to stay close to their domestic clients; or they have young families they don't wish to uproot; or their children are grown, and they want to be close to the grandkids; or the right person never even gets asked.

So you come up with creative (for which read mind-boggling) solutions. An oft-seen one is taking a much-respected partner out of semi-retirement. This will often be a genial figure, delighted to be living abroad, happy to come into the new office, take the lawyers to lunch and regale them with anecdotes about long-ago and faraway exploits. This person will usually know a great deal about the home office and be very helpful with information about the firm, but his or her contribution is not likely to advance the cause of building the practice.

One otherwise sensible firm decided to send its *pro bono* partner to its new London office. This partner, who was doing a wonderful job running the firm's *pro bono* practice back home, but who otherwise had no clients of her own, would have been utterly at sea in this new environment and would have brought nothing to the table for the lawyers in the new office. Even worse, sending her was tantamount to sending the message that the firm did not consider it worthwhile to assign a revenue-generating partner to the office.

In another instance, a firm sent a litigation partner to a busy corporate finance office in Hong Kong. With no litigation business he was qualified to handle in that part of the world, and with no particular cultural fit or language skills, the young man was consigned to sitting in his office, widely assumed by his local colleagues to be serving as the eyes and ears of firm management and therefore to be avoided at all costs.

Each of the situations described above resulted in a potential existential crisis for the foreign office involved. In two cases the problem was resolved and the office salvaged. In the third ... that chapter is still being written, but the office has had a series of departures and is experiencing declining revenues in an otherwise dynamic market.

11. It's my way or the highway

Even when the right person – meaning one with the appropriate skills and practice interests – is transferred to the new office from the home jurisdiction, there is always an excellent opportunity for making a mess of it. Absence of cultural sensitivity can be a tripping-up point, as in the case of the US managing partner of an East European office, who invited the office staff to his home for a barbecue, only to be told that socialising with 'superiors' was considered work and therefore an unconscionable invasion of what otherwise would be deemed free time.

Usually the problem has less benign origins than a friendly barbecue. This normally has to do with the importation of procedures from the home office. If the partner assigned to the new foreign office has no ability or authority to adapt the rules to local realities, confusion will reign. This isn't just about imposing onerous requirements like 2,200 billable hours (which to this author's knowledge is more urban legend than reality). It's about having a centralised billing system that is unable to prepare invoices in local currency. It's about associate reviews conducted on the telephone by people who have never met or worked with the lawyers being assessed. It's about not understanding that for some lawyers feng shui considerations can influence career decisions, and even decisions about which way office furniture should face.

Simply dictating compliance with rules because 'that's how we do it back home', when those rules do not conform with local practices, is a sure way to alienate and create resentment among your foreign lawyers. And if they are seen to be flouting the rules, then the lawyers in the home jurisdiction will sour on the foreign office, and quite possibly on the whole international practice: 'They just don't get how we do business. We'll never make it work.'

So what don't you understand about 2,200 billable hours?

12. This land is my land

Even if the cultural sensitivity quotient is all in order, that does not mean other sensitivities are being attended to. No one appreciates the colonial approach, where the foreign office is treated as a sort of playground or travel agency for visiting dignitaries from the home jurisdiction. Many local managing partners have had weekends spoiled by that breathless call from home, announcing that retired partner Buford B Buford IV was coming to visit their city and would dearly love circus tickets, a stretch limo and Turkish takeaway arranged for his arrival. A favourite of this author is the request to a Shanghai managing partner from the heads of the firm's real estate practice group to arrange for escorts to take them to art gallery openings, specifying that the ladies be … tall.

Management by remote control also falls into the neo-colonial mindset. Once the foreign office has been established and is more or less humming along, management of growth (revenue and personnel) and of careers, particularly the advancement of younger lawyers, become crucially important. A sure-fire formula for undercutting the authority and self-esteem of the local partners is for the home office to conduct further recruitment without soliciting their advice and participation. Another way is to make unilateral partnership and compensation decisions in that foreign office. Sideline or minimise the roles your foreign colleagues play in the development of their office, and you can be sure they will look for greener pastures.

13. It's good to be the king

Your clients don't really care about all the legal niceties, so long as their deal gets done, their case gets won and their product gets sold, right? So the important thing for your foreign presence is contacts, access, 'who you know not what you know'. So bring on the former ministers, ambassadors, generals, tribal chiefs and shamans, to run your office the way it should be run in their country. How grand it will be to have the inside track!

The trouble is that generals need armies, ministers need factotums and shamans need acolytes. Before you know it, your foreign office will be the principality of a person used to the trappings of power and accustomed to demanding more. Of course he or she must have a chauffeur. Certainly if the computer system breaks down the IT guy should be flogged. By all means make sure His Excellency has an office larger than a football field. And if they demand to be paid a king's ransom, why just imagine how influential they must be.

This is not to say that employing a distinguished public servant to represent your foreign office is necessarily ill-advised. You are fortunate if you find a talented and prominent figure who has your firm's best interests in mind. But beware the celebrity biding his time while plotting his return to power, and look out for fallen stars seeking to relive their glory days. Your office will be enmeshed in controversy, your reputation will suffer, and you will expose your partners to professional risk.

14. Best of breed

There is really no great mystery to recruiting the right people for your new international office. It's downright easy, and you don't need to find any out-of-work bureaucrats either. The trick is to swoop on the most successful local firm and grab some of their best people. It may cost a lot – these people are not leaving the most prestigious firms in their country for a pittance – but it will all work out when the business starts flowing.

Except that the business does not start flowing, as more than one US firm found out in London when raiding Magic Circle firms. They did bring in remarkably talented and successful lawyers, but they had not realised that, in too many cases, the work that had kept these individuals busy, happy and well paid, came from their firms' institutional clientele. Yes, the lawyers could move … but the clients weren't budging. By the time the two-year/three-year salary guarantees expired, the magic had worn off.

But, one might say, law is a personal service business. Clients want the lawyer, not the firm. That's also true, in part. Ideally, there is a close relationship between the lawyer and her client, which is further enhanced by the services and personnel the lawyer's firm is able to bring to servicing the client's needs. When the relationship is predominantly institutional, there is no one lawyer in the firm who is crucial to the client. When the relationship is predominantly personal, then the client will not feel strongly about the identity of the firm – provided of course that the firm can supply the support the client needs.

It is at this end of the scale that the notion of 'portable' business becomes pertinent. Every firm wants laterals to come with portable business. But if the business is so portable that it has already made its rounds to several firms before landing on your doorstep, you have to wonder. How long before the next portability exercise? Is this work just the same set of balls being juggled by this lawyer year after year, or has there been an effort to expand the scope of representation? Is the work the lateral team is bringing just the last hurrah before it peters out, or is there a realistic prospect of it continuing and expanding into other practice areas of the firm? Sometimes all 'portable' means is 'easy come, easy go'.

15. My silo is bigger

Not sure what your Almaty office does? Then chances are they don't know what your office does either. Or maybe you didn't even know you had an office in Almaty, and why should you? You have a nice energy practice in São Paulo: what could interest you in Kazakhstan, one of the world's leading oil and gas producers? As long as you get along with headquarters, you don't need to understand what these other offices are all about, much less go out of your way to develop relationships.

If the only time you meet the lawyers from other countries is at your firm's annual golf outing; if you maintain that your practice area has no need to hold regular discussions with international colleagues engaged in the same area; if you prize your referral relationship with a foreign firm over your own firm's office in the same city; if you fail to seek out opportunities for cross-selling; if in other words your firm has not made global integration an absolute priority and held you accountable for your share in the effort ... The truth is, if all that happened, the world would not come to an end, because these are common occurrences within international firms. Firms need to deal with integration issues, and some are better at it than others; but it is unrealistic to expect busy professionals to devote too much time to global harmonisation. But firms send the wrong message to their partners when they allow an out-of-sight-out-of-mind mentality to develop. And if that happens, why bother going international in the first place? You might have been better off staying home.

16. Conclusion

This chapter has sought to provide a guide to law firms for making a mess of their international expansion efforts. It is sincerely hoped that these suggestions will be found instructive, timely and cost-efficient. It may also be useful, however, to attempt to distil from the foregoing some rules for getting it right. Here are a few:

- Know your business: how did you get where you are, what makes your firm what it is, how do you keep and grow it?
- Know your partners: what do their clients and practices require now and in the years to come?

- Create and communicate an internal process for evaluating international opportunities, and involve the principal opinion leaders of the firm.
- Ensure the partners are aware you are working up a strategy, without inducing fear or exuberance.
- Make decisions based on tomorrow's needs, not today's fads.
- Find the right people, and conduct extensive due diligence.
- Place practice skills, track record, work ethic and cultural fit above contacts.
- Set compensation fairly, with an upside for success, but no lavish packages or guarantees.
- Understand the pricing tolerance of the local market for legal services.
- Set achievable goals – and then some – and then stick with them.
- Maximise the exposure of the new team to the legacy firm: create global practice groups and industry sectors; ensure the new team's visibility in every office; establish secondment and exchange programmes for younger lawyers among the offices.
- Balance the need to have consistent performance and compensation criteria across all offices against the new team's historical experience.
- Make clear where and how the new team fits into the rest of the firm's current practices and aspirations.
- Open management and leadership opportunities to the new team.
- If things start going wrong, be prepared to make changes promptly and decisively.

Professionalising the pricing and procurement processes

Richard Burcher
Validatum® and Virtual Pricing Director®
Silvia Hodges Silverstein
Buying Legal Council and Columbia Law School

Senior executives in many companies demand that legal departments improve control of spend. From management's point of view, legal departments are cost centres and need to be managed as such. To satisfy their shareholders and owners, companies scrutinise legal spend in ways never experienced before. The view is that the legal department has to be a better corporate citizen; no more 'legal is different' explanations are accepted. In practice, this means that lawyers need to budget and stick to the forecasts, and no longer just manage risk and give legal advice. Like the rest of the organisation, the legal department is expected to be efficient, do more with less, reduce risk and save money, and achieve desired outcomes such as:

- operational efficiency;
- predictability of spend;
- enhanced client–attorney relationship; and
- strategic perspective on the state of the business.

1. Aligning interests

Outside counsel and clients share a common goal – to manage matters effectively and achieve a successful outcome by applying their legal expertise. But their goals and priorities can conflict: in-house counsel must find ways to manage legal matters effectively while staying within their budgets; outside counsel need to run their firms and maintain, if not increase, their profitability. In the case of litigation, if outside counsel are paid for their time regardless of the outcome of the case, clients fear they may bring the case even when it is not in the best interest of the client, spend more hours working on the case than the client would want, and reject a settlement when the client would be better off were it accepted. Alternatively, if outside counsel are compensated according to the conventional contingency fee arrangement, they are paid only a fraction of any trial award or settlement, but bear all of the cost of litigation. In this situation, clients fear that outside counsel may have insufficient incentive to bring the case, spend too little time working on it if it is brought, and encourage a settlement when the client would be better off going to trial.[1] It is, therefore, important to find ways that align the interests of law firms and their clients.

2. Introducing business professionals: pricing directors, legal operations and procurement

These new demands necessitate support on both sides: more and more clients now work with legal operations experts, data analysts and legal procurement managers, while firms work with pricing professionals.

- Legal operations professionals help improve the legal department's processes and efficiencies;
- Data analysts collect, organise and analyse data for the legal department;
- Legal procurement professionals oversee the selection, purchasing, budgeting and invoicing of legal services; and
- Pricing directors help law firms figure out the cost and price for services to ensure profitability for the firm and determine ways to deliver the service for the agreed price.

Business professionals' tools include:

- pricing: alternative fee arrangement (AFA) programme development and establishment of AFA 'playbooks';
- procurement: management of outside counsel, controlling and monitoring of purchasing activities and contracts, as well as sourcing, bidding and requests for proposal and reverse auctions;
- analytics: legal spend analytics to gain insight into how much money a company spends on what types of services, using UTBMS codes;[2]
- benchmarking: comparing the department with industry best practice;
- technology: e-billing,[3] matter management etc;

---

1 Polinsky, A Mitchell and Rubinfeld, Daniel L, "Aligning the Interests of Lawyers and Clients", *Stanford Law and Economics* Olin Working Paper No 223 (April 2002) at: http://ssrn.com/abstract=281628.

2 UTBMS stands for the Uniform Task Based Management System, a series of codes used to classify the legal services performed by a law firm in an electronic invoice submission. More information can be found at www.utbms.com.

3 E-billing or electronic bill payment and presentment, as it is also referred to, is the electronic submission of invoices by outside counsel over the internet, using software. Clients pay these bills electronically. E-billing is common practice in more and more countries today.

- outside counsel guidelines;
- reporting, scorecards and dashboards; and
- alternative resources: legal process outsourcing (LPO) and contract lawyers.

In this chapter, we will discuss the first two tools: pricing and procurement.

3. Pricing

Pricing is the process of determining what a law firm will receive in exchange for its services. Pricing in the legal sector used to be straightforward. For the longest time, law firms billed by the hour. Some argue that the process for determining price is not based on sound business practices: "Firms look at the rates charged by other lawyers with similar years in practice at other firms they'd like to compete with – and then they add on whatever the partners want to make in increased profit per equity partner."[4] While this approach is focused entirely on the firm, it disregards the firm's costs to produce the service and ignores what the market will bear and what their clients will pay.

Now more and more clients demand an alternative fee arrangement (AFA).[5] AFAs are also called 'value-based fee arrangements', 'alternative billing arrangements' (ABAs), or even 'appropriate fee arrangements'.

AFAs are meant to align the company's interests with those of its law firm, promote efficiency and accurate budgeting, and reward results rather than effort, thereby shifting some risk to the law firm.

Although the concept of AFAs is not new, the push to AFAs has never been more prevalent in the legal sector as it is today. A recent Buying Legal Council study found that 83% of participants already used AFAs, while an additional 15% plan to do so in the future.[6]

Fee arrangements come in three main categories: hourly based, fixed fee and value based. Arrangements can be applied to an entire matter, distinct stages of a matter, or across a group of matters.

---

4 Hackett, Susan, "Reconnecting Law Firm Pricing to Cost, Profit, and Value", *Corporate Counsel* (25 September 2012) at: www.law.com/corporatecounsel/PubArticleFriendlyCC.jsp?id=1202572446358.

5 AFAs are billing methods based on metrics other than the number of hours worked. AFAs include fixed fees, flat fees, retainers, contingency fees, capped fees, collared arrangements, capped fees, blended rates etc.

6 Data available in the 2019 Market Intelligence Report at www.buyinglegal.com.

Table 1. Advantages of AFAs

Advantages for legal departments	Advantages for law firms
AFAs represent an opportunity to: • save money • manage legal spend • buy value rather than hours • improve the predictability of legal spend • reduce budgetary pressure • align the interests of the law firm with those of the client • share the risk of lawyer's fees and costs	AFAs represent a chance to: • prove their willingness to innovate • partner with clients • improve profitability by rewarding efficiency and quality work

3.1 Hourly based AFAs

Hourly based AFAs are technically not pure AFAs, but discounts and blended rates are often referred to as AFAs nevertheless:

- *Straight discounts* are rate reductions for a single matter.
- *Volume discounts* are reduced rates based on the amount of work a client gives a firm. They are often utilised in addition to other AFAs. They may ensure work for the firm, but significantly cut into the firm's profits and may even endanger the firm's value proposition.
- *Blended rates* set one hourly rate for all lawyers working on a matter, regardless of their seniority or status. This simplifies billing and eliminates the 'penalty' for work done by more senior partners. On the flipside, clients might fear that blended rates incentivise law firms to be 'too efficient' and have more junior lawyers or paralegals do as much work as possible. The feared result is too little senior advice for clients. In fact, blended rates have been called arguably the least effective AFA because the firm's incentive is to push work down to the lowest-rate biller, typically a junior associate,

who is in turn incentivised to run up the number of billable hours on a given matter.[7]

- *Capped fees* limit the maximum legal spend by imposing a ceiling under which the firm bills the client hourly. The client is not charged for fees above that amount. Capped fees limit the total cost of an agreed amount of work and provide clients with greater certainty and predictability than hourly billing. This arrangement may signal to the client that the firm does not really need to charge as much for its billable hours as its standard fee suggests. Capped fees typically benefit the client more than the law firm; however, some firms see them as a way to get new work. In effect, firms may use capped fees as a (potential) loss leader to retain or win market share. Of all hourly based AFA models, capped fees offer the most incentive for firms to work efficiently and/or use outsourcing options. Determining the cap is critical to the success of this model. Clients often distrust caps, as they perceive the fees as coming in above the cap and seldom, if ever, below. Firms often dislike capped fees because their lawyers do not necessarily operate more efficiently than they would if the matter were being billed using normal hourly fees and therefore ignore the cap. As a result, firms believe they lose money because their realisation rates go down.
- *Collared fee or risk-collared arrangements* are similar to capped fees. Clients guarantee to pay a minimum amount for a particular group of cases, while the firm guarantees it will not bill the client more than a maximum amount. This creates both a fee floor and a ceiling, and reduces the risk for both parties.
- Under *outcome-dependent holdbacks*, firms agree to discount or 'hold back' a portion of their fees with the provision that the client will pay a bonus if the firm meets agreed criteria related to case outcomes. Client and firm establish a metric defining a successful outcome, by reference to quantitative and/or qualitative factors. Work is billed at an hourly rate, but a portion of the fees billed is held in reserve for future payment

7 Kozubek, Michael, "Alternative Fee Arrangements Vary in Effectiveness, Experts Say", *Inside Counsel* (April 2010) at: www.insidecounsel.com/2010/04/01/alternative-fee-arrangements-vary-in-effectiveness-experts-say (website no longer operational).

to the firm according to the metric or at the client's discretion. A holdback is a type of partial contingency arrangement in which the law firm is guaranteed part of its fees, but the other part is contingent upon the outcome. Since success is defined at the outset, holdbacks facilitate risk sharing, which clients strongly prefer. For example, a firm may receive 80% of its normal rates while a matter is underway. At the end, it may receive the remaining 20%, or less, depending on the client's satisfaction with the result. This type of arrangement may also be combined with a success fee that provides a bonus for a positive outcome.[8]

- When using *budget/time-dependent holdbacks*, firm and client establish a metric based upon the perceived cost of the matter or the timeframe within which the client wants it resolved. Work is billed hourly, but an agreed amount is held in reserve, payable to the firm for its successful achievement of budgetary or timing objectives. Given the focus on time and money, firms have an incentive to optimise workflow and explore outsourcing options and other efficiencies. A greater amount of risk is shared because the client has a larger role in defining successful results. Since estimating cost and timing is essential, only firms that possess the necessary tools or experience should consider this approach.
- *Contingency fees (or conditional fees)* contemplate payment only if the firm achieves an agreed result for the client. This arrangement aligns the firm's and the client's interests. Traditionally used by plaintiffs' lawyers in litigation, contingency fees can also be used for transactional matters. However, many jurisdictions prohibit the use of such contingency fees generally, or for certain types of legal services. The fee is typically a percentage of the money recovered, saved or won at trial or on settlement. The client generally pays nothing unless the legal action is financially successful. Such arrangements provide clients who are willing to forego a large portion of a positive result with protection from a bad result. Contingency fees may be appropriate for cases that have a high likelihood of success and a success fee significantly higher than estimated standard hourly billing

8 Hassett, Jim, "The Nine Most Common Types of Alternative Fees", Legal Business, *LexisNexis* (28 September 2011) at: www.lexisnexis.com/legalnewsroom/legal-business/b/finance/posts/the-nine-most-common-types-of-alternative-fees.

revenues. It is important to note that success might mean different things to different clients. In the case of litigation, a client may value a quick resolution over a win following a lengthy trial. Contingency fees encourage firms to work efficiently and provide a risk-sharing mechanism. Results can be drastically disproportionate: windfalls occur when the firm's share greatly exceeds the corresponding hourly fees, or when the cost to the client is far less than the value of the representation. The drawback is that clients might be suspicious and assume that if a firm is willing to assume the risk, the lawyers must think they will win, and billing hourly might cost the client significantly less.

- *Success fees (or partial contingency fees)* set a bonus that the firm receives in addition to its hourly, flat or capped-fee arrangement if the result meets agreed criteria. This may be defined as level of success, speed of resolution or cost savings. This type of AFA is typically used in transactional matters outside of defence litigation work or in high-stakes work. Success fees may be the best example of value billing, where client and firm interests are, on the face of it, aligned. Problems result if the firm must determine whether to advise a client against a particular course of action (because it is not in its best interests from a legal perspective) but stands to gain financially if the client takes that course of action. In such cases, the success fee may lead to a conflict of interest or lack of independence.

3.2 Fixed fees and flat fees

Fixed fees and flat fees set an agreed amount for a distinct scope of work. Firms typically calculate them by applying a mark-up to the firm's estimation of resources for that type of matter ('cost-plus calculation').

- *A fixed fee* can be used when a firm handles a single case (or case portion) for a pre-specified, negotiated amount.[9] Establishing a flat rate for litigation poses challenges due to the uncertainties. This can be reduced, if not circumvented, by

9 In some countries like Taiwan, clients expect fixed-fee billing and are, generally, uncomfortable with hourly billing. Fixed-fee billing is the norm, not an AFA. See Easton, Paul C, "Legal Project Management is Key to Fixed-fee Billing", *Legal Project Management* (31 August 2009) at: http://legalprojectmanagement.info/blog/2009/08/legal-project-management-is-key-to-fixed-fee-billing.html#.Xrp8fi-ZN-U.

breaking a case into specific well-defined phases, and setting a flat fee for each. For example, the firm can set one fee to draft and file a complaint, and an additional fee to cover subsequent stages of litigation.[10] On the transactional side, a flat fee can be agreed for each phase from preliminary agreements to due diligence to drafting the principal documents etc.

- *A flat fee* is an agreed total for multiple similar cases (eg, for all cases within a jurisdiction or geographical area, or of particular exposure or risk). There may be a specific number of cases, or the agreement may cover all cases of a specific type that occur during a set time period. Recurring matters, such as routine loan closings, leases and collections, lend themselves to flat fee agreements. These matters often involve a well-defined scope of work and limited complexity, and may be handled in volume. This is important to the law firm to ensure an aggregate profit. When using flat fees for litigation matters, firms must handle many of the same type of cases, as the firm will make a profit on some and lose out on others.

Fixed and flat fees give clients incentives for firms to work efficiently by removing the correlation between time expended and profit. Firms need to work with the client in advance to understand and define the scope of the matter as thoroughly as practicable to ensure accurate pricing, cost control and profitability. Both parties must agree to the assumptions and qualifications that govern the matter and the fee. Fixed and flat fees and performance-based bonuses have been said to be most effective at reducing cost and improving client satisfaction.[11]

Once the project is underway, the firm must carefully manage it, constantly reviewing assumptions and qualifications. Factors outside the control of the client and the firm (eg, changed economic conditions, acts of government agencies such as competition or antitrust regulators, unforeseeable reactions by the counterparty), and factors within client control (eg, the client changes some element of a deal's tax structure) may affect

10 Leach, Chris, "Alternative Fee Arrangements with Law Firms Can Be Beneficial", Special supplement to the *Denver Business Journal* (12 October 2008) at: www.bizjournals.com/denver/stories/2008/10/13/focus4.html?s=print.

11 Kozubek, Michael, "Alternative Fee Arrangements Vary in Effectiveness, Experts Say", *Inside Counsel* (April 2010) at: www.insidecounsel.com/2010/04/01/alternative-fee-arrangements-vary-in-effectiveness-experts-say (website no longer operational).

the integrity of the fee arrangement. Regular communication between the firm and the client is essential. For such a fee arrangement to work, each party must be confident that the other will not take advantage.

- *Flat fees with shared savings* set a flat fee for a matter but include a safety valve by tracking the cost of the work on an hourly basis. At the conclusion of the matter, the client and firm share the difference if the fee based on hourly rates is lower than the flat fee.
- *A fixed-fee menu* provides a list of fees for related services or for segments of a particular matter. For example, a fee of $5,000 might be quoted for a particular type of real estate transaction. Then charges would accrue for different situations, such as plus $5,000 for assumption of an existing loan and $7,500 for new financing.[12]
- *Portfolio fixed fees* set a single price for a large number of matters, such as all of a large company's annual labour and employment cases in a particular jurisdiction. Again, success for a law firm depends on having a large volume of matters, so that there will be enough profitable matters to offset any losses the law firm may incur on others. For this arrangement to work, the desire for predictability shifts to the law firm since it will want to have some reassurance as to the number and timing of cases.
- In a *bundling arrangement*, the firm receives a large number of matters simultaneously that it handles for a specific fee.
- *Subscriptions and retainers* allow clients to 'buy access' to certain firm lawyers, or to the entire firm, for a monthly fee. Agreements can include all types of matters or exclude more complex work that will be priced separately. Both client and firm must be clear about which services are included and which are not. Since clients are more likely to call the firm because they will not be charged for every call, firms may develop a more intense relationship and learn more about the client than they would when the firm is used only for discrete projects. This may lead to additional work outside the subscription/retainer. Therefore, some firms see subscriptions and retainers as marketing tools and use them as loss leaders.

---

12 Hassett, Jim, "The Nine Most Common Types of Alternative Fees", Legal Business, *LexisNexis* (28 September 2011) at: www.lexisnexis.com/legalnewsroom/legal-business/b/finance/posts/the-nine-most-common-types-of-alternative-fees.

Firms hope that, eventually, clients will begin to see the difference in quality and become willing to pay higher fees for higher-quality work. This arrangement also sensitises clients to paying their invoices as they are billed on a monthly basis.

3.3 Value-based billing arrangements

Value-based billing arrangements seek to reflect a firm's contribution to a case. They assume that the hours spent were not necessarily a relevant indicator of that contribution and may actually create an incentive to distort billings. Value billing must not be confused with flat or fixed-fee pricing. To the client it 'looks' the same in that it results in a set fee; however, the price is arrived at in the opposite manner: by an open discussion of the value to be delivered by the firm. The value determines the price, and the cost (or project management plan) is based on the value proposition.

- The *Fuselage Pricing Model* is a mix of value billing and retainer. It allows clients to choose first-class, business-class and coach-class pricing. The model works with standard business counselling and corporate matters. Similar to airlines differentiating the level of service flight attendants provide to passengers, clients receive different levels of service from the firm. For example, the firm's best people in every area of expertise are always at the first-class client's disposal. Coach-class clients, by contrast, do not have on-demand access, and work only with a single, highly trained lawyer. While this lawyer will provide sound legal advice, he or she may not have the same depth of experience and knowledge in any particular area.[13]
- *Packaging* high-value representation with low-value work helps secure interesting, lucrative work for the firm while enabling it to handle lower-value work at a price point that is acceptable to the client. Historically, this work would be sent to a lower-cost firm for servicing. In other words, the firm would have lost this business if it had not accommodated the client based on value. Such arrangements consolidate a larger amount of work with the firm, offsetting any economic risk from the low-value matters with the high-value matters, while

13 Lamb, Patrick J, "Alternative Fee Arrangements: Value Fees and the Changing Legal Market", Ark Group (2010). Exemplar Law Group's CEO Christopher Marston created the Fuselage Pricing Model.

providing the client with quality representation at a saving. It also allows the firm to determine how to manage low-value matters efficiently and cost effectively, and to manage its own costs (and risk) associated with the provision of legal services to the particular client.

- *Secondments* provide in-house legal departments with temporary assistance. Placement of a lawyer on-site with the client is an alternative to handling the work traditionally and billing at hourly rates. The basic premise of a secondment is that if a client has enough of the 'right' type of work (eg, in terms of volume, skill and experience required), but not enough to make permanent recruitment feasible, taking a lawyer on secondment will be cheaper than paying for that lawyer on an hourly rate basis. In return, the law firm gets guaranteed utilisation of the lawyer, a degree of certainty of revenue and predictable cash flow. In-house counsel are said to love secondments.[14] Clients may rely on the lawyer's specialised skillset that they cannot afford to recruit, on getting help with the 'heavy lifting' on a big deal, or on providing its small in-house team broader access to their external law firm's resources than otherwise possible. Law firms benefit from the stronger relationship with the client and the secondees' invaluable experience and perspective. The insight secondees get from working in the client's environment cannot be gained from researching the company. Secondments provide an opportunity to understand the client's inner culture and pressure points, as well as the opportunity to build broader and deeper relationships – not just with the in-house teams, but also with their internal clients. When an ongoing secondment programme is established, it is likely to build a very strong connection over time between firm and in-house team, giving the firm a powerful competitive advantage.

  Pricing secondments is a challenge for firms. Due to the intense competition among firms, particularly since the economic downturn, the price clients will pay for secondees has decreased drastically. Firms typically charge 'at cost'. As firms restructured and struggled to find work for their lawyers, farming them out to clients allowed them to retain

---

14 Smith, Mark, "The Joy of Secs (secondments), Legal Business", *LexisNexis* (22 September 2011) at: www.lexisnexis.com/legalnewsroom/legal-business/b/people/posts/the-joy-of-secs-secondments.

good people and keep clients happy. However, firms struggle to define 'at cost'. For example, is it salary cost including benefits and bonus, or a proportion of the overhead?

Due to the potential for unpredictability when using AFAs, firms often want to discuss safety valves, look backs and savings clauses with their clients. These safeguards are meant to allow firms pre-negotiated 'outs' if the unanticipated occurs, but not eliminate all risks. Rather than exercising the safeguard option too quickly and negatively impacting the lawyer–client relationship, discussions about safeguards should encourage regular communication between client and firm.

4. Setting up an AFA

When setting up an AFA, firms need to discuss the boundaries of a project with the client and analyse the results it is likely to produce. It is important to understand the scope of a matter, which could include:

- client expectations, including best and worst case assumptions;
- metrics used by the client and their respective weight and importance; and
- perspectives of the client's stakeholders, as well as business objectives.

Firms also need to determine the known state of past performance so they can measure and compare:

- The firm analyses similar litigation matters – including by phase – utilising both internal and external data in terms of cost, duration, timekeeper allocation, rates, number of parties involved, pleadings etc.
- The firm scopes the matter based on the client's communicated assumptions to determine the likely number of hours by timekeeper role, phase and tasks.
- The firm fleshes out the possible division of labour between the client and the firm and suggests milestones. What work will the client do in-house? What will the firm handle?

In addition, firms need to gain intelligence into how others provide the same services and value:

- Understand their direct competitors for the particular type of work: do only a few firms have the expertise necessary for this type of matter, or is it of the 'garden variety' type?

Finally, firms need to ensure their offer aligns the firm's goals with those of the client:

- What is important to the client and the client's different stakeholders, particularly the final decision maker(s)?
- How are decision makers measured and compensated? What is their autonomy in terms of decision making?
- How will the case outcome influence the decision maker's career?
- What level of risk sharing is the firm willing to accept?

In the end, successful pricing needs to be based on trust and real business partnership. Both law firm and client must be certain that the other party will not take advantage of them. Pricing is also both art and science. It is important to understand your firm's own costs, market prices and your clients' preferences. Successful pricing requires your firm to understand its own processes, and to show a willingness to examine these processes to improve efficiency.

5. Legal procurement

As mentioned at the outset, more and more legal departments collaborate with their colleagues in procurement when hiring and managing outside counsel. Legal procurement applies its experience and insight into efficient and effective spending for the legal department:

> *In 2008, when the CEO came in for the annual 'save money' talk, they didn't take 'I can't' for an answer from the General Counsel (GC). Instead, the CEO introduced procurement to the GC and let them know they were there to help.*[15]

This shift is particularly seen at the initial instruction phase, when procurement professionals help evaluate providers and negotiate fee structures. When involved in the purchasing of legal services, procurement typically negotiates on behalf of the legal department, measures value and provides more objective comparisons.

Procurement professionals are 'buyers' in the classic sense: they are responsible for the engagement letter/retainer or framework agreement and negotiations. Procurement professionals are influencers; they try to affect the outcome decisions with their opinion. Additionally, procurement professionals act as gatekeepers

15 Brown, Toby, "Procurement's Role in Purchasing Legal Services: A Counterpoint ... to a Degree", in *Buying Legal: Procurement Insights and Practice* (2012), p70.

for the legal category – they help manage and direct the flow of information between the service provider and client. When effectively using procurement, legal departments do not simply hand over all power to their procurement colleagues. Procurement is rarely the final decision maker. Selecting law firms is still the legal department's prerogative. Rather, procurement is mainly responsible for managing the sourcing process; for negotiation and contract development; pre-purchase evaluation of outside counsel (which may or may not be traditional law firms); as well as developing sourcing criteria and purchasing strategies.

More and more procurement professionals are involved not only in purchasing routine services and legal 'commodities', but also in complex and high-value legal services. Exceptions may be emergency situations, where procurement's timeframe does not fit.

Clients now regularly use procurement tools such as issuing requests for proposal when selecting law firms and other legal services providers. They send the request for proposal to potential sellers of legal services, asking them to bid for the service and specifying service requirements: the company develops a document identifying the need (ie, the type of service they need and why) and specifications. It also lays out the bidding process – how the process will work and how outside counsel will be scored (eg, how different skills are weighed), as well as rules for the bidding process. If an electronic auction is included, the company will invite potential suppliers to register online and opens the event for a specific time for bidding. The company awards the contract to one of the bidders. The decision can be based on price or other factors such as skills, experience, geographic reach, fit or 'bench depth'.

6. Multi-sourcing

It is frequently difficult, if not impossible, for a law firm to meet cost-effectively all of the client's needs. This is not a function of law firms overcharging, but rather elements of their cost structure precluding the delivery of some services at a price point that clients considered to be fair value.

Clients now expect firms more imaginatively and creatively to resource the delivery of their work for optimal cost effectiveness but still preserving the firm's ability to deliver the work profitably. This has seen the emergence of multi-sourcing options for the delivery of the full range of services that clients will often expect from the law firms, from the mundane and routine through to strategic and mission-critical.

The emergence of both technological solutions and different delivery models has greatly enhanced firms' ability to accommodate this expectation. For example, many large firms now have lower-cost production centres, well away from the high-cost basis to be found in the centre of major metropolitan cities.

Subcontracting of work to alternative legal service providers and the use of smart technology for tasks such as initial document review are also playing a key role in driving down production cost and pricing.

7. Data and management information

Law firms and their clients are increasingly amassing huge volumes of data and management information. More sophisticated practice management systems and related software applications enable a large number of metrics, input costs and key performance indicators to be captured and analysed.

Data on its own is of very limited value though. The key to effective use of the data is the ability to analyse and present it in a way that provides actionable insights. If this conceptual and technical hurdle could be overcome to a point where both parties can achieve highly granular visibility into issues around scoping, resourcing and related input costs, more intelligent and informed decisions can be made collaboratively around the strategy and tactics for the management of the project.

Conversely, the lack of insights means that too many decisions are currently a function of guesswork or are simply left to chance; a state of affairs that is increasingly unacceptable to both firms and their clients.

This management information is valuable in its own right, but where it really delivers significant benefits is when it has the ability to deliver insights into trends and patterns. For example, it can help firms and clients decide whether from a cost-effectiveness and risk/reward point of view, based on a large number of historical examples, it is better to proceed to trial or, alternatively, indicate the optimal point in the proceedings to settle.

These expectations have given rise to new technical and skills requirements; for example, the rise in deployment of machine learning (a subset of artificial intelligence) and data scientists.

At present, firms and clients capture data in different formats, on different platforms and with differing levels of detail. The information held by both is often asymmetric in terms of quantity and usability. Increased collaboration between law firms and clients around the collection, analysis and deployment of management information will go a long way towards service delivery and pricing solutions that work for both.

8. Pricing technology

For most practitioners wanting to bring some rigour to pricing calculations, the spreadsheet has been the go-to tool of choice, given its ubiquitous presence and a broad level of understanding and usage capability. As the legal profession increasingly embraces the potential offered by artificial intelligence (including machine learning, big data and natural language processing), spreadsheet tools on their own are exposed as having serious limitations.

As noted earlier, an increasingly sophisticated approach to the pricing function in law firms has seen the emergence over the last five years in particular of roles such as pricing director. However, in even the largest and best-resourced law firms, the pricing director and his or her team are spread very thinly across the firm's professionals and are therefore often only utilised in the context of major bids and a comparatively small number of the firm's key client relationships.

This leaves the average partner in the invidious position of having to cope with little or no support. The new breed of pricing software helps to address this deficit by intelligently guiding lawyers through the pricing function, drawing on historical data and risk/probability projections, and simulating individual and personalised support for partners through partner-friendly data insights, 'intelligent' pricing templates and 'Siri-like' interaction through chat bots and avatars.[16]

8. Conclusion

Both new pricing and the influence of procurement have changed the way lawyers need to manage their firms and provide their services. Neither using AFAs nor working with procurement means that firms will no longer make money. It is better to understand these changes and be prepared to work in this new way, as the competition will not become less fierce any time soon. Now is the time to embrace change!

---

16 For example, Virtual Pricing Director® (www.virtualpricingdirector.com).

About the authors

Mats Anderson
Justice, Supreme Administrative Court (Sweden)
mats.anderson@dom.se

Mats Anderson was previously head of the Linklaters Nordic tax team. He also ran the consultancy Clear Blue Water AB, focusing on strategic development of larger law firms in the Nordic region, continental Europe and the United Kingdom.

Mr Anderson had his initial management-to-change experiences in the mid-1990s in his then Swedish law firm. Since then, he has been involved as a partner in relevant firms or as a consultant in a number of projects, such as mergers, the opening up of greenfield offices in new markets, and general strategy projects.

Mr Anderson started with Swedish law firm Lagerlöf & Leman in 1991. This firm merged with the international firm Linklaters in 2001, in which Mr Anderson was a partner until 2007 when he left to start his consultancy. He was appointed Justice in 2018.

Robert C Bata
Principal, WarwickPlace Legal LLC
rbata@warwickplace.com

Robert C Bata is the principal of WarwickPlace Legal, LLC, a consultancy exclusively focused on advising law firms on the formulation, development and execution of international strategy. His clientele ranges from some of the world's largest multinational law firms to regional and national firms, including midsize and small independent firms around the world seeking to enhance their international capabilities. Prior to founding WarwickPlace Legal in 2010, Mr Bata spent more than 30 years practising cross-border M&A and dispute resolution with Sullivan & Cromwell, Mayer Brown and a predecessor firm of Dentons. A seasoned law firm leader, he established and successfully led offices for his firms in New York, London, Central and Eastern Europe and China. He is a frequent speaker at law firm retreats and various bar association events, and conducts workshops on international strategy for law firm management committees and practice groups. Mr Bata currently serves as co-chair of the International Bar Association's Senior Lawyers Committee.

Mr Bata earned his BA in Russian and East European Studies from Yale University and his JD from the University of Texas School of Law.

Richard Burcher

Managing director, Validatum®
Chairman, Virtual Pricing Director®
richard.burcher@validatum.com

Richard Burcher is a former New Zealand practising lawyer and managing partner with nearly 40 years' experience, including post-graduate study in professional services pricing.

Mr Burcher is a regular speaker at national and international conferences, including International Bar Association global conferences (Dublin, Ireland and Seoul, South Korea), the Commonwealth Law Conference (Hyderabad, India), the VQ Virtual Intelligence Knowledge and Strategy Forum (Stockholm, Sweden) and the Canadian Bar Association Managing Partners Forum (Calgary, Canada).

In 2018 Mr Burcher was appointed a teaching fellow (pricing) on the faculty of the Australian College of Law, master of legal business (MLB) qualification, and in 2019 was inducted as a fellow of the US College of Law Management.

His legal services pricing research and commentary have been widely published and he has worked with a broad cross-section of law firms with turnovers of between £10 million ($15 million) and £900 million ($1.5 billion) on pricing governance and process, partner training and pricing software.

E Leigh Dance

Founder and managing partner, ELD International LLC
Founder and executive director, Global Counsel Leaders
eldance@eldinternational.com

E Leigh Dance and her consultancy ELD International help global law firms and corporate legal/compliance functions to perform better and achieve goals faster. Through projects in over 30 countries on all continents, Ms Dance is known in legal and business circles as a skilled strategist, thought leader, change manager, connector and speaker. Law firms and legal networks retain ELD International to reality-check their marketing and business development strategies and actions with international clients, for market research, and to implement successful programmes with the world's largest legal service buyers. Ms Dance lives and works from bases in New York and Brussels and speaks English, French and Italian. Her articles can be found in publications including *The Wall Street Journal, Financial Times, Legal Week* and *American Lawyer*. Ms Dance's *Global In-House* column is published in American Lawyer Media's *Corporate Counsel*. In 2010 she founded the highly regarded Global Counsel Leaders Circle elite group of in-house leaders, www.GlobalCounselLeaders.com.

Felix Dette

Partner, METIS Rechtsanwälte PartGmbB
felix.dette@metis-legal.de

Felix Dette is a partner (corporate/M&A) in the boutique law firm METIS in Frankfurt, Germany. Dr Dette specialises in private M&A and general corporate law, with a focus on stock corporations and corporate groups. He also advises on corporate restructurings and joint ventures. He has broad experience in advising national and international corporate clients and family-owned businesses in Germany.

Dr Dette studied law at the universities of Heidelberg and Lund/ Sweden and was scholar of the German Economy Foundation. During legal training he spent three months with the law firm Clayton Utz in Perth, Australia. Prior to joining METIS, Dr Dette spent close to five years working in the Frankfurt office of the international law firm Freshfields Bruckhaus Deringer LLP.

Dr Dette holds a doctoral degree from the Mannheim University. Besides his role at METIS, he is a lecturer in corporate law at the Mannheim Business School.

Ignaz Fuesgen
Managing director, smartvokat
ignaz.fuesgen@smartvokat.com

Ignaz Fuesgen is a managing director at smartvokat, a legal innovation company based in Germany. Prior to joining smartvokat, Mr Fuesgen held executive and senior roles at leading international law firms and management consultancies in Germany and South Africa, including KPMG Consulting, BearingPoint, Clifford Chance, Allen & Overy, Webber Wentzel and Deloitte Legal. His advisory clients include law firms, alternative legal services providers, in-house departments and legal tech providers. An author, public speaker, mentor and entrepreneur, he is passionate about legal innovation and digital transformation, as well as any new ideas nurturing access to justice for all people.

Mr Fuesgen is a certified legal project practitioner (LPP) and accredited trainer of the International Institute of Legal Project Management (IILPM) and certified Scrum Master (ScrumAlliance). He completed an Executive MBA from Carlson School of Management (Minneapolis, USA) with distinction and a master's degree in Social and Economic Sciences from the Vienna University of Business and Economics (Vienna, Austria).

Heidi K Gardner
Distinguished fellow, Harvard Law School
hgardner@law.harvard.edu

Heidi K Gardner, PhD, is a distinguished fellow at Harvard Law School and faculty chair in the school's executive programmes. Previously she was a professor at Harvard Business School. Dr Gardner's book *Smart Collaboration: How Professionals and Their Firms Succeed by Breaking Down Silos* became a *Washington Post* bestseller. Named by Thinkers50 as a 'Next Generation Business Guru', Dr Gardner co-founded the research and advisory firm Gardner & Co.

Dr Gardner has authored more than 70 books, chapters, case studies and articles. Her books include *Smart Collaboration for In-house Legal Teams* (2020), *Leadership for Lawyers* (2nd edition, 2019) and *Smart Collaboration for Lateral Hiring* (2018).

Dr Gardner has lived and worked on four continents, including as a Fulbright fellow and for McKinsey & Co and Procter & Gamble. She earned her BA in Japanese from the University of Pennsylvania, a master's degree from the London School of Economics and PhD from London Business School.

Dina Gracheva
Independent strategy consultant
gracheva.consulting@gmail.com

Dina Gracheva is an expert in strategic management and innovation, with experience in working as a marketing director of a law firm, as well as a consultant on strategy and business development for law firms and governmental institutions. Working in international environments outside of the legal industry, she also promotes the view that law firms can learn from other businesses and adapt various instruments to achieve success in a professional services world.

Wolf-Peter Gross
Management consultant, Law Firm Change Consultants
wpg@lawfirmchange.com

Wolf-Peter Gross is management consultant at Law Firm Change Consultants, the leading consulting firm for law firms and legal departments in Europe. He is lawyer, systemic organisational consultant, leadership coach and business mediator. He was general counsel in the telecommunication and system integration industry and has many years of experience as managing director in international businesses. Since 2005 Dr Gross has worked as a consultant with a focus on the development of professional service firms and law departments in the fields of strategy, organisation, culture, leadership and change processes. He is the author of several articles and books.

William S Harvey
Professor of management and associate dean of research, University of Exeter Business School
william.harvey@exeter.ac.uk

William Harvey is professor of management and associate dean of research at the University of Exeter Business School. He researches on reputation, talent management and leadership within organisations. Professor Harvey received a first class degree from the University of Durham, an MPhil with distinction and a PhD from the University of Cambridge. He has worked at the University of Oxford, the University of British Columbia, the University of Sydney and the University of Exeter. He has held visiting posts in Australia, France, Germany, Norway, India and the United States. Professor Harvey has researched and worked with leaders across the world in a variety of sectors, including consulting, defence, education, energy, finance, government, healthcare, insurance, manufacturing and retail.

Silvia Hodges Silverstein
CEO, Buying Legal Council
Adjunct professor, Columbia Law School
silvia@buyinglegal.com

Dr Silvia Hodges Silverstein is the CEO of the Buying Legal Council, the international trade organisation for legal procurement, and adjunct professor at Columbia Law School.

She co-authored the Harvard Business School case studies GlaxoSmithKline: Sourcing Complex Professional Services on the company's legal procurement initiative and Riverview Law: Applying Business Sense to the Legal Market on the new model law firm.

Dr Hodges Silverstein has authored many articles on law firm management, including *The Georgetown Journal of Legal Ethics'* "I didn't go to law school to become a salesperson" and the *South Carolina Law Review*'s "What we know and need to know about Legal procurement". She is also the author/editor of several books, including the *Legal Procurement Handbook and Buying Legal: Procurement Insights and Practice*. She is the publisher of *Winning Proposals – The Essential Guide for Law Firms and Legal Services Providers*.

She earned her PhD at Nottingham Law School (United Kingdom), holds a master's degree in business from Universität Bayreuth (Germany) and Warwick Business School (United Kingdom), and an undergraduate degree (economics) from Universität Bayreuth.

Bente R Løwendahl
Former professor, BI Norwegian Business School

Bente R Løwendahl was professor of strategic management at BI Norwegian Business School, Department of Strategy and Logistics. Her research interests were the strategic management of knowledge-intensive firms, with a particular focus on professional service firms (PSFs). Her book *Strategic Management of Professional Service Firms* (1997, third edition, CBS Press, 2005) is widely cited by researchers as well as practitioners in this field. Her research has also appeared in academic journals such as *Strategic Management Journal, Human Relations, Organisation Studies, Scandinavian Journal of Management, and California Management Review*. She contributed to a number of books, including, but not limited to, a Norwegian textbook on strategy for Bachelor-level students (third edition, Cappelen Damm, 2010) and the *Handbook of Research on Entrepreneurship in Professional Services*, edited by Markus Reihlen and Andreas Werr (E Elgar, 2012).

Ms Løwendahl held degrees in economics and business administration (MSc), as well as strategy/applied economics (PhD – The Wharton School, University of Pennsylvania).

Ivan Matviak
Co-founder, Gardner & Co
ivan@gardnerandco.co

Ivan Matviak is a co-founder of Gardner & Co, a research and advisory firm, and an investor/adviser to venture-backed technology companies. Mr Matviak has co-authored several publications on collaboration and professional service firm strategy.

Previously he was an executive vice president at State Street Bank, where he led the bank's insurance sector and served as president/chairman of three of the bank's FinTech subsidiaries. Prior to State Street Mr Matviak led the Bank of Scotland's small business commercial banking operations for the United Kingdom. Earlier in his career Mr Matviak was a consultant with Bain & Co's strategy and private equity groups in London and Johannesburg, and led strategy, product, marketing and sales functions at the Walt Disney Company (London and Paris) and Proctor & Gamble.

He holds an MBA and MA in international studies from the Wharton School of Business/Lauder Institute and a BA in international relations from the University of Pennsylvania.

Robert Millard
Director, Cambridge Strategy Group
robert.millard@camstrategy.com

Robert Millard advises law firms on evolving their strategies and business models in response to the challenges posed by digitalisation. His clients include forward-thinking firms of all types and sizes, ranging from some of the world's leading premium global law firms to some quite modest-sized businesses, across many countries.

Mr Millard is a former co-chair of the International Bar Association (IBA) Law Firm Management Committee. He is currently engaged with a doctoral research project into value creation in large US and UK law firm mergers. He is also an active member of the American Bar Association, the Academy of Management and the Strategic Planning Society. In 2017–2018 he served on the steering committee of the IBA President's Task Force on the Future of Legal Services. He has co-authored nine books over the past eight years on topics related to law firm strategy, partner compensation, digital transformation and developing high-performance business models.

Timothy Morris
Professor of management studies, Saïd Business School, University of Oxford
tim.morris@sbs.ox.ac.uk

Timothy Morris is professor of management studies at Saïd Business School, University of Oxford. His research on professional firms focuses on reputation, innovation and change as well as the processes by which these firms can build and sustain competitive advantage. His other area of research work concerns the changing nature of the role and capabilities of CEOs. His scholarly research has been published in the leading American and European journals and has been featured in *The Economist* and the *Financial Times*. He studied at the University of Cambridge and has a master's and doctorate from the London School of Economics.

Michael Smets
Professor of management, Saïd Business School, and fellow of Green Templeton College, University of Oxford
michael.smets@sbs.ox.ac.uk

Michael Smets is professor of management at the Saïd Business School and a fellow of Green Templeton College, University of Oxford. Professor Smets studies and advises professional service firms, especially in law, accounting, consulting and engineering. His research focuses on their leadership, innovation, internationalisation and career structures. Thinkers50 have included him as the "up and coming voice on leadership" on their 2019 'Radar' of management scholars to watch and his research is regularly featured in the *Financial Times*, Forbes, Bloomberg, CNN, CNBC, the *Guardian* and other international media outlets. Professor Smets has studied at Cologne University in Germany and holds a master's and doctorate from the University of Oxford.

Lisa R Smith
Principal, Fairfax Associates
lisa.smith@fairfaxassociates.com

Lisa Smith is a founding principal of Fairfax Associates and heads the Washington, DC office. She is a leading consultant to law firms and advises firms in the United States and globally on strategy development and execution, growth strategy and mergers, management and governance, partner compensation and structure, leadership development and firm financial performance. She is a thought leader in the industry and has written a number of books and articles, including the monthly *Fairfax Insights*, is a frequent speaker at legal industry conferences and law firm retreats, co-chairs the annual Fairfax Partner Compensation Workshop and has taught in executive education programmes at both Georgetown University Law Center and George Washington University. She earned her MBA from the Tuck School at Dartmouth College.

Christoph H Vaagt
Managing partner, Law Firm Change Consultants
CHV@lawfirmchange.com

Christoph Vaagt is the founder and managing partner of the consulting firm for law firms and legal departments, Law Firm Change Consultants, based in Munich. He holds a degree in law, and worked as a consultant across various industries and as a lawyer in Munich before turning to consulting for law firms and legal departments.

Prior to the foundation of his own firm in 2005, Mr Vaagt was a consultant with major US law firm consultancy, Hildebrandt International. Having worked with consultants such as Brad Hildebrandt and Alan Hodgart for leading US and UK law firms on projects ranging from devising international strategies to arranging mergers, he has acted for major German, Austrian, Swiss and other top European firms. He specialises in change management techniques, focusing on the strategy and culture of law firms.

Mr Vaagt is author of the first benchmark study of the German law firm market and has edited the first editions of *Law Firm Strategies for the 21st Century* and *General Counsel in the 21st Century*, both published by Globe Law and Business on behalf of the International Bar Association. He has also contributed to German-speaking publications on law firm management and legal department management.

Tomasz Wardyński
Founding partner, Wardyński & Partners
tomasz.wardynski@wardynski.com.pl

Tomasz Wardyński, CBE, is an advocate and founding partner of Wardyński & Partners, one of the largest and most recognised legal firms in Poland. He has been closely involved with its management and development for 30 years.

Mr Wardyński handles arbitration proceedings involving foreign and domestic entities, while also practising civil, commercial and competition law. He is a member of the ICC Commission on Arbitration and ADR and served as a member of the ICC International Court of Arbitration in Paris.

In 2001 Her Majesty Queen Elizabeth II appointed him an Honorary Commander of the British Empire.

The International Bar Association (IBA) has been an important part of his activity for many years. He has served as the Polish Bar's representative there and at present is also a member of the advisory board of the IBA Senior Lawyers Committee. He is also a member of the American Bar Association.

About Globe Law and Business

Globe Law and Business was established in 2005, and from the very beginning, we set out to create law books which are sufficiently high level to be of real use to the experienced professional, yet still accessible and easy to navigate. Most of our authors are drawn from Magic Circle and other top commercial firms, both in the UK and internationally.

Our titles are carefully produced, with the utmost attention paid to editorial, design and production processes. We hope this results in high-quality books which are easy to read, and a pleasure to own. All our new books are also available as ebooks, which are compatible with most desktop, laptop and tablet devices. We have recently expanded our portfolio to include a new range of journals and Special Reports, available both digitally and in hard copy format, and produced to the same high standards as our books.

We'd very much like to hear from you with your thoughts and ideas for improving what we offer. Please do feel free to email me at sian@globelawandbusiness.com with your views.

Sian O'Neill
Managing director
Globe Law and Business
www.globelawandbusiness.com